Here's some spiel about GCSE German...

AQA GCSE German is tricky, that's for sure. Luckily, this CGP Revision Guide will make things a whole lot easier for you. It's brimming with crystal-clear notes for every topic, plus brilliant coverage of all the vocab and grammar you'll need.

But that's not all. We've also packed in plenty of exam-style reading, writing, translation, speaking and listening questions — with **free audio files** available from this page:

www.cgpbooks.co.uk/GCSEGermanAudio

How to access your free Online Edition

You can read this entire book on your PC, Mac or tablet, with handy links to all the online audio files. Just go to **cgpbooks.co.uk/extras** and enter this code:

4035 5276 3066 9750

By the way, this code only works for one person. If somebody else has used this book before you, they might have already claimed the Online Edition.

CGP — still the best! ☺

Our sole aim here at CGP is to produce the highest quality books — carefully written, immaculately presented and dangerously close to being funny.

Then we work our socks off to get them out to you
— at the cheapest possible prices.

CONTENTS

CONTENTS

Published by CGP

Editors:
Izzy Bowen
Lucy Forsyth
Rose Jones
Cathy Lear
Heather McClelland
Ali Palin

Contributors:
Angela Blacklock-Brown
Miriam Mentel
Ben Merritt
Gaynor Tilley

With thanks to Glenn Rogers, Margit Grassick and Peter Tyson for the proofreading.
With thanks to Jan Greenway and Ana Pungartnik for the copyright research.

Acknowledgements:

Audio produced by Naomi Laredo of Small Print.

Recorded, edited and mastered by Graham Williams of The Speech Recording Studio,
with the assistance of Andy Le Vien at RMS Studios.

Voice Artists:
Bernd Bauermeister
Oliver Janesh Christiansen
Lena Lohmann
Indira Varma

AQA material is reproduced by permission of AQA.

With thanks to iStock.com for permission to use the image on page 55.

Abridged and adapted extract from 'Effi Briest', on page 16, by Theodore Fontane.

Abridged and adapted extract from 'Der Wolf und die sieben jungen Geißlein', on page 31, by the Brothers Grimm.

ISBN: 978 1 78294 552 9
Printed by Elanders Ltd, Newcastle upon Tyne.
Clipart from Corel®

Numbers and Quantities

No two ways about it, you've got to know the numbers — so get cracking.

Eins, zwei, drei — *One, two, three*

0	null	13	dreizehn	
1	eins	14	vierzehn	
2	zwei	15	fünfzehn	
3	drei	16	sechzehn	
4	vier	17	siebzehn	
5	fünf	18	achtzehn	
6	sechs	19	neunzehn	
7	sieben			
8	acht			
9	neun			
10	zehn			
11	elf			
12	zwölf			

The teens use numbers three to nine with 'ten' on the end — so thirteen is 'three' and 'ten' stuck together ('drei' + 'zehn'). But watch out — 16 and 17 are a bit different.

21	einundzwanzig
22	zweiundzwanzig
23	dreiundzwanzig

You say the in-between numbers backwards — 'one and twenty' for 'twenty-one'.

20	zwanzig	60	sechzig	100	hundert	
30	dreißig	70	siebzig	1000	tausend	
40	vierzig	80	achtzig	2000	zweitausend	
50	fünfzig	90	neunzig	1 000 000	eine Million	

For years before 2000, you say, e.g. 'neunzehnhundert...' (*nineteen hundred*...). For a 'normal' number, not a year, you say 'tausendneunhundert...' (*one thousand, nine hundred*...).

1967	neunzehnhundertsiebenundsechzig
2005	zweitausendfünf

Erste, zweite, dritte — *First, second, third*

1) For most numbers between <u>1 and 19</u>, add '<u>-te</u>'. The exceptions are in green.

2) From <u>20 onwards</u>, just add '<u>-ste</u>'.

The article won't always be 'das'.

In German, '1st' is written '1.'

1st	das erste	8th	das achte
2nd	das zweite	9th	das neunte
3rd	das dritte	10th	das zehnte
4th	das vierte	20th	das zwanzigste
5th	das fünfte	21st	das einundzwanzigste
6th	das sechste	70th	das siebzigste
7th	das siebte	100th	das hundertste

Grammar — number endings

The <u>endings</u> of number words <u>change</u> depending on the <u>case</u> of the <u>noun</u>. See p.58-59 for more on cases.

Ich möchte den <u>ersten</u> Hund.
I would like the <u>first</u> dog.

Wie viele? — *How many?*

einige	*some / a few*	eine Menge	*a lot of / lots of*
mehrere	*several*	ein Dutzend	*a dozen*
viele	*many*	ein paar	*a few*

Ich habe genug Äpfel.
I have enough apples.

Der Bäcker hat anderthalb Brötchen.
The baker has one-and-a-half rolls.

READING

German risk assessments cover 11 rules on elf and safety...

Read this text and then answer the questions in German — write the numbers out in full.

Heinrich ist neunzehn Jahre alt. Er hat zwei Schwestern, die siebzehn und fünfundzwanzig Jahre alt sind. Ihre Großmutter ist achtundneunzig Jahre alt — fast ein Jahrhundert!

e.g. Wie alt ist Heinrich? **Er ist neunzehn Jahre alt.**

1. Wie alt sind Heinrichs Schwestern? [1]

2. Wie alt ist ihre Großmutter? [1]

3. Wie viel älter ist ihre Großmutter als Heinrich? [1]

Times and Dates

You have to know how to say the time, as well as the days and months — examiners just love this stuff. Luckily, it'll be useful for organising your German social life too. What do you mean you don't have one?

Wie viel Uhr ist es? — *What time is it?*

1) There are lots of ways to <u>ask the time</u> and <u>say the time</u> in German. You'll need to get the hang of them.

Wie viel Uhr ist es?	*What time is it?*	Wie spät ist es?	*What time is it?*

2) Here are some <u>responses</u> to questions about the time. Learn to understand and use them yourself.

Something o'clock	
Es ist ein Uhr.	*It's 1 o'clock.*
Es ist zwei Uhr.	*It's 2 o'clock.*
Es ist zwanzig Uhr.	*It's 8pm.*

'Quarter to' and 'past', 'half past'	
Viertel nach zwei	*quarter past two*
halb drei	*half past two* ←
Viertel vor drei	*quarter to three*

Be careful — 'halb drei' means 'half to three' (i.e. half past two), not 'half past three'.

'... past' and '... to'	
zwanzig nach sieben	*twenty past seven*
fünf nach acht	*five past eight*
zehn vor zwei	*ten to two*

The 24-hour clock	
drei Uhr vierzehn	*03:14*
zwanzig Uhr zweiunddreißig	*20:32*
neunzehn Uhr fünfundfünfzig	*19:55*

Die Woche — *The week*

Montag	*Monday*
Dienstag	*Tuesday*
Mittwoch	*Wednesday*
Donnerstag	*Thursday*
Freitag	*Friday*
Samstag	*Saturday*
Sonntag	*Sunday*

Grammar — on Mondays

To say '<u>on Monday</u>', use '<u>Montag</u>' or '<u>am Montag</u>'.

To talk about something that happens regularly '<u>on Mondays</u>', use '<u>montags</u>'. Use the other days in the same way.

heute	*today*
morgen	*tomorrow*
gestern	*yesterday*
übermorgen	*the day after tomorrow*
vorgestern	*the day before yesterday*
die Woche	*week*
das Wochenende	*weekend*

Januar, Februar, März, April...

Januar	*January*	Juli	*July*
Februar	*February*	August	*August*
März	*March*	September	*September*
April	*April*	Oktober	*October*
Mai	*May*	November	*November*
Juni	*June*	Dezember	*December*

die Jahreszeit	*season*
der Frühling	*spring*
der Sommer	*summer*
der Herbst	*autumn*
der Winter	*winter*

For Lesley and Ian, summer was a state of mind...

Ich fahre im August mit meiner Familie nach Köln.	*I'm going to Cologne in August with my family.*
Es gab letzten Winter viel Eis und Schnee.	*Last winter, there was lots of ice and snow.*

in March — im März
this summer — diesen Sommer

On Wednesday — Am Mittwoch
The day before yesterday — Vorgestern

Times and Dates

You can put it all together to say the date. You can also say how often you do things.

Der Wievielte ist heute? — *What's the date today?*

Watch out for dates in German — make sure you use the <u>correct case</u>. See p.58-59 for more on cases.

In German, a date is written as a number with a dot after it. Der 4. April is said 'der vierte April'.

Es ist der 4. April.   *It's the 4th April.*

Ich komme am 20. Oktober.   *I'm coming on the 20th October.*

the 8th June — der 8. Juni

on the 14th August — am 14. August

You say this as 'am vierzehnten August'. This ending is used because it's in the dative case.

Morgen — *Tomorrow...* Gestern — *Yesterday...*

heute Morgen	*this morning*
heute Abend	*this evening*
morgen früh	*tomorrow morning*
diese Woche	*this week*
letzte Woche	*last week*
alle zwei Wochen	*every two weeks*
jeden Tag	*every day*
am Wochenende	*at the weekend*
neulich	*recently*
selten	*rarely, seldom*

Carolina ging letzte Woche in die Bibliothek.
Carolina went to the library last week.

Question

Wie oft fährst du mit dem Bus?
How often do you travel by bus?

Simple Answer

Ich fahre jeden Tag mit dem Bus.
I travel by bus every day.

Extended Answer

Ich fahre jeden Tag mit dem Bus zur Schule. Wenn das Wetter aber schön ist, fahre ich lieber mit dem Fahrrad.
I travel by bus every day to get to school. But when the weather's nice, I prefer to cycle.

Sentences can start with a time phrase...

...but if they do, remember to <u>switch the word order</u>.

Um Viertel nach zwei habe ich eine Prüfung.   *At quarter past two, I have an exam.*

At half past ten — Um halb elf

Montags besuchen wir unsere Großmutter.   *On Mondays, we visit our grandmother.*

Every two weeks — Alle zwei Wochen

Am 12. Juni zweitausendsiebzehn werde ich nach Irland fahren.   *On the 12th of June 2017, I will go to Ireland.*

At the weekend — Am Wochenende

See p.1 for help with writing numbers.

LISTENING TRACK 01

Want to learn some German time phrases? — *it's a date!*

Helena, Jan and Lisa are catching up on what they've been doing.
Listen to what they have to say and answer the questions in **English**.

e.g. When did Helena go to the museum?   on Saturday

1. Who did she go to the museum with? [1]
2. What did she think of the exhibits? [1]
3. What did Helena do the day before yesterday? [1]

4. What did Jan do at the weekend? [1]
5. How often does he play with his team? [1]
6. When is Jan's birthday? [1]
7. Where will they go for the party? [1]

Questions

You've got to be able to understand questions. You might have to ask them too.

Wann? Wo? Warum — *When? Where? Why?*

wann?	*when?*	wohin?	*where (to)?*	wie viele?	*how many?*
warum?	*why?*	woher?	*where (from)?*	was?	*what?*
wieso?	*why?*	wie?	*how?*	wer / wen / wem?	*who / whom?*
wo?	*where?*	wie viel?	*how much?*	welche/r/s?	*which (one)?*

See p.74 for when to use 'wer / wen / wem' and p.67 for more about 'welche'.

Wohin **fährst** du in Urlaub?
*Where **are you going** on holiday?*

Wie viel **Geld** hast du?
*How much **money** do you have?*

Warum **kommt** Hannelore **nicht**?
*Why **isn't** Hannelore **coming**?*

Mit **wem** sprichst du?
*With **whom** are you talking?*

All Rex could ask was 'why?'

Reverse word order to ask a question

To ask a question, just <u>change the word order</u>.

Ich kann **mitkommen.**
*I can **come along.***

→ Kann ich **mitkommen?**
*Can I **come along?***

Dein Bruder kommt **auch.**
*Your brother is coming **too.***

→ Kommt dein Bruder **auch?**
*Is your brother coming **too?***

Grammar — questions

In English, you change '<u>I can go</u>' to '<u>Can I go?</u>' to make it into a question — you can in German too. Put the <u>verb first</u> and then the <u>verb's subject</u> to show it's a question.

'Wo' can mean 'where', but it sometimes means 'what'

You can write '<u>wo</u>' in front of some <u>prepositions</u> to make lots of handy question words.

See p.75-76 for more prepositions.

<u>Wo</u>mit schreibst du? — *<u>What</u> are you writing <u>with</u>?*
<u>Wo</u>rauf läuft er? — *<u>What</u> is he walking <u>on</u>?*
<u>Wo</u>rüber sprechen Sie? — *<u>What</u> are you talking <u>about</u>?*
<u>Wo</u>zu brauche ich es? — *<u>What</u> do I need it <u>for</u>?*

Grammar — prepositions

If the preposition starts with a <u>vowel</u> — like '<u>über</u>' or '<u>auf</u>' — you need to add an '<u>r</u>' <u>between</u> it and the '<u>wo</u>'.

Learn how to say 'isn't it?'

The most common words used for this are '<u>nicht (wahr)?</u>', '<u>ja?</u>' and '<u>oder?</u>'. Just stick them on the end of a statement with a comma first and bung a question mark on the end — lovely.

Gut, nicht?
Good, isn't it?

Es ging gut, ja?
It went well, didn't it?

Du schlugst die Fliege, oder?
You hit the fly, didn't you?

Questions

In the speaking exam, you'll have to ask a question — a chance to quiz your teacher, finally.

Darf ich eine Frage stellen? — *May I ask a question?*

It's time to put the question words from page 4 into practice.

Wann kommt Emilie?
When is Emilie coming?

Warum bist du müde?
Why are you tired?

Wo ist unser Lehrer?
Where is our teacher?

Wie sagt man das auf Deutsch?
How do you say that in German?

Wie viel kostet es?
How much does it cost?

Verkaufen Sie Briefmarken?
Do you sell postage stamps?

Weißt du die Antwort?
Do you know the answer?

Hast du ein Fahrrad?
Do you have a bicycle?

Spielt ihr Tennis?
Are you playing tennis?

Woher kommen sie?
Where do they come from?

Möchten Sie eine Tüte?
Would you like a bag?

Müssen wir tanzen?
Do we have to dance?

Darf ich mehr Milch haben?
May I have more milk?

Soll sie das machen?
Should she do that?

Willst du Spanisch lernen?
Do you want to learn Spanish?

Question

Wie viele Schüler gibt
es in deiner Klasse?

*How many pupils are
there in your class?*

Simple Answer

Es gibt fünfundzwanzig Schüler.
There are twenty-five pupils.

Extended Answer

Es gibt fünfundzwanzig Schüler in meiner Klasse.
Es gibt zehn Mädchen und fünfzehn Jungen.

There are twenty-five pupils in my class.
There are ten girls and fifteen boys.

In meiner Klasse gibt es nur vierzehn Schüler.
Meine Klasse ist ziemlich klein, nicht wahr?

In my class there are only fourteen pupils.
My class is quite small, isn't it?

Gudrun often posed some rather
hair-raising questions...

SPEAKING

Knock, knock. Wer ist da? *Your German teacher...*

Here's a role-play that Finn did with his teacher.

Teacher: Was ist dein Lieblingssport, Finn?

Finn: Ich mag Eishockey.

Teacher: Das ist **ungewöhnlich**[1].
Spielst du das oft?

Finn: Ich spiele Eishockey jeden Samstag.

Teacher: Du musst sehr gut sein.
Was denkst du über Sport?

Finn: Meiner Meinung nach ist Sport sehr gut
für die **Gesundheit**[2]. Es macht auch
viel Spaß. Und Sie, mögen Sie Sport?

Teacher: Nicht so sehr — ich bin nicht sportlich.

Finn: Was machen Sie in Ihrer **Freizeit**[3]?

Teacher: Ich koche sehr gern für meine Freunde.

Grade
6-7

[1]unusual
[2]health
[3]free-time

See p.91 for more
tips on the role-play.

Tick list:
✓ tenses: present
✓ opinion phrase
✓ correct time phrase
✓ correctly formed question

To improve:
+ add a few more complex
structures, e.g. weil, dass

*Use the instructions below to prepare your
own role-play. Address your teacher as 'Sie'
and speak for about two minutes.* [15 marks]

Du sprichst mit deinem Lehrer über Sport.
- *Lieblingssport — was*
- *wie oft*
- *!*
- *? Meinung über Sport*
- *Freizeit verbringen — wie*

'!' means you'll need to answer a question you haven't prepared.
When you see '?', you need to ask a question.

Being Polite

Being polite helps you make friends and get marks. It's a win-win situation, so it's time to turn on the charm.

Learn how to start and end a conversation

To <u>reply</u> to a greeting, just <u>say it back</u>. If someone says 'Guten Tag' to you, say 'Guten Tag' to them.

Guten Morgen	*Good morning*	Auf Wiedersehen	*Goodbye*
Guten Tag	*Good day*	Bis bald	*See you later*
Guten Abend	*Good evening*	Tschüss	*Bye (informal)*
Grüß dich	*Hello (informal)*	Auf Wiederhören	*Goodbye*

'Auf Wiederhören' is used for ending telephone conversations.

Wie geht's? — *How are you?*

Grammar — formal and informal 'you'

There are <u>four</u> different ways to say '<u>you</u>' in German:

Informal 'you'

① Use '<u>du</u>' for a person who's a member of your <u>family</u>, a <u>friend</u>, or someone <u>your own age</u>.

② Use '<u>ihr</u>' for <u>two or more</u> people that you <u>know</u> well.

Formal 'you'

③ Use '<u>Sie</u>' for someone you <u>don't know</u>, or someone <u>important</u>, or someone <u>older</u> than you.

④ '<u>Sie</u>' is also used for a group of <u>two or more</u> people you <u>don't know</u>.

'Wie geht es (dir)?' is often shortened to 'Wie geht's?'.

Wie geht es dir?	*How are you? (inf.)*
Wie geht es Ihnen?	*How are you? (frml.)*
Wie geht es euch?	*How are you? (inf. plu.)*

Mir geht's...	*I'm...*
...(sehr) gut.	*...(very) well.*
...klasse / super.	*...great.*
...nicht so gut.	*...not so well.*
...(sehr) schlecht.	*...(very) ill.*

Here's what these short forms mean:
inf. ➔ informal
frml. ➔ formal
plu. ➔ plural
If you see 'sing.', it means 'singular'.

Ich hätte gern — *I would like*

1) It's more polite to say '<u>ich hätte gern</u>' (*I would like*) than '<u>ich will</u>' (*I want*).

2) Here's how to say you would like <u>a thing</u>:

Ich hätte gern das Salz.
I would like the salt.

a coffee — einen Kaffee
a book — ein Buch

See p.88 for more info on the grammar behind these phrases.

3) Here's how to say you would like <u>to do</u> something:

Sie würden gern lesen.
They would like to read.

to chat — plaudern
to travel — reisen

Ich würde gern singen.
I would like to sing.

to fly — fliegen
to paint — malen

Darf ich — *May I*

Use '<u>darf ich</u>' rather than '<u>kann ich</u>' to ask for something. It's a <u>bit more polite</u>.

May I express my sympathy for Rex on page 4...

Darf ich die Milch haben?
May I have the milk?

the newspaper — die Zeitung
the scissors — die Schere

Darf ich mich hinsetzen?
May I sit down?

play with you — mitspielen
have something to drink — etwas zu trinken haben

Being Polite

Introducing yourself properly is really important. Apologising is too — add a few tears for extra effect.

Darf ich Petra vorstellen? — *May I introduce Petra?*

Dies ist Petra.	*This is Petra.*
Herzlich willkommen!	*Welcome!*
Schön, es freut mich, Sie kennen zu lernen.	*Pleased to meet you. (frml.)*
Kommen Sie herein. Setzen Sie sich.	*Come in. Sit down. (frml.)*

Setzen Sie sich, Herr Müller!

Bitte und danke — *Please and thank you*

1) When someone says '<u>danke</u>', it's polite to say '<u>bitte</u>' or '<u>bitte schön</u>'.

bitte	*please*
danke / danke schön	*thank you*
bitte schön / bitte sehr	*you're welcome*
nichts zu danken	*it was nothing*

2) Learn these <u>phrases</u> too:

Alles Gute!	*All the best!*
Prost!	*Cheers!*
Viel Glück!	*Good luck!*

Es tut mir leid — *I'm sorry*

If you find yourself lost or you make a disastrous gaffe, don't worry — we've got some phrases for you.

Es tut mir leid.	*I'm sorry. (when you've done something wrong)*
Entschuldigung/Entschuldigen Sie!	*Excuse me. (when you want to ask someone something)*

Herzlich willkommen, Jens. Kommen Sie herein. Es tut mir leid, dass ich nicht da war.	*Welcome, Jens. Come in. I'm sorry that I wasn't there.*
Kein Problem. Es freut mich, Sie kennen zu lernen. Danke für die Einladung. Das war nett von Ihnen.	*No problem. Pleased to meet you. And thank you for the invitation. That was nice of you.*

If you're using the informal 'you', say 'Komm herein' instead.

To say 'that was nice of you' to a friend, use 'dir' instead of 'Ihnen'.

WRITING — Please may I do a writing question? Why, certainly...

Lisa has asked Josef to play in a football match on Sunday. Josef sends this email reply.

Liebe Lisa,

Grade 6-7

wie geht's? Danke, dass du mich gefragt hast, am Sonntag in der Fußballmannschaft zu spielen.

Ich würde sehr gern Fußball spielen, aber ich habe meinen Fuß **verletzt**[1]. Er ist nicht **schwer**[2] verletzt, aber ich darf keinen Sport machen.

Ich möchte aber die Mannschaft **unterstützen**[3]. Wie viel kosten die Tickets? Darf ich am Sonntag mit dir zum Fußballplatz fahren?

Es tut mir leid, dass ich nicht mitspielen kann.

Bis bald,

Josef

[1]injured
[2]badly
[3]support

Tick list:
✓ variety of polite phrases
✓ correct forms of address
✓ correctly formed questions
✓ correct word order

To improve:
+ develop each idea a bit further
+ vary sentence structure more

*Josef feiert seinen Geburtstag. Du schreibst ihm eine E-Mail. Schreib, dass du zu seiner Geburtstagsfeier nicht kommen kannst. Du musst ungefähr **40** Wörter auf **Deutsch** schreiben.* [8 marks]

Opinions

To get a decent mark, you've got to say what you think about things — anything from movies to Lederhosen.

Magst du...? — *Do you like...?*

Was hältst du von...?	*What do you think of...?*
Wie findest du...?	*How do you find...?*
Was denkst du über...?	*What do you think about...?*
Denkst du das auch?	*Do you agree?*
Was meinst du?	*What do you think?*

> The verb comes straight after 'Meiner Meinung nach' (see p.62), and it goes to the end after 'dass' (see p.64).

Meiner Meinung nach...	*In my opinion...*
Ich denke, dass...	*I think that...*
Ich halte ... für...	*I think... is...*
Ich bin für...	*I am in favour of...*

Wie findest du Fußball?	*How do you find football?*
Ich meine, dass Fußball spannend ist.	*I think that football's exciting.*

What do you think of — Was hältst du von

I believe that — Ich glaube, dass

PRO

Deine Meinung — *Your opinion*

Ich mag... (nicht)	*I (don't) like...*
Ich liebe...	*I love...*
Ich interessiere mich für...	*I'm interested in...*
Ich finde... toll.	*I find... great.*
Ich stimme zu.	*I agree.*

...interessiert mich nicht.	*...doesn't interest me.*
Ich hasse...	*I hate...*
Ich bin gegen...	*I am against...*
Ich bin (nicht) für...	*I am (not) in favour of...*
Das stimmt (nicht).	*That's (not) right.*

Grammar — '...gefällt mir (nicht)'

'Das gefällt mir' means 'I like that'.
'Gefallen' is a dative verb, so you need to use the dative case for articles and pronouns.

Fußball gefällt mir.	***I like football.***
Putzen gefällt mir nicht.	***I don't like cleaning.***

Diese Zeitschrift interessiert mich nicht.	
This magazine doesn't interest me.	

Ich halte sie für langweilig.	
I think it is boring.	

If you've got a masculine or a neuter noun, you need 'ihn' or 'es' instead.

You might not have an opinion on something, so use one of these phrases to sit on the fence:

Ich bin mir nicht sicher.	*I'm not sure.*	Es geht.	*It's all right.*
Ich bin dafür und dagegen.	*I'm for and against it.*	Es ist mir egal.	*I don't mind / care.*

Ich spiele lieber Tennis — *I prefer to play tennis*

You can add more detail by saying what you prefer. Just put in 'lieber'.

Fisch schmeckt mir nicht.	*I don't like fish.*
Ich esse lieber Fleisch.	*I'd rather eat meat.*

cheese — Käse

Ulrich spielt gern Schach.	*Ulrich likes playing chess.*
Aber er treibt lieber Sport.	*But he prefers to do sport.*

he prefers to listen to music — er hört lieber Musik

Wir hassen Hausaufgaben.	*We hate homework.*
Wir sehen lieber fern.	*We prefer to watch TV.*

We prefer to go to the cinema. — Wir gehen lieber ins Kino.

The photographer said 'Cheese!' and the lads were quick to oblige...

Opinions

This is your chance to rant about that band you hate or that film you really can't stand.

Common opinion topics

dieses Buch	*this book*
diese Zeitschrift	*this magazine*
diese Zeitung	*this newspaper*
diese Fernsehsendung	*this TV programme*
dieser Film	*this film*
dieser Schauspieler / diese Schauspielerin	*this actor / this actress*
diese Musik	*this music*
diese Band	*this band*
dieser Sänger / diese Sängerin	*this male / female singer*
diese Mannschaft	*this team*
dieses Café	*this cafe*
dieses Restaurant	*this restaurant*

Question

Was hältst du von diesem Film?
What do you think of this film?

Simple Answer

Dieser Film ist prima.
This film is great.

Extended Answer

Dieser Film ist prima, weil die Schauspieler gut sind.
This film is great because the actors are good.

Toll — *Great...* Furchtbar — *Terrible...*

Use lots of different, interesting <u>adjectives</u> to say what you think about things and pick up plenty of marks.

toll / prima	*great*	amüsant / lustig	*amusing / funny*	anstrengend	*strenuous*
gut	*good*	wunderbar	*wonderful*	kompliziert	*complicated*
schön	*lovely*	spannend	*exciting*	furchtbar / schlimm	*terrible*
wunderschön	*beautiful*	interessant	*interesting*	schlecht / schlimm	*bad*
freundlich	*friendly*	nett	*nice (person)*	entsetzlich	*terrible*
ausgezeichnet	*excellent*	(un)sympathisch	*(not) likeable (person)*	langweilig	*boring*
fantastisch	*fantastic*	billig	*cheap*	schwierig	*difficult*
fabelhaft	*fabulous*	entspannend	*relaxing*	teuer	*expensive*

Ich mag diese Band. Ich finde sie toll.
I like this band. I find it great.

Der Rock gefällt mir. Er ist sehr schick.
I like the skirt. It's very smart.

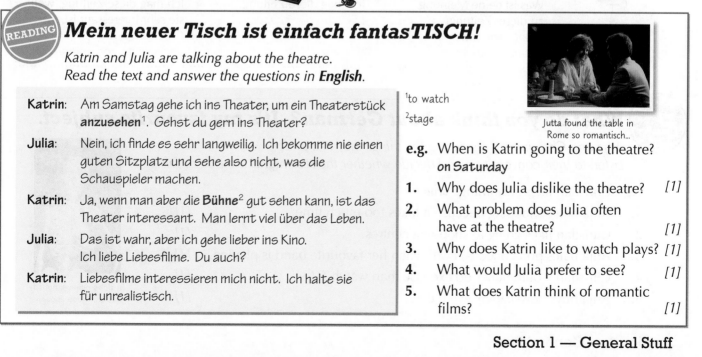

READING Mein neuer Tisch ist einfach fantasTISCH!

Katrin and Julia are talking about the theatre.
*Read the text and answer the questions in **English**.*

Katrin: Am Samstag gehe ich ins Theater, um ein Theaterstück **anzusehen**[1]. Gehst du gern ins Theater?

Julia: Nein, ich finde es sehr langweilig. Ich bekomme nie einen guten Sitzplatz und sehe also nicht, was die Schauspieler machen.

Katrin: Ja, wenn man aber die **Bühne**[2] gut sehen kann, ist das Theater interessant. Man lernt viel über das Leben.

Julia: Das ist wahr, aber ich gehe lieber ins Kino. Ich liebe Liebesfilme. Du auch?

Katrin: Liebesfilme interessieren mich nicht. Ich halte sie für unrealistisch.

[1]to watch
[2]stage

Jutta found the table in Rome so romantisch...

e.g. When is Katrin going to the theatre?
on Saturday

1. Why does Julia dislike the theatre? [1]
2. What problem does Julia often have at the theatre? [1]
3. Why does Katrin like to watch plays? [1]
4. What would Julia prefer to see? [1]
5. What does Katrin think of romantic films? [1]

Opinions

You've got to explain your views for the best marks. Add one of these nifty words to extend your sentences.

'Weil' — *Because*

'Weil' means '<u>because</u>'. When you use '<u>weil</u>', the <u>verb</u> in that part of the sentence gets shoved to the <u>end</u>.

Der Film gefällt mir. Er ist interessant.	Der Film gefällt mir, weil er interessant ist.
I like the film. It is interesting.	*I like the film because it is interesting.*
Ich finde sie sehr nett. Sie ist freundlich.	Ich finde sie sehr nett, weil sie freundlich ist.
I find her very nice. She is friendly.	*I find her very nice because she is friendly.*

'Denn' — *Because*

> You've always got to put a comma before 'weil' and 'denn'.

'Denn' means '<u>because</u>' too, but it <u>doesn't</u> change the word order.

Ich mag ihn, denn er ist wirklich nett.	*I like him because he is really nice.*
Ich liebe dieses Buch, denn es ist sehr spannend.	*I love this book because it is very exciting.*

lively — lebhaft
generous — großzügig

funny — lustig
entertaining — unterhaltsam

Don't confuse 'denn' with 'dann', which means 'then'.

Putting it all together

Include an <u>opinion phrase</u> and a super <u>adjective</u> or two — then <u>justify your view</u>.

Meiner Meinung nach ist er der beste Schauspieler, weil er talentiert ist.	Ich mag Kohl nicht, weil er geschmacklos ist. Ich esse lieber Tomaten.
In my opinion, he's the best actor because he is talented.	*I don't like cabbage because it is tasteless. I prefer eating tomatoes.*

Question	Simple Answer	Extended Answer
Was ist deine Meinung zu dieser Zeitung?	Ich mag diese Zeitung.	Ich mag diese Zeitung, weil sie sehr interessant ist.
What's your opinion of this newspaper?	*I like this newspaper.*	*I like this newspaper because it's very interesting.*

TRACK LISTENING 02 What do you think about German? It's my favourite subject.

Anja and Christian are discussing the things they like to do.
Listen to their conversation and decide whether the statements are true or false.

e.g. Christian likes swimming. **true**

1. Anja hates shopping because it takes too much time. [1]
2. Christian likes going to shopping centres. [1]
3. Anja hates pop concerts, even when her favourite band is playing. [1]
4. Christian would rather do exercise than watch TV. [1]
5. Anja buys newspapers every day. [1]

In Bob's opinion, nobody was ever good enough...

About Yourself

You never get a second chance at a first impression. So when introducing yourself in German, make sure you do it correctly. And also that the other person understands German...

Über Dich — *About Yourself*

sich vorstellen	*to introduce oneself*	buchstabieren	*to spell*
der Vorname	*first name*	geboren (am)	*born (on)*
der Familienname	*last name*	der Geburtstag	*birthday*
der Spitzname	*nickname*	das Geburtsdatum	*date of birth*
der Buchstabe	*letter (of the alphabet)*	der Geburtsort	*birthplace*

Herbert always had a whale of a time on his birthday...

Wie heißt du?
Ich heiße **Abi**.

What are you called?
I am called Abi.

My first name is... —
Mein Vorname ist...
My nickname is...—
Mein Spitzname ist...

Wie alt bist du?
Ich bin fünfzehn Jahre alt.

How old are you?
I am fifteen years old.

Wann hast du Geburtstag?
Ich habe am 1. Mai Geburtstag.

When is your birthday?
My birthday is on 1st May.

in a town —
in einer Stadt
in the countryside
— auf dem Land
near to... —
in der Nähe von...

Wo wohnst du?
Ich wohne in Leicester.

Where do you live?
I live in Leicester.

You might be asked to <u>spell</u> your name or another word. So here's how to pronounce the <u>alphabet</u>.

A — *aah*	H — *haah*	O — *ohh*	T — *tey*
B — *bay*	I — *ee*	P — *pay*	U — *ooh*
C — *tsay*	J — *yot*	Q — *kooh*	V — *fow*
D — *day*	K — *kaah*	R — *air*	W — *vey*
E — *ay*	L — *ell*	S — *ess*	X — *iks*
F — *eff*	M — *em*	ß — *ess tsett / scharfes ess*	Y — *oohpsilon*
G — *gay*	N — *en*		Z — *tsett*

Grammar — umlauts

An <u>umlaut</u> is <u>two dots</u> above a <u>vowel</u> — it's a type of <u>accent</u>. It's only used above <u>three</u> of the vowels ('<u>a</u>', '<u>o</u>' and '<u>u</u>'). It changes their sound:

a — *aah* → ä — *ay*
o — *ohh* → ö — *urr*
u — *ooh* → ü — *ew*

Words can <u>change</u> their <u>meaning</u> if they have an umlaut, for example:

sch<u>o</u>n   *already*   sch<u>ö</u>n   *beautiful*

SPEAKING

Ladies and gentlemen, please put your hands together for...

Read the question and Frank's response.
Kannst du dich der Klasse vorstellen?

[1] on the coast
[2] the beach

Guten Tag, die Klasse! Ich möchte mich vorstellen. Ich heiße Frank. Das buchstabiert man eff - air – aah - en - kaah. Ich bin jetzt sechzehn Jahre alt und ich habe am ersten Februar Geburtstag. Ich bin in Cardiff geboren. Früher habe ich in Bangor in Wales gewohnt, was schön war, weil es **an der Küste**[1] liegt und ich **den Strand**[2] liebe! Es freut mich aber sehr jetzt in Österreich zu wohnen.

Grade 6-7

Tick list:
✓ tenses: present, simple past, perfect, conditional
✓ good, clear answer

To improve:
+ use more tenses, e.g. the future
+ give reasons for all opinions

Now answer the question yourself.
You should try to talk for about two minutes. [10 marks]

My Family

It's a wonder examiners don't get bored hearing about people's siblings — family's a common exam topic...

Meine Familie — *My Family*

die Eltern	*parents*	der Bruder	*brother*	der Enkel	*grandson*
der / die Verwandte	*relative*	die Schwester	*sister*	die Enkelin	*granddaughter*
der Vater	*father*	Stief...	*step...*	der Onkel	*uncle*
die Mutter	*mother*	Halb...	*half...*	die Tante	*aunt*
der Sohn	*son*	der Großvater	*grandfather*	der Cousin	*male cousin*
die Tochter	*daughter*	die Großmutter	*grandmother*	die Cousine	*female cousin*

Grammar — compound words

In German, you can put words <u>together</u> to make <u>new</u> ones — these are called <u>compound words</u>. The <u>gender</u> of the new word is <u>determined</u> by the gender of the <u>last</u> noun.

'Stief' + 'Vater' = 'Stief<u>vater</u>'   *stepfather*

'<u>Vater</u>' is <u>masculine</u>, so it's '<u>der</u> Stiefvater'.

Sie hat zwei Brüder und eine Schwester.	*She has two brothers and a sister.*
Meine Familie ist groß. Ich habe fünfzehn Cousins!	*My family is big. I have fifteen cousins!*
Ich mag meinen Stiefvater. Er ist sehr nett.	*I like my stepfather. He's very nice.*

Wie ist deine Familie? — *What's your family like?*

You don't need to list every family member — just say something interesting about <u>a few</u> of them.

Question	Simple Answer	Extended Answer
Beschreib deine Familie.	Ich wohne bei meinen Eltern. Ich bin ein Einzelkind.	Ich habe einen Bruder. Er und seine Freundin haben eine Tochter, also bin ich Tante. Ich besuche oft meine Nichte.
Describe your family.	*I live with my parents. I'm an only child.*	*I have one brother. He and his girlfriend have a daughter, so I am an auntie. I often visit my niece.*

The German words for 'boyfriend' and 'girlfriend' are the same as for 'friend': 'Freund' and 'Freundin'. See p.15 for how to differentiate them.

Ich wohne bei meinem Vater und meiner Stiefmutter. Jedes zweite Wochenende besuche ich meine Mutter.	*I live with my dad and my stepmum. Every other weekend, I visit my mum.*
Meine Großeltern wohnen im Ausland, deswegen kann ich sie nur selten besuchen.	*My grandparents live abroad, so I can't visit them very often.*
Ich habe zwei Nichten. Die sind die Kinder meiner Schwester.	*I have two nieces. They are my sister's children.*

my stepdad — meinen Stiefvater

my half-sister — meine Halbschwester

siblings — Geschwister

nephews — Neffen

I don't see my aunt's second cousin's grandad very often...

Joachim has written about himself and his family. Translate the passage into **English***. [9 marks]*

Hallo, ich bin Joachim und ich bin in Leipzig geboren. Ich wohne mit meiner Frau, ihren zwei Töchtern und meinem Sohn. Er studiert Medizin und er will in der Zukunft Arzt werden. Eine meiner Stieftöchter hat ein Kind, das Georg heißt. Wir werden bald seinen zweiten Geburtstag feiern.

You don't need to change the names — Georg stays as Georg, not George. Look out for false friends too, e.g. 'will'.

Describing People

People come in all shapes and sizes. So here's how to describe what they look like...

Beschreiben — *To describe*

klein	*small / short*	blau	*blue*	rot	*red / ginger*		
groß	*big / tall*	grau	*grey*	die Augen	*eyes*		
dünn	*thin*	grün	*green*	die Haare	*hair*		
dick	*fat*	braun	*brown*	aussehen	*to look like*		
lang	*long*	hell	*light*	der Bart	*beard*		
kurz	*short*	dunkel	*dark*	der Schnurrbart	*moustache*		
glatt	*straight (hair)*	blond	*blonde*	die Brille	*glasses*		

Does my left eye look big in these?

Question

Wie sehen deine Familienmitglieder aus?

What do your family members look like?

Simple Answer

Meine Eltern sind groß, aber mein Bruder ist klein.
Wir alle haben rote Haare und braune Augen.

My parents are tall, but my brother is short.
We all have red hair and brown eyes.

Grammar — plurals

Some words that are <u>plural</u> in English are singular in German...
> **Sie <u>trägt</u> eine Brille.**   *She <u>wears</u> glasses.*
> **Meine Hose <u>ist</u> rot.**   *My trousers <u>are</u> red.*

...and some are <u>singular</u> in English but <u>plural</u> in German.
> **Seine Haare <u>sind</u> braun.**   *His hair <u>is</u> brown.*

Extended Answer

Meine Mutter hat lange glatte Haare und ihre Augen sind hellblau.
Mein Vater ist dünn und er hat einen Schnurrbart. Er trägt eine Brille.

My mum has long straight hair and her eyes are light blue.
My dad is thin and he has a moustache. He wears glasses.

Adjectives have to agree if they come before a noun, but they don't have to if they're after one — look at the first sentence in the extended answer. See p.66 for more.

Das Aussehen — *Appearance*

See p.68 for how to compare things.

You can extend your descriptions by <u>comparing</u> two people or saying what someone <u>doesn't have</u>.

Deine Schwester ist größer als mein Bruder.	*Your sister is taller than my brother.*	shorter — kleiner
Meine beste Freundin Sina hat kurze blonde Haare. Sie hat auch eine Tätowierung.	*My best friend Sina has short blond hair. She also has a tattoo.*	freckles — Sommersprossen
Unser Großvater hat keinen Bart, aber er hat einen grauen Schnurrbart.	*Our grandad doesn't have a beard, but he has a grey moustache.*	thick — dicken
		black — schwarzen

Listen very carefully — I shall say this only once...

TRACK LISTENING 03

*Your exchange partner Jamal is talking about his siblings. Answer the questions in **English**.*

1. How many brothers does Jamal have? [1]
2. What is his sister's hair like? [1]
3. What does Jamal's half-sister look like? Give **two** details. [2]
4. What does he think of his brother's moustache and why? [2]

Personalities

Read on for how to tell your examiner you're a hard-working, confident, helpful and generous person...

Die Persönlichkeit — *Personality*

frech	*cheeky*	schüchtern	*shy*	selbstbewusst	*self-confident*
höflich	*polite*	streng	*strict*	selbstständig	*independent*
witzig	*funny*	zuverlässig	*reliable*	unternehmungslustig	*adventurous*
lebhaft	*lively*	egoistisch	*selfish*	großzügig	*generous*
lästig	*annoying*	hilfsbereit	*helpful*	gut gelaunt	*good-tempered*

Question	**Simple Answer**	**Extended Answer**	**Grammar — adverbs**
Wie würdest du dich selbst beschreiben? *How would you describe yourself?*	Ich bin nett und großzügig, aber manchmal egoistisch. *I'm nice and generous but sometimes selfish.*	Ich weiß, dass ich manchmal gemein sein kann. Ich versuche aber, höflich und gut gelaunt zu sein. *I know that I can sometimes be mean. But I try to be polite and good-tempered.*	Using underlined adverbs is a good way to make your sentences more interesting. They're words like '<u>sehr</u>' *(very)* and '<u>ziemlich</u>' *(quite)*. See p.69 for how to <u>use</u> them.

Der Mensch — *Person*

Meine Halbschwester ist absolut zuverlässig.

My half-sister is completely reliable.

Obwohl meine Großmutter manchmal ziemlich schüchtern ist, ist sie auch lebhaft.

Although my grandmother is sometimes quite shy, she is also lively.

Mein Vater ist oft streng, also versuche ich immer höflich und hilfsbereit zu sein.

My dad is often strict, so I try to always be polite and helpful.

Meiner Meinung nach bin ich selbstbewusst und großzügig. Mein Bruder meint aber, dass ich egoistisch bin.

In my opinion, I'm self-confident and generous. But my brother thinks that I'm selfish.

hard-working — fleißig

serious — ernst

quiet — ruhig

impatient — ungeduldig

honest — ehrlich

conceited — eingebildet

WRITING

You can always rely on my sister to be annoying...

Dagmar has written an email to her British exchange partner describing her family.

Hallo,

ich dachte, dass ich dir eine kurze E-Mail schreiben würde, um dir Informationen über meine wirklich liebe Familie zu geben! Meine Mutter ist immer **äußerst**[1] gut gelaunt und geduldig, was wichtig ist, weil mein Vater echt faul ist. Ich war früher oft frech. Ich bin aber höflicher geworden. Zwei Geschwister habe ich auch — einen älteren Halbbruder, der Max heißt, und eine kleinere Schwester namens Julia. Beide sind ziemlich hilfsbereit und nett. Und bei dir? Wie ist deine Familie?

Liebe Grüße,

Dagmar

Grade 8-9

[1]extremely

Tick list:
- ✓ tenses: present, perfect, simple past, conditional
- ✓ good use of intensifiers
- ✓ complex sentences

To improve:
+ use the future tense

Du schreibst eine E-Mail über deine Familie an deine Freundin aus Deutschland. Schreib:

- *wie viele Familienmitglieder du hast*
- *etwas über ihre Persönlichkeiten*
- *was deine Meinungen über ihre Persönlichkeiten sind*
- *wie deine Persönlichkeit war, als du jünger warst*

*Du musst ungefähr **90** Wörter auf **Deutsch** schreiben. Schreib etwas über alle Punkte der Aufgabe. [16 marks]*

Relationships

Time to use a whole load of reflexive verbs to tell the examiner how well you get on with your friends. Fun...

Die Beziehung — *Relationship*

das Verhältnis	*relationship*
die Freundschaft	*friendship*
kennen lernen	*to get to know*
sich verstehen (mit)	*to get on (with)*
auskommen (mit)	*to get on (with)*
unterstützen	*to support*
sich kümmern (um)	*to look after*
sorgen (für)	*to care (for)*
sich fühlen	*to feel*
das Gefühl	*feeling*
sich streiten (mit)	*to argue (with)*
der Streit	*argument*
sich ärgern (über)	*to be annoyed (about)*
auf die Nerven gehen	*to get on one's nerves*

Grammar — reflexives (sich + verb)

Reflexives use 'sich'. 'Sich' changes for different people.

ich — mich	wir — uns
du — dich	ihr — euch
er / sie / es — sich	Sie — sich

Ich verstehe **mich** gut mit Finn. *I get on well with Finn.*

See p.79 for more on reflexive verbs.

Grammar — Freund / Freundin

'Freund/in' can mean 'friend' or 'boyfriend' / 'girlfriend'. It's usually obvious which, but if you want to make it clear:
- say 'mein Freund / meine Freundin' for boyfriend / girlfriend
- use 'ein Freund / eine Freundin von mir' for a friend

Eng befreundet sein — *To be close friends*

Sie verstehen sich ganz gut mit ihren Stiefgeschwistern.

They get on very well with their step-siblings.

← argue — streiten sich

Obwohl ich normalerweise gut mit meinen Eltern auskomme, ärgere ich mich manchmal über ihre strengen Regeln.

Although I usually get on well with my parents, I sometimes get annoyed about their strict rules.

← I sometimes just want to be alone — möchte ich manchmal einfach allein sein

Ich bin der Meinung, dass Freundschaften sehr wichtig sind. Ich fühle mich glücklich, wenn ich mit Freunden zusammen bin.

In my opinion, friendships are very important. I feel happy when I'm with friends.

← good / comfortable — wohl

relaxed — entspannt

 ## Friends are for life, not just for GCSE German...

Read the questions and the sample answers.

1. Was kannst du auf dem Foto sehen?

Ich sehe zwei Mädchen auf dem Foto. Sie sehen sehr glücklich aus, da sie viel lachen. Vielleicht hat eins einen Witz erzählt.

Grade 8-9

2. Verstehst du dich gut mit deinen Freunden? Warum (nicht)?

Ab und zu geht meine beste Freundin mir auf die Nerven, weil sie oft ärgerlich ist. Letzte Woche haben wir uns gestritten. Normalerweise verstehen wir uns aber sehr gut.

3. Ist es wichtig, gute Freundschaften zu haben? Warum (nicht)?

Ja, es ist wichtig, weil meine Freunde mich unterstützen. Aber es ist mir noch wichtiger, ein gutes Verhältnis mit meiner Familie zu haben. Sie werden immer für mich sorgen.

Tick list:
✓ tenses: present, perfect, future
✓ opinions justified

To improve:
+ use the subjunctive
+ use more connectives, e.g. 'obwohl'

Now try responding to questions 2 and 3 yourself. Speak for about 2 minutes. [10 marks]

Partnership

Marriage might seem a long way off at the mo, but it's not long till you might have to talk about it in the exam...

Die Partnerschaft — *Partnership*

in einem Verhältnis sein	*to be in a relationship*	heiraten	*to marry*
ledig	*single*	verheiratet	*married*
sich verloben	*to get engaged*	die Hochzeit	*wedding*
der / die Verlobte	*fiancé(e)*	sich trennen	*to separate*
die Ehe	*marriage*	getrennt	*separated*
die gleichgeschlechtliche Ehe	*same-sex marriage*	sich scheiden lassen	*to get divorced*
die zivile Partnerschaft	*civil partnership*	geschieden	*divorced*

Das Eheleben — *Married life*

Question	Simple Answer	Extended Answer
Möchtest du heiraten?	Ich glaube, dass ich heiraten will. Ich bin aber noch jung.	Ich bin noch nicht sicher, ob ich heiraten will. Meiner Meinung nach kann man jemandem treu bleiben, ohne verheiratet zu sein.
Do you want to get married?	*I think that I want to get married. But I'm still young.*	*I'm still not sure if I want to get married. In my opinion, you can stay faithful to someone without being married.*

Grammar — future

The <u>future</u> tense can be made with a form of '<u>werden</u>' and an <u>infinitive</u> verb.

Ich <u>werde</u> ihn <u>heiraten</u>.
I <u>will marry</u> him.

Wir <u>werden</u> ledig <u>bleiben</u>.
We <u>will stay</u> single.

See p.84 for more.

Ich denke, dass ich wahrscheinlich in der Zukunft ledig bleiben werde.	*I think that I will probably remain single in the future.*
Ich bin geteilter Meinung über die Ehescheidung.	*I have mixed opinions about divorce.*
Es ist mir wichtig, dass homosexuelle Leute auch heiraten dürfen.	*It's important to me that homosexual people are also allowed to marry.*

unmarried — unverheiratet

same-sex partnership — die gleichgeschlechtliche Partnerschaft

single parenthood — alleinstehende Elternschaft

READING

I do, I do, I do have an opinion on marriage... honest...

Lies diesen Ausschnitt aus dem Buch 'Effi Briest', geschrieben von Theodor Fontane. Sag, ob die Aussagen richtig (R), falsch (F) oder nicht im Text (NT) sind.

Danach ging Effi zu ihren Freundinnen; die Zwillinge warteten schon auf sie im Garten.

„Nun, Effi", sagte Hertha, während alle drei zwischen den blühenden Blumen spazierten, „nun, Effi, wie geht es dir eigentlich?"

„Oh, ganz gut. Wir nennen uns schon du und beim Vornamen. Er heißt Geert."

„Ich mache mir aber Sorgen um dich. Ist er denn **der Richtige**[1]?"

„Natürlich ist er der Richtige. Das verstehst du nicht, Hertha. Jeder ist der Richtige. Natürlich muss er **von Adel**[2] sein und gut aussehen."

„Bist du wirklich ganz glücklich?"

„Wenn man zwei Stunden verlobt ist, ist man immer ganz glücklich. Wenigstens denk ich es mir so."

[1] 'the one'
[2] noble

e.g. Die Zwillinge sitzen im Wohnzimmer. **F**

1. Effi kennt Geert seit einem Jahr. [1]

2. Effis Freundin Hertha ist ängstlich um sie. [1]

3. Die Liebe ist das Wichtigste für Effi. [1]

4. Effi freut sich auf die Hochzeit. [1]

Music

Music's a great topic to talk about, so make sure you get this page stuck in your head like an annoyingly catchy tune — known as 'ein Ohrwurm' *(an earworm)* in German. Fun fact.

Die Musik — *Music*

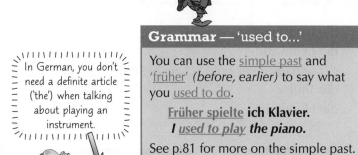

spielen	*to play*
singen	*to sing*
hören	*to listen to*
das Instrument	*instrument*
der Musiker / die Musikerin	*musician*
der Sänger / die Sängerin	*singer*
bevorzugen	*to prefer*
teilnehmen an	*to take part in*
die Band	*band*
der Chor	*choir*
das Orchester	*orchestra*
das Konzert	*concert*
abonnieren	*to subscribe to*

In German, you don't need a definite article ('the') when talking about playing an instrument.

Grammar — 'used to...'

You can use the simple past and 'früher' *(before, earlier)* to say what you used to do.

Früher spielte ich Klavier.
I used to play the piano.

See p.81 for more on the simple past.

Ich spiele Geige in einem Orchester.	*I play the violin in an orchestra.*
Ich singe oft in einem Chor.	*I often sing in a choir.*
Wir nehmen an einem Konzert teil.	*We're taking part in a concert.*

Question	**Simple Answer**	**Extended Answer**
Spielst du ein Instrument?	Ja, ich spiele Gitarre und Trompete.	Ja, ich spiele Querflöte seit vier Jahren. Als ich jünger war, spielte ich Klarinette und ich sang in einer Band.
Do you play a musical instrument?	*Yes, I play the guitar and the trumpet.*	*Yes, I've been playing the flute for four years. When I was younger, I played the clarinet and I sang in a band.*

Der Musikgeschmack — *Taste in music*

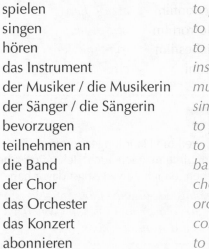

Here are a few sentences for talking about your taste in music:

Ich höre am liebsten Rockmusik.	*I like listening to rock music the most.*
Er hörte früher Popmusik, aber jetzt mag er Volksmusik.	*He used to listen to pop music, but now he likes folk music.*
Am allerliebsten höre ich Musik auf meinem Handy.	*More than anything else, I like listening to music on my mobile.*
Je öfter ich in einem Orchester spiele, desto mehr mag ich klassische Musik.	*The more often I play in an orchestra, the more I like classical music.*

pop music — Popmusik
rap — Rapmusik
classical music — klassische Musik
streams — überträgt / streamt
CD player — CD-Spieler
in a brass band — in einer Blaskapelle

LISTENING TRACK 04

You've got to listen to a load of spiel about music now...

A group of music pupils are introducing themselves and talking about their tastes in music. Match each of them with one of the statements below.

e.g. Johanna... *G*

1. Johanna... *[1]*
2. Preethi... *[1]*
3. Jürgen... *[1]*

A. ...has a sister who likes pop music.
B. ...hates listening to rock music.
C. ...thinks classical music is relaxing.
D. ...finds rock concerts too loud.
E. ...likes classical music for ballet.
F. ...found a rap song terrible.
G. ...went to a rock concert.
H. ...enjoys playing the same songs.

Cinema

Give your German some Hollywood glamour by learning this page so you can talk about your favourite films.

Das Kino — *Cinema*

die Eintrittskarte	*ticket*	die Werbung	*advert(s)*
die Leinwand	*screen*	der Actionfilm	*action film*
der Schauspieler / die Schauspielerin	*actor / actress*	der Horrorfilm	*horror film*
der Trailer	*trailer*	der Liebesfilm	*romantic film*
die Handlung	*plot*	der Krimi	*crime film*

Und bitte!

Question

Was für Filme siehst du gern?

What kind of films do you like watching?

Simple Answer

Liebesfilme gefallen mir am besten, weil sie immer ein Happy End haben.

I like romantic films best because they always have a happy ending.

Extended Answer

Ich sehe gern Krimis, weil die Handlungen immer spannend sind. Actionfilme mag ich auch. Ich würde aber keinen Horrorfilm sehen, da ich zu viel Angst davor habe.

I like watching crime films because the plots are always exciting. I also like action films. But I wouldn't watch a horror film because I'm too scared of them.

Obwohl die Werbung mich ärgert, gehe ich gern ins Kino.

Although the adverts annoy me, I like going to the cinema.

Die Trickeffekte sind immer beeindruckend.

The special effects are always impressive.

Grammar — ins / im Kino

'In' is a preposition. It can take the accusative or the dative case.

If there's movement, use the accusative. 'Ins' is short for 'in das'.

Wir gehen ins Kino. *We're going to the cinema.*

If there's no movement, use the dative. 'Im' is short for 'in dem'.

Wir sind im Kino. *We're in the cinema.*

See p.76 for more on cases and prepositions.

Gehst du gern ins Kino? — *Do you like going to the cinema?*

Adjectives are useful when you're giving your opinion of a film. Luckily, we've written a few below...

Ich habe einen Horrorfilm gesehen.

I have watched a horror film.

Den Film fand ich sehr bewegend.

I found the film very moving.

Ich gehe gern ins Kino, da ich es besser finde, Filme auf der Kinoleinwand zu sehen. Die Eintrittskarten sind aber teuer.

I like going to the cinema because I find it better to watch films on the big screen. But the tickets are expensive.

a sci-fi film — einen Science-Fiction-Film	
a comedy — eine Komödie	
a romcom — eine romantische Komödie	

boring — langweilig	
fascinating — faszinierend	
scary — gruselig	
entertaining — unterhaltsam	

WRITING *Exams...if only they were fantasy films...*

Translate the following passage into **German**. *[12 marks]*

I like going to the cinema. Last weekend, I went to the cinema with my friend and we watched an action film. I found the film really exciting although it was a little bit scary. Next week, I will watch a comedy with my sister because she prefers funny films. In the future, I would like to be an actor.

Lisa didn't get the advert job — it was a no-frills product...

TV

From the big screen to the small... Don't be a couch potato — learn the vocab so you'll do well in the exam...

Das Fernsehen — *Television*

fernsehen	*to watch television*	die Nachrichten	*news*
der Sender	*TV channel*	der Dokumentarfilm	*documentary*
die Sendung	*TV programme*	der / die Promi	*celebrity*
die Serie	*series*	umschalten	*to switch channels*
die Seifenoper	*soap opera*	senden	*to broadcast*

Mein Bruder sieht gern die Nachrichten, aber ich würde lieber einen Krimi sehen.

My brother likes watching the news, but I would rather watch a crime show.

a quiz show — eine Quizsendung
a reality show — eine Reality-Show

Man kann viel von Dokumentarfilmen lernen.

You can learn a lot from documentaries.

Ich sehe lieber Serien ohne Werbung, deswegen bevorzuge ich die Sender, die keine Werbung zeigen.

I prefer watching series without adverts, so I prefer the TV channels that don't show adverts.

You can also use 'anschauen' for 'to watch'. It's a separable verb — see below.

Was kommt im Fernsehen? — *What's on TV?*

Question

Was hast du neulich im Fernsehen angeschaut?

What have you watched recently on TV?

Simple Answer

Ich schaute gestern einen interessanten Dokumentarfilm an.

I watched an interesting documentary yesterday.

Extended Answer

Die Nachrichten schaue ich jeden Tag an, da es wichtig ist zu wissen, was in der Welt passiert.

I watch the news every day because it's important to know what's happening in the world.

Grammar — fernsehen

'Fernsehen' *(to watch TV)* is a separable verb. It splits into two parts — 'fern' and 'sehen'.

Ich sehe fern.   *I watch TV.*

In the perfect tense, the 'ge-' prefix is added to the start of the second part to make the past participle. The verb is written as one word.

Ich habe ferngesehen.   *I have watched TV.*

If it's used in the infinitive form, it's not separated.

Ich will fernsehen.   *I want to watch TV.*

See p.86 for more on separable verbs.

Blimey, I've got 'Quadrataugen'* after all that...

Read Marlene's opinions about TV, then decide if each statement is true, false or not in the text.

Ich sehe regelmäßig fern, meistens abends oder am Wochenende. Am liebsten sehe ich Musiksendungen oder Quizsendungen, weil ich sie unterhaltsam finde. Leider gibt es auch viele langweilige Sendungen im Fernsehen, wie zum Beispiel die Nachrichten oder Sportsendungen. Die interessieren mich überhaupt nicht. Auch finde ich die Werbung im Fernsehen furchtbar. Ich schalte dann schnell auf eine andere Sendung um. Meine Schwester sitzt stundenlang vor dem Fernseher, obwohl meine Mutter dann **schimpft**[1], weil es nicht gut für die Augen ist. Aber das ist ihr egal. Ich glaube, dass sie **fernsehsüchtig**[2] ist.

[1]complains   [2]addicted to television

e.g. Marlene rarely watches TV.   **false**

1. She doesn't like news or sports programmes.   *[1]*

2. Marlene finds adverts on TV very interesting.   *[1]*

3. Her sister doesn't spend much time watching TV.   *[1]*

4. Marlene never watches TV with her sister.   *[1]*

*'Quadrataugen' means 'square eyes'.

Food

Apologies, this page is pretty heavy on vocab. But it's all about food, so that makes it more palatable...

Das Essen — *Food*

das Gemüse	*vegetables*	das Fleisch	*meat*	die Wurst	*sausage*
die Tomate	*tomato*	das Rindfleisch	*beef*	die Bratwurst	*fried sausage*
die Karotte	*carrot*	das Schweinefleisch	*pork*	das Hähnchen	*chicken*
der Pilz	*mushroom*	der Schinken	*ham*	das (Wiener) Schnitzel	*veal / pork cutlet*
die Zwiebel	*onion*				
die Kartoffel	*potato*	der Fisch	*fish*	das Brot	*bread*
die Erbsen	*peas*	der Lachs	*salmon*	das Brötchen	*bread roll*
das Obst	*fruit*	der Thunfisch	*tuna*	der Reis	*rice*
der Apfel	*apple*	die Meeresfrüchte	*seafood*	die Nudeln	*pasta*
die Birne	*pear*			die Pommes frites	*chips*
die Banane	*banana*	lecker	*tasty*	die Suppe	*soup*
die Apfelsine	*orange*	ekelhaft	*disgusting*		
die Ananas	*pineapple*	scharf	*hot / spicy*	die Milch	*milk*
die Nuss	*nut*	süß	*sweet*	der Käse	*cheese*

die Butter *butter*   das Ei *egg*

Was isst du gern? — *What do you like eating?*

Question	**Simple Answer**	**Extended Answer**
Was isst du am liebsten?	Ich esse sehr gern Fisch, allerdings mag ich keinen Lachs.	Mein Lieblingsgericht ist Reis mit Tomatensoße und Erbsen. Ich finde es lecker. Da ich Vegetarier bin, esse ich kein Fleisch.
What do you like eating the most?	*I really like eating fish. However, I don't like salmon.*	*My favourite meal is rice with tomato sauce and peas. I find it tasty. Because I'm a vegetarian, I don't eat meat.*

Grammar — essen *(to eat)*

'Essen' is irregular. Here are its forms in the present tense:

ich esse   **wir essen**
du isst   **ihr esst**
er / sie / es isst   **Sie / sie essen**

In the simple past, the stem is 'aß'. The past participle in the perfect tense is 'gegessen'.

Ich finde, dass Rindfleisch ekelhaft schmeckt. — *I find that beef tastes disgusting.*   *delicious* — köstlich

Ich mag kein scharfes Essen. — *I don't like hot / spicy food.*   *salty* — salziges / *sweet* — süßes / *fatty* — fettiges

Ich esse gern Bananen, aber Ananasse sind zu süß für meinen Geschmack. — *I like eating bananas, but pineapples are too sweet for my taste.*

Ich habe Hunger und ich habe Durst. — *I'm hungry and I'm thirsty.*   You can also say 'ich bin hungrig / durstig'.

I've always been a bit Lachs about healthy eating...

(TRACK LISTENING 05)

Elsa, Sonja and Moritz are discussing their food preferences. Complete the sentences.

e.g. Elsa has decided not to eat... A. fatty food. B. vegetables. C. meat and fish. **C**

1. Elsa particularly likes...   A. apples. B. pineapples. C. bananas. *[1]*
2. Sonja's favourite food is... A. sausages. B. pork. C. roast potatoes. *[1]*
3. Sonja doesn't usually like... A. red meat. B. fried food. C. pork. *[1]*
4. Moritz enjoys...   A. cooking. B. eating out. C. eating healthily. *[1]*

Eating Out

And for dessert, a page on eating out. Restaurants are a popular topic for the role-play, so get learning...

Das Restaurant — *Restaurant*

reservieren	*to book*
die Kneipe / das Gasthaus	*pub*
das Café	*café*
die Karte	*menu*
die Vorspeise	*starter*
das Hauptgericht	*main course*
die Nachspeise	*dessert*
bestellen	*to order*
der Kellner / die Kellnerin	*waiter / waitress*
die Selbstbedienung	*self-service*
bezahlen	*to pay*
die Rechnung	*bill*
Bedienung inbegriffen	*service included*
das Trinkgeld	*tip*

Grammar — asking questions

To ask questions, reverse the order of the verb and the subject.
Du hast den Lachs bestellt. *You ordered the salmon.*
Hast du den Lachs bestellt? *Did you order the salmon?*
Question words like 'wie viel' *(how much)* are also handy:
Wie viel kostet das Bier? *How much does the beer cost?*
See p.4-5 for more on asking questions.

Ich hätte gern die Suppe.	*I would like the soup.*
Könnte ich bitte die Rechnung haben?	*Could I please have the bill?*
Ich würde gern bezahlen.	*I would like to pay.*

Was möchten Sie essen? — *What would you like to eat?*

Zum Hauptgericht hätte ich gern das Tagesgericht.

For the main course, I would like the dish of the day. ← the steak — das Steak

Ich esse gern im Restaurant, weil man Speisen probieren kann, die man zu Hause nie kochen würde. Letzte Woche habe ich chinesisches Essen probiert.

I like eating in restaurants because you can try dishes that you would never cook at home. Last week, I tried Chinese food. → Indian — indisches / Thai — thailändisches

Ich will mich beschweren. Die Suppe ist kalt.

I want to complain. The soup is cold. ← burnt — angebrannt

 SPEAKING

Time for the reckoning — let's ask for the bill...

Here's an example role-play. Ciara is ordering food in a restaurant.

Kellner: Guten Abend. Haben Sie eine Reservierung? *Grade 6-7*

Ciara: Leider habe ich keine Reservierung. Haben Sie einen Tisch frei? Ich würde gern am Fenster sitzen.

Kellner: Natürlich. Was nehmen Sie?

Ciara: Ich hätte gern ein großes Glas stilles Mineralwasser und eine Bratwurst mit Pommes frites. Das finde ich immer sehr lecker.

Kellner: Sonst noch etwas?

Ciara: Ja, ich nehme auch dazu eine Portion Erbsen.

Kellner: Möchten Sie auch gleich die Nachspeise bestellen?

Ciara: Nein. Das werde ich später machen. Vielen Dank.

Tick list:
✓ variety of tenses
✓ correct question

To improve:
+ use the past tense
+ use a subordinate clause

Prepare the role-play card below. Use 'Sie' and speak for about two minutes. [15 marks]

Sie sind in einem Restaurant.
- *Tisch reserviert — für wie viele Personen*
- *Schon hier gegessen — wann*
- *Etwas zu trinken (ein Detail)*
- *? Tagesgericht*
- *!*

Sport

Whether you're sporty or not, you need to know some sporty vocab. Ready? On your marks, get set, GO!

Der Sport — *Sport*

spielen	*to play*	der Fußball	*football*	der Basketball	*basketball*
gewinnen	*to win*	das Rugby	*rugby*	Fahrrad fahren	*to cycle*
verlieren	*to lose*	das Tennis	*tennis*	segeln	*to sail*
trainieren	*to train*	der Federball	*badminton*	Ski fahren	*to ski*
joggen / laufen	*to run*	das Hockey	*hockey*	spazieren gehen	*to go for a walk*
schwimmen	*to swim*	der Korbball	*netball*	wandern	*to hike*

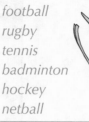

Question
Wie oft treibst du Sport?

How often do you do sport?

Simple Answer
Ich treibe ziemlich selten Sport. Ich wandere aber gern — ich wandere jedes Wochenende.

I don't do sport very often. I like hiking though — I go hiking every weekend.

Extended Answer
Ich bin Mitglied einer Fußballmannschaft. Wir trainieren dreimal pro Woche und jeden zweiten Samstag spielen wir ein Match. Letztes Mal haben wir gewonnen und ich habe ein Tor geschossen.

I'm a member of a football team. We train three times a week, and every other Saturday, we play a match. Last time, we won and I scored a goal.

Welche Sportarten treibst du? — *What sports do you do?*

It's useful to talk about <u>where</u> and <u>how often</u> you do sport, as well as what you <u>think</u> of different sports.

das Schwimmbad	*swimming pool*
das Stadion	*stadium*
der Sportplatz	*sports field*
das Sportzentrum	*sports centre*
das Fitnessstudio	*gym*
der Verein	*club*
die Mannschaft	*team*
das Training	*training*
das Rennen	*race*
der Wettbewerb	*competition*

Grammar — adverbs of time

<u>Adverbs of time</u> are words like '<u>now</u>' and '<u>rarely</u>'. You use them to say <u>when</u> and <u>how often</u> you do something. They usually go <u>after</u> the <u>first verb</u> in a German sentence.

Ich spiele <u>regelmäßig</u> Hockey.   *I play hockey <u>regularly</u>.*

Wir haben <u>immer</u> verloren.   *We <u>always</u> lost.*

You can also put them at the <u>beginning</u> of a sentence to emphasise <u>when</u> something happens.

   <u>Gestern</u> **bin ich geschwommen.**   <u>*Yesterday*</u>, *I swam.*

For more about adverbs of time, see p.70.

Ich bin Mitglied eines Fahrradvereins.

I'm a member of a cycling club. ← of a gymnastics club — eines Turnvereins

Auf dem Sportplatz treibe ich Leichtathletik. Wir trainieren zweimal pro Woche.

On the sports field, I do athletics. We train twice a week. ← I play cricket — spiele ich Kricket

Ich spiele Hockey, weil ich es mag, Mitglied einer Mannschaft zu sein.

I play hockey because I like being a member of a team. ← I prefer training with other people — ich lieber mit anderen Leuten trainiere

Wenn wir ein Match im Stadion spielen, bin ich immer nervös.

When we play a match in the stadium, I'm always nervous. ← I'm usually excited — bin ich normalerweise begeistert

Ich bevorzuge es, Sport draußen zu treiben. Deswegen gehe ich nie ins Fitnessstudio.

I prefer to do sport outside. Therefore, I never go to the gym. ← in the fresh air — an der frischen Luft

Sport

Here's another page on sport — get stuck in so you can win a gold medal in your exam...

Was hältst du von Sport? — *What do you think about sport?*

Meiner Meinung nach ist Sport super, weil er mich nach dem Schulstress entspannt.

In my opinion, sport is great because it relaxes me after the stress of school.

it helps me to stay healthy — er mir hilft, gesund zu bleiben

Ich halte Sport für fantastisch, da ich ihn mit meinen Freunden treiben kann.

I think sport is fantastic because I can do it with my friends.

Sport treiben interessiert mich überhaupt nicht, obwohl ich gern Fußball im Fernsehen sehe.

Doing sport doesn't interest me at all although I like watching football on TV.

the Olympics — die Olympischen Spiele

Grammar — word order

Think about <u>word order</u> when you use <u>conjunctions</u>. The order stays the <u>same</u> with <u>coordinating conjunctions</u>, e.g. '<u>aber</u>' (but).

Ich mag Hockey, <u>aber</u> ich <u>finde</u> Rugby langweilig.
I like hockey, <u>but</u> I <u>find</u> rugby boring.

The order <u>changes</u> with <u>subordinating conjunctions</u>, e.g. '<u>weil</u>' (because). The <u>verb</u> moves to the <u>end</u>.

Ich mag Hockey, <u>weil</u> es spannend <u>ist</u>.
I like hockey <u>because</u> it <u>is</u> exciting.

For more on word order, see p.62.

Question

Schaust du Sport im Fernsehen an?
Do you watch sport on TV?

Simple Answer

Ja, ich finde ihn total spannend!
Yes, I find it really exciting!

Extended Answer

Ich schaue Sport fast nie im Fernsehen an, da ich es ein bisschen langweilig finde. Ich denke aber, dass es nützlich ist, weil man viel von den Profis lernen kann.

I hardly ever watch sport on TV because I find it a bit boring. But I think it's useful because you can learn a lot from the pros.

WRITING ## Be a good sport and have a go at this exam question...

Your exchange partner Martin has sent an email discussing which sports he does and why.

Hallo,

Grade **8-9**

wie geht's? Ich treibe im Moment ziemlich viel Sport, weil er mich entspannt und mir total Spaß macht. Ich spiele jeden Mittwoch mit meinen Freunden Fußball auf dem Sportplatz und **außerdem**[1] gehe ich regelmäßig Rad fahren und schwimmen. Früher war ich Mitglied in einem Tennisverein, aber jetzt interessiere ich mich mehr für Mannschaftssport, da ich sehr **kontaktfreudig**[2] bin. In der Zukunft möchte ich öfter Ski fahren gehen, weil ich nur zweimal in meinem Leben Ski gefahren bin. Und du? Treibst du oft Sport?

Liebe Grüße,

Martin

Du schreibst eine E-Mail über Sport. Schreib:

- welche Sportarten du machst
- wie oft du Sport treibst
- was deine Meinungen über diese Sportarten sind
- ob es einen Sport gibt, den du in der Zukunft ausprobieren möchtest

Du musst ungefähr **90 Wörter** auf **Deutsch** schreiben. Schreib etwas über alle Punkte der Aufgabe. [16 marks]

[1] in addition
[2] sociable

Tick list:
✓ tenses: present, perfect, simple past, conditional
✓ adverbs
✓ opinions justified

To improve:
+ use more adjectives

Technology

Technology is a hot topic — it's always changing. Examiners love talking about it, so revise this section carefully. There's a lot of specific vocab, and you need to be able to talk about the pros and cons of technology.

Die Technologie — *Technology*

der Computer	*computer*	die Kamera	*camera*	hochladen (sep.)	*to upload*
der Laptop	*laptop*	schicken	*to send*	herunterladen (sep.)	*to download*
der Tablet-PC	*tablet*	simsen	*to text*	löschen	*to delete*
das Handy	*mobile phone*	empfangen	*to receive*	(aus)drucken	*to print (out)*
das Smartphone	*smartphone*	anrufen	*to call*	der Drucker	*printer*

Mir ist es wichtig, mein Handy immer dabei zu haben.

It's important to me to always have my phone with me.

Ich simse, um mit meinen Freunden in Kontakt zu bleiben.

I text in order to stay in contact with my friends.

Grammar — um... zu...

You can use the '<u>um...zu...</u>' construction to say '<u>in order to...</u>' or '<u>to...</u>' something. '<u>Zu</u>' goes near the <u>end</u> of the sentence, just before the <u>infinitive</u>.

Ich benutze mein Handy, <u>um</u> mit meinen Freunden <u>zu</u> chatten.
I use my mobile phone <u>to</u> chat with my friends.

Question

Ist es dir wichtig, das neueste Smartphone zu haben?

Is it important to you to have the latest smartphone?

Simple Answer

Ja. Heutzutage entwickelt sich die Technologie so schnell. Man braucht das Neueste, um aktuell zu bleiben.

Yes. These days technology develops so fast. You need the latest one to stay up to date.

Extended Answer

Nein. Ich habe schon ein Smartphone. Es hat keinen Sinn, ein neues mit einer Kamera zu kaufen, die nur ein kleines bisschen besser ist oder womit man schneller das Internet surfen kann.

No. I already have a smartphone. It doesn't make sense to buy a new one with a camera that's only slightly better or one that you can surf the Internet faster with.

Auf meinem Laptop — *On my laptop*

Ich mache meine Hausaufgaben auf meinem Laptop.

I do my homework on my laptop.

Meiner Meinung nach sind Tablet-PCs viel praktischer als Laptops, denn sie sind so viel kleiner.

In my opinion, tablets are much more practical than laptops because they're so much smaller.

Ich lade Fotos auf meinen Laptop hoch, die ich mit meiner Kamera gemacht habe.

I upload photos onto my laptop that I've taken with my camera.

Ich lösche die Fotos, die ich nicht mag, und ich drucke den Rest aus.

I delete the photos that I don't like and I print out the rest.

I play video games — Ich spiele Videospiele

they have touchscreens — sie haben Touchscreens

they're not as heavy — sie sind nicht so schwer

my tablet — meinem Tablet-PC

my smartphone — meinem Smartphone

save — speichere

Question

Verbringst du zu viel Zeit auf deinem Laptop?

Do you spend too much time on your laptop?

Simple Answer

Ja vielleicht, aber ich brauche ihn für meine Hausaufgaben.

Yes, perhaps, but I need it for my homework.

Extended Answer

Ja, ich verbringe ungefähr drei Stunden pro Tag auf meinem Laptop. Ich sollte mich mehr bewegen.

Yes, I spend around three hours a day on my laptop. I should get more exercise.

Technology

As for the Internet... who can imagine life without it now? Make sure you learn the technical vocab below so you can give accurate opinions. You're just one click away from mastering this page...

Das Internet — *Internet*

die Website	*website*
die Startseite	*homepage*
online	*online*
die (E-)Mail	*email*
die E-Mail-Adresse	*email address*
das Konto	*account*
erforschen	*to research*
streamen	*to stream*
das Netzwerk	*network*
das WLAN	*Wi-Fi*
das Passwort	*password*
schützen	*to protect*
die Sicherheit	*security*

Punctuation is useful for spelling out an email or webpage address.

der Punkt	*full stop*
der Bindestrich	*hyphen*
der Schrägstrich	*forward slash*
der Unterstrich	*underscore*

Hannes would protect his mailbox to the bitter end...

Es geht mir auf die Nerven, wenn das Netzwerk nicht funktioniert.

It gets on my nerves when the network doesn't work.

Die Sicherheit online ist sehr wichtig. Man braucht ein Passwort, um sein Postfach zu schützen.

Security online is very important. You need a password to protect your mailbox.

Wofür benutzt du das Internet? — *What do you use the Internet for?*

Question

Könntest du ohne das Internet leben?

Could you live without the Internet?

Simple Answer

Nein, ich benutze das Internet für alles, zum Beispiel Einkaufen.

No, I use the Internet for everything, for example shopping.

Extended Answer

Schon als Kind habe ich das Internet benutzt, also finde ich es schwer, mir das Leben ohne Internet vorzustellen. Aber ich könnte es schaffen.

Even as a child, I used the Internet, so I find it hard to imagine life without it. But I could do it.

Ich benutze Suchmaschinen, um Informationen zu finden.

I use search engines in order to find information.

visit lots of web pages — besuche viele Webseiten

Ich verbringe viel Zeit beim Internetsurfen.

I spend a lot of time on the Internet.

waste — verschwende

Ich spiele Videospiele online. Das kann ich mit Leuten auf der ganzen Welt tun.

I play video games online. I can do this with people all over the world.

chat in forums — chatte in Foren

Man kann im Internet viel erforschen. Das finde ich nützlich, wenn ich meine Hausaufgaben mache.

You can research a lot on the Internet. I find that useful when I do my homework.

find out — herausfinden

read the news online — lese die Nachrichten online

Ich streame Musik.

I stream music.

WRITING — *Ah, the Internet — only useful for watching cat videos really...*

Translate the text into **German**. [12 marks]   Have a look at the grammar box on p.26 for help.

I have a mobile and a tablet. I use the Internet every day. I use it to do my homework. I recently downloaded lots of films. I text twenty or thirty times per day. In future, I will try to use my phone less often and do more sport.

Social Media

Ah, social media... wonderful for procrastination. Unfortunately, you do have to revise it as well...

Das soziale Netzwerk — *Social network*

das Konto	*account*
chatten	*to chat online*
die Nachricht	*message*
das Postfach	*mailbox*
teilen	*to share*
das Video	*video*
das Foto	*photo*
gehören zu	*to belong to*
die Gruppe	*group*
bloggen	*to blog*

Grammar — hochladen, herunterladen

'Laden' *(to load)* is an irregular verb, so 'hochladen' *(to upload)* and 'herunterladen' *(to download)* are irregular too. You can put 'hoch' or 'herunter' in front of 'laden'. Learn the forms of 'laden'.

ich lade	*I load*	wir laden	*we load*
du lädst	*you load*	ihr ladet	*you load*
er / sie / es lädt	*he / she / it loads*	Sie / sie laden	*you / they load*

Make sure you can use it in the past tense too:

Ich lud die Fotos hoch. *I uploaded the photos.*

Wir haben es heruntergeladen. *We have downloaded it.*

So oft wie möglich chatte ich mit meinen Freunden. | *As often as possible, I chat online with my friends.*

Ich bin Blogger(in) und gehöre zu mehreren sozialen Netzwerken. Ich teile Fotos von meinen Ferienreisen. | *I am a blogger and I belong to several social networks. I share photos of my travels.*

Die Vorteile sind... — *The advantages are...*

You need to be able to discuss the pros of social networks. Think about your own opinion.

Ich bin der Meinung, dass soziale Netzwerke nützlich sind, weil man ganz einfach mit Freunden und Familie in Kontakt bleiben kann. | *In my opinion, social networks are useful because you can really easily stay in contact with friends and family.*

Es gefällt mir, dass man zu verschiedenen Gruppen gehören kann. | *I like that you can belong to different groups.*

Ich schicke fast keine E-Mails mehr, weil ich mit meinen Freunden chatte. | *I hardly send emails any more because I chat online with my friends.*

organise an event — eine Veranstaltung organisieren

meet people who share the same interests — Leute, die die gleichen Interessen teilen, kennen lernen

keep up to date with important news — auf dem Laufenden über wichtige Neuigkeiten bleiben

READING *Got the message? Let's move on... to some questions...*

Read Brigitte's email about her use of social media and then answer the questions below.

Hallo,

ich wollte dir meine Meinungen über soziale Netzwerke geben. Meiner Meinung nach sind soziale Netzwerke sehr nützlich, um in Kontakt mit Familie und Freunden zu bleiben. Obwohl ich nur mit fünfzig Leuten auf einem sozialen Netzwerk befreundet bin, ist das genug. Ich chatte nur mit Leuten, die ich persönlich kenne. Ich genieße es sehr und bin abends immer online. Meine Eltern denken aber, dass ich zu viel Zeit auf dem Computer verbringe.

Und wie ist es bei dir? Bist du oft online?

Brigitte

e.g. Why does Brigitte think social networks are useful?

Because they help her to stay in contact with family and friends.

1. How many friends does she have on a social network? [1]

2. Whom does she chat to? [1]

3. When is she online? [1]

4. What do her parents think? [1]

The Problems with Social Media

This page is going to sound a bit like your parents going on about how dangerous social media is — sorry!

Soziale Medien — *Social media*

RISK OF OVERSHARING

der Vorteil	*advantage*	die Einstellung	*setting*	gefährlich	*dangerous*
der Nachteil	*disadvantage*	das Privatleben	*private life*	missbrauchen	*to abuse / misuse*
die App	*app*	das Risiko	*risk*	das Cyber-Mobbing	*cyber-bullying*

Question

Denkst du, dass soziale Netzwerke gefährlich sein können?

Do you think that social networks can be dangerous?

Simple Answer

Ich glaube, dass man vorsichtig sein muss. Im Allgemeinen sind sie allerdings nicht gefährlich.

I think that you have to be careful. In general, however, they're not dangerous.

Extended Answer

Solange man die Einstellungen vorsichtig verändert, muss man nicht alles teilen. Daher kann man sicher sein. Aber es ist nicht möglich, das Cyber-Mobbing zu kontrollieren.

As long as you carefully change the settings, you don't have to share everything. Therefore, you can be safe. But it's not possible to control cyber-bullying.

Die Nachteile sind... — *The disadvantages are...*

Ein Nachteil von sozialen Netzwerken ist, dass es schwierig ist, das Privatleben zu schützen.

Allerdings ist es möglich, die Einstellungen zu verändern, sodass niemand auf persönliche Informationen zugreifen kann.

Es gibt immer ein Risiko, dass jemand ein soziales Netzwerk missbrauchen könnte. Manche Leute benutzen sie für Cyber-Mobbing.

A disadvantage of social networks is that it's difficult to protect your private life.

However, it's possible to change the settings so no one can access personal information.

There's always a risk that someone could misuse a social network. Some people use them for cyber-bullying.

SPEAKING — *Procrastinating on Fakebook? Tell your parents it's revision...*

Read Rohan's answer to this question.

Was sind für dich die Vor- und Nachteile sozialer Medien?

Wie viele Leute meiner Generation bin ich **abhängig**[1] vom Internet und ich benutze jeden Tag soziale Netzwerke. Für Jugendliche sind soziale Netzwerke wichtiger als E-Mail. Meine Freunde und ich teilen viele Fotos und Neuigkeiten, was ich sehr mag, weil ich immer auf dem Laufenden über ihre Leben bin. Wenn ich von zu Hause wegziehe, wird es noch nützlicher sein.

Allerdings weiß ich, dass ich immer vorsichtig sein muss, da es ein Risiko gibt, dass **Fremde**[2] meine Fotos sehen könnten. Ich versuche, mein Konto sicher zu halten, indem ich regelmäßig die Einstellungen kontrolliere. Ein Freund von mir war letztes Jahr **Opfer**[3] des Cyber-Mobbings. Es war furchtbar.

Grade 8-9

[1]dependent
[2]strangers
[3]victim

Tick list:
✓ varied word order
✓ good relevant vocab
✓ complex structures, e.g. 'indem...'

To improve:
+ use more adjectives if relevant

Now try answering these questions. Try to talk for about two minutes. [10 marks]

- *Wie benutzt du soziale Netzwerke?*
- *Was sind deiner Meinung nach die Vorteile sozialer Netzwerke?*
- *Und was sind die Nachteile?*

Helmut was enthralled by his wife's social media posts...

Festivals in German-Speaking Countries

You might not feel too festive with all this revision, but read on and you'll find out how to jazz up your next celebration with some groovy traditions from the German-speaking world. Viel Spaß....

Frohe Weihnachten! — *Merry Christmas!*

Heiliger Abend	*Christmas Eve*	schmücken	*to decorate*
Weihnachten	*Christmas*	der Weihnachtsbaum	*Christmas tree*
Heilige Drei Könige	*Epiphany*	der Adventskranz	*advent wreath*
feiern	*to celebrate*	anzünden	*to light*
bekommen	*to receive*	die Kerze	*candle*
das Geschenk	*present*	die Weihnachtslieder	*Christmas carols*
sich freuen auf	*to look forward to*	die Weihnachtskarte	*Christmas card*

Viele Familien gehen am Heiligen Abend in die Kirche.

Lots of families go to church on Christmas Eve.

have a big festive meal — haben [...] ein großes Festessen

Ich singe gerne Weihnachtslieder.

I like singing Christmas carols.

decorate the Christmas tree — schmücken den Weihnachtsbaum
invite the whole family — laden die ganze Familie ein

Meine Eltern stellen die Geschenke unter den Weihnachtsbaum.

My parents put the presents under the Christmas tree.

Weihnachten in Deutschland — *Christmas in Germany*

Christmas is a bit <u>different</u> in Germany. On 6th December, <u>Sankt Nikolaus Tag</u> (*St Nicholas' Day*) is celebrated. Children leave their shoes at the door, and if they've been good, they are filled with <u>treats</u>.

Deutsche Kinder stellen ihre Schuhe vor die Tür, damit Sankt Nikolaus ihnen Süßigkeiten und Nüsse schenken kann.

German children put their shoes at the door so that St Nicholas can give them presents of sweets and nuts.

In Deutschland packt man die Geschenke am Heiligen Abend aus.

In Germany, people unwrap the presents on Christmas Eve.

Grammar — sich freuen auf

Use '<u>sich freuen auf</u>' + <u>accusative</u> to say you're <u>looking forward to</u> something. Don't forget to choose the right <u>reflexive pronoun</u>.

Ich <u>freue mich auf</u> den Lebkuchen.
I <u>am looking forward to</u> the gingerbread.
Er <u>freut sich auf</u> den Weihnachtsmarkt.
He's <u>looking forward to</u> the Christmas market.

Oh I wish it could be Weihnachten every day...

Read the passage about Werner's Christmas and answer the questions in **English**.

Bei uns beginnt die Weihnachtsfeier am Anfang Dezember. Jedes Jahr macht meine Mutter einen Adventskranz mit vier Kerzen. Jede Woche zünde ich eine Kerze an und die Letzte zündet meine Schwester am Heilgen Abend an. Mein Vater kauft uns immer einen großen Weihnachtsbaum und wir alle helfen, den Baum zu schmücken. Meine Oma backt Lebkuchen und Kekse mit Sternen und Herzen aus Schokolade darauf.

e.g. When do Werner's family start celebrating Christmas? **at the beginning of December**

1. What does his mother do every year? [1]
2. Who lights the last candle and when does this happen? [2]
3. What does Werner's father do? [1]
4. Who decorates the tree? [1]
5. Describe what Werner's grandmother bakes. [2]

Festivals in German-Speaking Countries

Now you're getting into the party mood, here are some other festivals to talk about. It's my gift to you...

Ostern — *Easter*

Karfreitag	*Good Friday*	die Auferstehung	*resurrection*	das Osterei	*Easter egg*
Ostersonntag	*Easter Sunday*	die Christen	*Christians*	verstecken	*to hide*
Jesu Tod	*Christ's death*	religiös	*religious*	der Osterhase	*Easter bunny*

Christen feiern Jesu Auferstehung.　　　　*Christians celebrate the resurrection of Christ.*

Der Osterhase bringt die Ostereier.　　　　*The Easter bunny brings the Easter eggs.*

Die Eltern verstecken die Schokoladeneier.　*Parents hide the chocolate eggs.*

Andere religiöse Feste — *Other religious festivals*

islamisch	*Muslim*	christlich	*Christian*
jüdisch	*Jewish*	hinduistisch	*Hindu*

Ich bin Jude / Jüdin.　*I am Jewish.* ← Sikh — Sikh　　*Hindu* — Hindu

Ich feiere Chanukka.　*I celebrate Hanukkah.* ← the festival of lights — das Lichterfest

Grammar — religions

In German, you need a different word for Christian, Muslim, Jewish etc. depending on whether it describes a person or a thing.

Ich bin Moslem(in). (*I am Muslim.*)

ein islamistisches Fest (*a Muslim festival*)

Question	Simple Answer	Extended Answer
Welche Feste feierst du?	Ich feiere das Fest des Fastenbrechens.	Zu Hause feiern wir das Fest des Fastenbrechens. Es kommt nach Ramadan, einer Fastenzeit, die einen Monat dauert. Wir laden unsere Verwandten zu einem Festessen ein.
Which festivals do you celebrate?	*I celebrate Eid.*	*At home we celebrate Eid. It follows Ramadan, a period of fasting, which lasts a month. We invite our relatives to a festive meal.*

Karneval / Fasching — *Carnival*

Karneval (or Fasching) is a celebration before Lent. There are carnival parades and parties. Some of the biggest events take place on Rosenmontag (*Rose Monday*), which is the Monday before Ash Wednesday.

Es gibt einen Umzug.　　　*There is a procession.*

Die Leute verkleiden sich.　*People put on fancy dress.*

 Life's just one long party when you're learning German...

Listen to this podcast about Karneval and answer the questions in **English**.

e.g. What other German names are there for Karneval? Fasching / Fastnachtszeit

1. In which countries is Karneval celebrated? *[3]*
2. How is Karneval described? *[2]*
3. Where are the biggest parties? *[1]*
4. What do most people do? *[1]*

Festivals in German-Speaking Countries

The German Bundesländer (Federal States) have a lot of say in which days are public holidays.

Der Tag der Deutschen Einheit — *The Day of German Unity*

Am 3. Oktober feiert man die Wiedervereinigung Deutschlands.

On the 3rd October, people celebrate the reunification of Germany.

Der Tag der Deutschen Einheit ist ein Feiertag.

The Day of German Unity is a public holiday.

Es gibt ein großes Feuerwerk.

There is a big fireworks display.

> Germany was divided into East and West Germany after the Second World War.
>
> Official reunification took place in 1990, creating the Bundesrepublik Deutschland (*Federal Republic of Germany*).

Weitere Feste — *More festivals*

Silvester	*New Year's Eve*
der Neujahrstag	*New Year's Day*
der Valentinstag	*Valentine's Day*
das Pfingsten	*Whitsuntide*
der Maifeiertag	*May Day*

Grammar — use 'zu...' for 'at...' or 'on...'

With <u>single</u> words like '<u>Pfingsten</u>' (*Whitsuntide*), German uses '<u>zu</u>' to say '<u>at</u>' or '<u>on</u>':

zu Silvester   **on** New Year's Eve

If the word ends in '<u>Tag</u>' or a <u>day of the week</u>, use '<u>am</u>':

am Neujahrstag   **on** New Year's Day

Der erste Januar ist ein Feiertag. Die meisten Leute arbeiten nicht.

The first of January is a public holiday. Most people don't work.

> Many shops are shut — Viele Geschäfte haben zu

Ich habe eine Einladung zu einer Party bei einem Freund bekommen.

I have received an invitation to a party at a friend's house.

> at my neighbour's house — bei meinem Nachbarn

Question	**Simple Answer**	**Extended Answer**
Was hältst du vom Valentinstag?	Ich finde ihn blöd und sinnlos.	Meiner Meinung nach ist Valentinstag zu kommerziell. Die Geschäfte wollen einfach Geld machen. Es ist völlig unnötig.
What do you think of Valentine's Day?	*I think it's stupid and pointless.*	*In my opinion, Valentine's Day is too commercial. The shops just want to make money. It's completely unnecessary.*

SPEAKING

Sid carries the gift nervously — it's the present tense...

Laura is talking to her teacher about festivals.

Grade 6-7

Teacher: Was ist dein Lieblingsfest?

Laura: Ich mag den Maifeiertag, weil alles schön bunt und laut ist. In meinem Dorf gab es dieses Jahr viele Feierlichkeiten.

Teacher: Kannst du mir ein deutsches Fest beschreiben?

Laura: Am 6. Dezember feiern die Deutschen den Sankt Nikolaus Tag. Die Kinder stellen ihre Schuhe vor die Tür und bekommen Süßigkeiten.

Teacher: Was hältst du von Karneval?

Laura: Es klingt sehr spannend. Ich würde gern daran teilnehmen. Welche Feste feiern Sie?

Teacher: Ich feiere immer das Lichterfest. Feierst du auch ein religiöses Fest?

Laura: Ich bin zwar nicht religiös, aber ich feiere Ostern mit meiner Familie.

Tick list:
- ✓ range of adjectives
- ✓ tenses: present, simple past, conditional

To improve:
- + use more subject-specific vocab
- + use more complex sentences

Now answer the questions yourself. Address your teacher as 'Sie' and talk for about 2 minutes. [15 marks]

The Home

Home sweet home; home is where the heart is; there's no place like home... you might not agree with the clichés, but you do need to be able to talk about your abode (humble or otherwise).

Wie ist dein Haus? — *What's your house like?*

das Haus	*house*	der Wohnblock	*block of flats*
die Wohnung	*flat*	das Einfamilienhaus	*detached house*
das Doppelhaus	*semi-detached house*	am Stadtrand	*on the outskirts*
das Reihenhaus	*terraced house*	im Stadtzentrum	*in the town centre*

Howard's new home ensured the perfect amount of company...

Ich wohne in einem alten Haus. — *I live in an old house.*

modern — modernen   *new* — neuen
big — großen   *small* — kleinen

Wir ziehen in ein Reihenhaus um. — *We're moving into a terraced house.*

farm house — Bauernhaus

Meine Wohnung liegt in der Nähe von einem Park und den Geschäften. — *My flat is near a park and the shops.*

the motorway — der Autobahn
a train station — einem Bahnhof

Wie sehen die Zimmer aus? — *What do the rooms look like?*

das Wohnzimmer	*living room*	die Vorhänge	*curtains*
das Badezimmer	*bathroom*	die Möbel	*furniture*
das Esszimmer	*dining room*	das Bett	*bed*
das Schlafzimmer	*bedroom*	das Etagenbett	*bunk bed*
die Küche	*kitchen*	der Schrank	*cupboard*
die Wände	*walls*	der Stuhl	*chair*
der Teppich	*carpet*	der Garten	*garden*

Grammar — identifying plurals

You can use grammatical <u>markers</u> like <u>articles</u> and <u>verb forms</u> to tell whether a noun is <u>plural</u> or not.

<u>Die</u> Zimmer <u>sind</u> schön.
The rooms <u>are</u> nice.

<u>Das</u> Zimmer <u>ist</u> schön.
The room <u>is</u> nice.

Die Küche ist hell und geräumig. — *The kitchen is bright and spacious.*

on the ground floor — im Erdgeschoss

Im Schlafzimmer habe ich einen riesigen Kleiderschrank. — *In the bedroom, I have a huge wardrobe.*

a double bed — ein Doppelbett

Mein Haus hat einen Garten. — *My house has a garden.*

a conservatory — einen Wintergarten

READING — Well, it's only a small mansion, but it's home...

*Read this extract from 'Der Wolf und die sieben jungen Geißlein' by the Brothers Grimm. Answer the questions in **English**.*

Wer aber hereinkam, war der Wolf. Die **Geißlein**[1] hatten Angst und wollten sich verstecken. Das erste sprang unter den Tisch, das zweite ins Bett, das dritte in den Ofen, das vierte in die Küche, das fünfte in den Schrank, das sechste unter die Waschschüssel, das siebente in den **Kasten**[2] der Wanduhr. Aber der Wolf fand sie und **verschluckte**[3] eins nach dem andern. Nur das jüngste in dem Uhrkasten fand er nicht.

[1](goat) kids
[2]case
[3]swallowed

e.g. What did the goat kids want to do?
They wanted to hide from the wolf.

1. Where did the first kid go? *[1]*
2. List three other hiding places mentioned. *[3]*
3. Which kid did the wolf **not** find? *[1]*

What You Do at Home

Whether you spring out of bed as soon as the alarm clock sounds, or huddle under the duvet for as long as possible, you need to be able to talk about your daily routine.

Mein Tagesablauf — *My Daily Routine*

aufwachen	*to wake up*	sich waschen	*to have a wash*	sich anziehen	*to get dressed*
aufstehen	*to get up*	sich rasieren	*to shave*	frühstücken	*to have breakfast*
sich duschen	*to have a shower*	sich schminken	*to put on make-up*	verlassen	*to leave (house)*

Ich stehe **um acht Uhr** auf.   *I get up at 8 o'clock.*

Oft **esse ich mit meiner**   *I often have lunch*
Familie zu Mittag.   *with my family.*

Nach dem Essen mache   *After the meal,*
ich meine Hausaufgaben.   *I do my homework.*

Grammar — reflexive verbs

Verbs like 'sich anziehen' are <u>reflexive</u> — they need a <u>pronoun</u> (mich, dich etc.). The pronoun needs to agree with the subject. See p.73 for more.

ich wasche <u>mich</u>	***I wash*** <u>*myself*</u>
du wäschst <u>dich</u>	***you wash*** <u>*yourself*</u>
wir waschen <u>uns</u>	***we wash*** <u>*ourselves*</u>

Was machst du zu Hause? — *What do you do at home?*

Josh needed specialist equipment to tidy his room.

putzen / sauber machen	*to clean*	den Tisch decken	*to lay the table*
vorbereiten	*to prepare*	kochen	*to cook*
aufräumen	*to tidy up*	die Mahlzeit	*meal / mealtime*
Staub saugen	*to vacuum*	abwaschen	*to wash up*
Staub wischen	*to dust*	(sich) kümmern (um)	*to look after*

Jeden Tag decke ich den Tisch.   *Everyday, I set the table.*

Am Wochenende putze ich das   *At the weekend, I clean*
Badezimmer und sauge Staub.   *the bathroom and vacuum.*

I look after my brother — kümmere ich mich um meinen Bruder

I cook dinner — koche ich das Abendessen

Question

Musst du zu Hause helfen?
Do you have to help at home?

Simple Answer

Ja, ich wische Staub und manchmal räume ich mein Zimmer auf.
Yes, I dust and sometimes, I tidy my room.

Extended Answer

Nachdem ich aufgestanden bin, muss ich an Schultagen das Frühstück für meinen Halbbruder vorbereiten. Ich dusche mich kurz danach, wasche ab und mache die Küche sauber. Abends koche ich für meine Familie. Ich Ärmster!

After I have got up, I have to prepare breakfast for my half-brother on schooldays. I have a shower shortly afterwards, wash up and clean the kitchen. In the evening, I cook for my family. Poor me!

READING — *I just need to tidy my sock drawer before I start revising...*

Translate this blog post into **English**. *[9 marks]*

Ich wohne bei meinen Eltern in einer Wohnung in Berlin. Ich muss jeden Tag zu Hause helfen. Das nervt mich. Nach der Schule putze ich die Wohnung. Ich muss auch für meine Eltern kochen, weil sie spät nach Hause kommen. Gestern räumte ich mein Zimmer auf. Ich hoffe, dass ich am Wochenende mehr Freizeit haben werde.

Talking About Where You Live

Oh! I do like to live beside the seaside... or up a hill... or in the country. Wherever — just gimme the marks.

Wo wohnst du? — *Where do you live?*

Don't forget to give an <u>opinion</u> about where you live — it'll help you impress the examiner.

auf dem Land	*in the countryside*	am Meer	*by the sea*	im Norden	*in the north*
an der Küste	*on the coast*	in den Bergen	*in the mountains*	die Großstadt	*city*
die Gegend	*region*	in der Nähe von	*near (to...)*	die Stadt	*town*

Ich wohne in einem Dorf im Süden.

I live in a village in the south.

> in a town — in einer Stadt

Meine Heimatstadt liegt in Nordwales.

My home town is in north Wales.

> in north-east England — in Nordostengland

Die Landschaft um mein Haus ist schön und grün.

The landscape around my home is beautiful and green.

> mountainous — bergig
> flat — flach

Ich finde meine Stadt sehr lebendig und interessant.

I think my town is very lively and interesting.

> boring — langweilig
> peaceful — ruhig

Was gibt es in deiner Stadt? — *What is there in your town?*

Es gibt viele Geschäfte, darunter eine Bäckerei und eine Metzgerei.

There are lots of shops, including a bakery and a butcher's.

> a chemist's — eine Drogerie

Der Hafen ist einen Besuch wert.

The harbour is worth a visit.

> The cathedral — Der Dom

Es ist immer was los.

There's always something going on.

> never — nie

Ich gehe oft zum Markt.

I often go to the market.

> to the library — in die Bibliothek

Es gibt ein paar historische Gebäude.

There are a few historic buildings.

> green spaces — Grünanlagen

 WRITING ## *My mum said not to tell strangers where I live, sorry...*

Ein Freund hat dir eine E-Mail geschickt, in der er seine Stadt beschreibt.

Grüß dich! Ich wohne in Köln, das eine schöne Großstadt in Westdeutschland ist. Es gibt hier so viel für Besucher zu tun, weil es riesig ist — wir haben über 1 000 000 Einwohner! Obwohl Köln in der Vergangenheit eine Industriestadt war, ist es jetzt viel sauberer und moderner, glaube ich. Wir haben viele Sehenswürdigkeiten, wie interessante Museen, einen beeindruckenden Dom und viele geräumige Grünanlagen, wo man spazieren gehen kann. Ich liebe das Leben hier, weil immer viel los ist. Wie ist dein Wohnort? Gibt es dort viel zu tun?

Grade 8-9

Tick list:
- ✓ tenses: present, simple past
- ✓ opinions justified using 'weil...'
- ✓ varied adjectives

To improve:
- + say what the town might be like in the future
- + use the conditional to say whether you'd recommend the town to visitors

Du schreibst eine Antwort auf die E-Mail. Schreib etwas über die folgenden Punkte:

- *wo du wohnst*
- *deine Meinung zu der Gegend und zu den Sehenswürdigkeiten.*

*Schreib ungefähr **90** Wörter auf **Deutsch**. Beantworte die beiden Teile der Frage. [16 marks]*

Clothes Shopping

Clothes — you might not be interested in them, but you'd be in trouble without them.

Ich brauche neue Klamotten — *I need new clothes*

das Hemd	*shirt*
das T-Shirt	*T-shirt*
der Pullover	*sweater*
das Kleid	*dress*
der Rock	*skirt*
die Hose (sing.)	*trousers*
die Jeans (sing.)	*jeans*
Schuhe	*shoes*
die Sportschuhe	*trainers*
die Klamotten	*clothes*
anprobieren	*to try on*
ausgeben	*to spend (money)*
Schlange stehen	*to queue*
pleite (sein)	*(to be) skint*
der Kunde	*(male) customer*
die Kundin	*(female) customer*

Im Einkaufszentrum kaufe ich Röcke und T-Shirts.
At the shopping centre, I buy skirts and T-shirts.

Ich gebe mein Geld für Schuhe und Kleider aus.
I spend my money on shoes and dresses.

Ich trage gern bunte Kleidungsstücke.
I like wearing colourful clothes.

Kleider stehen mir nicht. Ich trage lieber Hosen.
Dresses don't suit me. I prefer to wear trousers.

Grammar — stehen + dative

To say that something suits someone, use 'stehen' with the dative.

Die Farbe steht dir sehr gut. *The colour really suits you.*
Das rote Hemd steht ihm nicht. *The red shirt doesn't suit him.*

Gehst du gern einkaufen? — *Do you like going shopping?*

Ja, ich gehe jedes Wochenende einkaufen. *Yes, I go shopping every weekend.*

Einkaufen mit Freunden macht Spaß. *Shopping with friends is fun.*

from time to time — ab und zu

is boring — ist langweilig

Question

Gehst du gern einkaufen?

Do you like going shopping?

Simple Answer

Ja, Einkaufen gefällt mir sehr gut. Meistens kaufe ich Sportschuhe und Jeans.

Yes, I really like shopping. I mostly buy trainers and jeans.

Extended Answer

Ja, sehr gern. Ich gebe mein ganzes Geld für Klamotten aus. Gestern war ich in der Stadt unterwegs und habe viele schöne Sachen in den Geschäften gesehen. Schließlich habe ich mich für einen blauen Rock entschieden — ich werde ihn sehr oft tragen. Meine Eltern denken, dass ich Geld verschwende, aber Einkaufen macht mir Spaß!

Yes, absolutely. I spend all my money on clothes. Yesterday, I was out and about in town and saw lots of lovely things in the shops. In the end, I decided on a blue skirt — I'll wear it a lot. My parents think that I waste money, but I find shopping fun!

I'm not materialistic; I just like having loads of stuff...

TRACK LISTENING 07

Jana spricht über Einkaufen. Beantworte die Fragen auf **Deutsch**.

e.g. In welchem Geschäft ist Jana einkaufen gegangen?   **im Kaufhaus**

1. Welche zwei Kleidungsstücke hat Jana gekauft?   [2]
2. Was fand sie positiv im Geschäft?   [1]
3. Warum kann sie erst am Samstag einen Pullover kaufen?   [1]
4. Was würde Jana gern kaufen, wenn sie mehr Geld hätte?   [1]

'Erst' can be used to mean 'not until'.

Sebastian always had something up his sleeve...

Shopping

This page is positively awash with practical phrases you can use during your next German shopping spree.

Was möchten Sie? — *What would you like?*

das Kilo	*kilo(gram)*	die Schachtel	*box*
das Gramm	*gram*	eine Menge	*a lot of*
das Pfund	*pound*	ein paar	*a few*
die Scheibe	*slice*	ein bisschen	*a bit*
das Stück	*piece*	einige	*some*
die Flasche	*bottle*	mehrere	*several*
die Dose	*can / tin*	ungefähr	*about*
das Gewicht	*weight*	viel / viele	*a lot / many*

Sizes are different in some EU countries. E.g.:

Women's Clothes

Size	8	10	12	14	16	18
Größe	34	36	38	40	42	44

Men's Shoes (Rough equivalents)

Size	6	7	8	9	10	11
Größe	40	41	42	43	44	45

Ich möchte eine Hose. Meine Größe ist 36.   *I'd like a pair of trousers. I'm a size 10.*

Ich hätte gern eine Schachtel Pralinen.   *I'd like a box of chocolates.*

> Another way to say 'I would like...' is 'Ich hätte gern...'. See p.6 for more.

Ich hätte gern drei Kilo Käse — *I would like three kilos of cheese*

Question

Kann ich Ihnen helfen?

Can I help you?

Simple Answer

Ich möchte ein Kilo Orangen und eine Menge Kirschen.

I'd like a kilo of oranges and a lot of cherries.

Extended Answers

Ja, ich hätte gern ein großes Stück Käse, ein paar Eier und zwei Scheiben Schinken. Ich nehme bitte auch eine Dose Cola und eine Tüte Chips dazu.

Yes, I'd like a large piece of cheese, a few eggs and two slices of ham. I'll have a can of cola and a bag of crisps with that as well, please.

Ja, ich möchte hundert Gramm Erbsen, viermal Zwiebeln und einige Pilze, wenn Sie welche haben. Etwas Süßes wäre auch schön. Was für Kuchen haben Sie?

Yes, I'd like a hundred grams of peas, four onions and some mushrooms if you have any. Something sweet would be nice too. What sort of cake do you have?

Grammar — viel / viele

'Viel' (a lot of) is used with singular or uncountable nouns. 'Viele' (many) is used with plural nouns.

Ich brauche viel Obst.   *I need a lot of fruit.*

Ich möchte viele Kekse.   *I'd like many biscuits.*

WRITING — *OK, I'll admit it — the chocolate teapot was an impulse buy...*

Lies diese Kritik eines neuen Geschäfts.

Letzte Woche besuchte ich ein Geschäft und ich hatte viele Probleme. Ich hatte schon eine neue Hose gekauft. Aber ich wollte ein blaues Hemd anprobieren. Ich trage Größe 38. Der Verkäufer brachte mir aber ein Hemd, das viel zu groß war! Zehn Minuten später gab er mir ein weißes Hemd, das ich sehr hässlich fand. Ich bin mit diesem Kleidergeschäft gar nicht zufrieden.

Grade 6-7

Tick list:

✓ tenses: present, simple past, pluperfect

✓ variety of phrases

To improve:

+ use a 'weil' clause
+ add a future or conditional
+ use more adjectives

Schreib eine eigene Kritik eines Geschäfts.
Schreib etwas über die folgenden Punkte:

- *was du gekauft hast*
- *deine Meinung dazu*

*Schreib ungefähr **90** Wörter auf **Deutsch**.*
Beantworte die beiden Teile der Frage. [16 marks]

In the Shop

Once you've found that perfect novelty hat, you need to make sure you can actually pay for it.

Ein gutes Angebot — *A good deal*

Get your head around <u>euro coins</u> and <u>notes</u> in advance and avoid embarrassment at the till...

das Taschengeld	*pocket money*	die Kasse	*till*
anbieten	*to offer*	die Quittung	*receipt*
das Angebot	*offer*	wechseln	*to change (money)*
der Ausverkauf	*sale*	das Bargeld	*cash*
das Sonderangebot	*special offer*	das Kleingeld	*small change*
preiswert / günstig	*good value*	das Geldstück	*coin*
der Rabatt	*discount*	der Geldschein	*note*
kostenlos / gratis	*free of charge*	das Euro-Stück	*euro coin*
der Preis	*price*	der Euro-Schein	*euro note*

There are <u>100 cents</u> in a <u>euro</u>.

If something costs <u>5,50 €</u>, you say the price like this: <u>fünf Euro fünfzig Cent</u>.

Agnes could never resist a bargain, especially when it came to clogs...

Wie viel kostet das? — *How much does it cost?*

These phrases could come in handy if you get a <u>shopping role-play</u> in the speaking exam.

Kann ich mit Karte bezahlen oder akzeptieren Sie nur Bargeld?
Can I pay by card, or do you only accept cash?

Die Hose ist zu teuer, aber der Rock ist günstig.
The trousers are too expensive, but the skirt is good value.

Ich muss mein Geld in Euro wechseln.
I need to change my money into euros.

Ich will mein Geld zurück.
I want my money back.

Grammar — separable verbs

<u>Separable verbs</u> have <u>two</u> parts, e.g. 'anbieten' (*to offer*). See p.86 for more. In the <u>present</u> tense, the <u>separable prefix</u> goes to the <u>end</u> of the clause:

Der Laden bietet einen Rabatt an.
The shop offers a discount.

In the <u>perfect</u> tense, the 'ge' goes in the <u>middle</u> of the two parts of the verb:

Er hat es mir kostenlos angeboten.
He offered it to me free of charge.

SPEAKING *Do you accept magic beans...?*

Read the conversation below. Jonas is on holiday in Austria and wants to buy a few things.

Verkäufer: Guten Tag. Kann ich Ihnen helfen?

Jonas: Ich hätte gern vier Scheiben Käse, hundert Gramm Kartoffelsalat und zwei Brötchen, bitte. Ich nehme auch eine Flasche Wasser. Wie viel kostet das?

Verkäufer: Das macht zehn Euro fünfzig. Sonst noch etwas?

Jonas: Ja, kann ich bitte ein Stück Schokoladenkuchen haben? Er sieht lecker aus. Ich würde ihn gern probieren.

Verkäufer: Ja, natürlich.

Jonas: Darf ich bitte eine Quittung haben?

Verkäufer: Ja, bitte schön. Auf Wiedersehen.

Grade 6-7

Tick list:
✓ tenses: present, conditional
✓ opinion phrase
✓ correctly formed questions

To improve:
+ use conjunctions to link the sentences

Use the instructions below to prepare your own role-play. Address the assistant as 'Sie' and speak for about two minutes. [15 marks]

Sie sind am Markt in Österreich.
* *drei Produkte*
* *Ihre Meinung (zwei Punkte)*
* *? Rabatt*
* *!*
* *kein Kleingeld*

Giving and Asking for Directions

Feeling like you could do with a little direction? Look no further, my friend...

Wo ist...? — *Where is...?*

der Bahnhof	*train station*	das Kino	*cinema*	der Park	*park*
der Busbahnhof	*bus station*	die Post	*post office*	die Apotheke	*pharmacy*

liegen	*to be situated*	(nach) links	*(to the) left*	gegenüber	*opposite*
drüben	*over there*	(nach) rechts	*(to the) right*	neben	*near*
weg	*away*	geradeaus	*straight on*	bleiben	*to stay*
überqueren	*to cross (road)*	mitten in	*in the middle of*	nehmen	*to take*

Entschuldigung. Wo ist der Markt, bitte?

Gehen Sie hier links, gehen Sie geradeaus
und der Markt ist auf der rechten Seite.

Ich bin hier fremd. Wie
komme ich zu der Post?

Geh hier rechts und nimm
die erste Straße links.

Excuse me. Where is the market please?

*Go left here, go straight on and the
market is on the right-hand side.*

*I am a stranger here. How
do I get to the post office?*

*Go right here and take the
first street on the left.*

> Don't forget to use the polite form 'Sie' for people who are older than you.

Wie weit ist es? — *How far is it?*

Something had gone seriously
wrong with the satnav...

nah	*near*	weit	*far*	die Ecke	*corner*
in der Nähe	*nearby*	entfernt	*(far) away*	die Meile	*mile*

Die Bank ist zwei
Kilometer von hier.

Der Supermarkt ist
ganz in der Nähe.

Es ist gar nicht weit von hier.

Es ist um die Ecke.

Der Bahnhof ist zehn
Minuten von hier entfernt.

*The bank is two
kilometres from here.*

*The supermarket is
really close by.*

It's not at all far from here.

It's round the corner.

*The station is ten minutes
away from here.*

Grammar — prepositions and cases

Some prepositions take either the
accusative <u>or</u> the dative case.

If <u>movement</u> is involved, use the <u>accusative</u>:

Gehen Sie in die Stadt. (accusative)
Go <u>into town</u>.

If <u>no movement</u> is involved, use the <u>dative</u>:

Die Post ist in der Stadt. (dative)
The post office is <u>in town</u>.

TRACK LISTENING 08

I just don't know which way to turn...

*Listen to the dialogue. A tourist is asking for directions. Which three sentences are **true**? [3 marks]*

    A. The tourist is looking for the cinema.

    B. There are two cinemas nearby.

    C. The theatre is called 'Agora'.

    D. The tourist is not far from his destination.

    E. The destination is on the right-hand side.

Weather

Here's all you need to know to strike up a conversation at a bus stop in a German-speaking country.

Wie ist das Wetter? — *What's the weather like?*

Es...	*It is...*
schneit	*snowing*
regnet	*raining*
hagelt	*hailing*
donnert	*thundering*

Es ist...	*It is...*
heiß	*hot*
warm	*warm*
feucht	*damp*
nass	*wet*

windig	*windy*
sonnig	*sunny*
bedeckt	*overcast*
trocken	*dry*
nebelig	*foggy*

die Jahreszeit	*season*
der Sommer	*summer*
der Herbst	*autumn*
der Winter	*winter*
der Frühling	*spring*

Question	**Simple Answer**	**Extended Answer**
Wie ist das Wetter?	Es regnet, es ist windig und bewölkt.	Heute Morgen war es ziemlich wolkig und es hat geschneit, aber jetzt regnet es und es ist windig. Es hat ungefähr sechs Grad.
What's the weather like?	*It's raining, it's windy and cloudy.*	*This morning, it was fairly cloudy and it snowed, but now it's raining and it's windy. It's about six degrees.*

Die Wettervorhersage — *The weather forecast*

Am Wochenende wird es schneien.

At the weekend, it will snow.

it will be stormy — wird es Gewitter geben

Morgen wird es warm sein.

Tomorrow, it will be warm.

windy — windig

Im Süden wird es bedeckt sein.

In the south, it will be overcast.

fine and dry — heiter und trocken

Im Osten wird die Sonne scheinen.

In the East, the sun will shine.

In the West — Im Westen

Grammar — the future tense

Use the <u>future tense</u> to say what the weather <u>will be like</u>. Use the correct form of '<u>werden</u>' and the <u>infinitive</u>. (See p.84.)

Morgen <u>wird</u> es <u>regnen</u>.
Tomorrow, it <u>will rain</u>.

Es <u>wird</u> heute Abend kalt <u>sein</u>.
It <u>will be</u> cold this evening.

READING *Sorry to dampen the mood, but here's an exam question...*

*Lies die Wettervorhersage. Sind die Aussagen **richtig**, **falsch** oder **nicht im Text**? [5 marks]*

Hier ist die Wettervorhersage für dieses Wochenende in Deutschland. Im Norden ist es im Moment sonnig, aber am Wochenende wird es wolkiger werden. Leider wird es auch in Ost- und Westdeutschland das ganze Wochenende bewölkt sein. Obwohl das Wetter im Süden des Landes wärmer sein wird, wird es auch Gewitter dort geben. Es wird regnerisch sein und wir werden einige Hagelschauer sehen.

e.g. Die Wettervorhersage ist für Samstag und Sonntag.   **richtig**

1. Es wird in Norddeutschland sonnig bleiben.

2. In Ostdeutschland wird es kälter als im Norden sein.

3. Im Süden von Deutschland wird es nicht so kalt sein.

4. Es wird in Süddeutschland nicht donnern und blitzen.

5. Es wird im Süden des Landes trocken sein.

No amount of snow could stop the Millers doing the conga...

Healthy Living

Learning five German words a day is really good for you — it's all part of a healthy lifestyle...

Die Gesundheit — *Health*

die Bewegung	*exercise*	aufgeben	*to give up*
sich bewegen	*to exercise*	aufhören	*to stop*
sich fit halten	*to keep yourself fit*	die Ernährung	*diet / nutrition*
in Form sein	*to be in good shape*	abnehmen	*to lose weight*
gesund	*healthy*	zunehmen	*to put on weight*

See p.22-23 for info on how to talk about sports.

Ich möchte in Form sein.　*I would like to be in good shape.*

a bit healthier — ein bisschen gesünder

Eine ausgewogene Ernährung ist wichtig für die Gesundheit.　*A balanced diet is important for your health.*

Regular exercise — Regelmäßige Bewegung

Question	**Simple Answer**	**Extended Answer**
Ist es dir wichtig, dich zu bewegen?	Ich finde es wichtig, mich zu bewegen, weil es gesund ist.	Es ist mir wichtig, mich fit zu halten, aber man muss sich auch entspannen, um völlig gesund zu sein.
Is it important to you to exercise?	*I find it important to exercise because it's healthy.*	*It's important to me to keep myself fit, but you also have to relax in order to be completely healthy.*

Um mich fit zu halten... — *To keep myself fit...*

Um mich fit zu halten, schwimme ich dreimal pro Woche.　*To keep myself fit, I swim three times a week.*

To stay in good shape — Um in Form zu bleiben

Ich stelle sicher, dass ich genug schlafe.　*I make sure that I sleep enough.*

drink — trinke

tired — müde

Ich versuche, mich nach der Schule zu entspannen, sodass ich nicht gestresst werde.　*I try to relax after school so that I don't get stressed.*

a balanced diet — eine ausgewogene Ernährung

Ich esse gesund — ich habe aufgehört, Süßigkeiten zu essen.　*I eat healthily — I have stopped eating sweets.*

given up chocolate — Schokolade aufgegeben

WRITING ***An apple a day keeps the examiner away — if only...***

Wadi has written a blog about how he keeps himself healthy.

Grade 6-7

[1]sugary

Um in Form zu sein, esse ich ein gesundes Frühstück. Ich trinke ein Glas fettarme Milch und ich esse Joghurt mit Müsli. Es ist wichtig, jeden Tag zu frühstücken. Als ich jünger war, habe ich viele Süßigkeiten und Schokolade gegessen. Aber ich habe aufgehört, so viel **zuckerhaltiges**[1] Essen zu essen. Ich spiele auch Basketball und ich fahre jeden Tag mit dem Fahrrad zur Schule. Ich hoffe, dass ich immer gesund bleiben werde.

Tick list:
✓ tenses: present, simple past, perfect, future
✓ good use of subordinating conjunctions, e.g. 'als'.

To improve:
+ use subjunctives like 'hätte' or 'wäre' in a 'wenn' clause.

Du schreibst ein Blog über gesundes Leben. Schreib:
- *was du machst, um gesund zu essen*
- *wie du dich fit hältst*
- *wie sich deine Gewohnheiten geändert haben*
- *wie du in Zukunft gesund bleiben wirst*

*Schreib ungefähr **150** Wörter auf **Deutsch**. Schreib etwas über alle Punkte der Aufgabe. [32 marks]*

Unhealthy Living

This page is all about obesity, drugs, smoking and binge drinking. It's cheerful stuff...

Gesundheitsschädlich — *Bad for your health*

der Alkohol	*alcohol*
betrunken	*drunk*
rauchen	*to smoke*
die Drogen	*drugs*
süchtig	*addicted*
die Fettleibigkeit	*obesity*
übergewichtig	*overweight*
schädlich	*harmful*

Grammar — modal verbs

Modal verbs are useful for discussing healthy living. P. 87 has more info.

dürfen	*to be allowed to*	müssen	*to have to*
können	*to be able to*	sollen	*to be supposed to*
mögen	*to like to*	wollen	*to want to*

These verbs are usually followed by a second verb in the infinitive.
Man darf nicht rauchen. *You are not allowed to smoke.*

Question

Ist Fettleibigkeit ein ernstes Problem?

Is obesity a serious problem?

Simple Answer

Ja. Ich vermeide Süßigkeiten, da ich nicht übergewichtig werden will.

Yes. I avoid sweets because I don't want to become overweight.

Extended Answer

Fettleibigkeit ist ein großes Gesundheitsproblem in unserer Gesellschaft. Mehr Leute sind übergewichtig als vorher.

Obesity is a serious health problem in our society. More people are overweight than before.

Die Sucht — *Addiction*

Ich habe nie geraucht. Das Rauchen ist für die Gesundheit sehr schädlich.

Ich werde Drogen immer vermeiden.

Es ist schwierig auf Partys, wenn man keinen Alkohol trinkt.

I have never smoked. Smoking is very harmful to your health.

I will always avoid drugs.

It's difficult at parties if you don't drink.

| taken drugs — Drogen genommen |
| cigarettes — Zigaretten |
| you're teetotal — man abstinent ist |

SPEAKING *Help, I'm addicted to learning German...*

Mia is talking to her teacher about young people and their health problems.

Teacher: Denkst du, dass Jugendliche zu viel Alkohol trinken?

Mia: Ja, ich glaube, dass viele Jugendliche oft zu viel trinken. Ich bin abstinent, aber viele meiner Freunde betrinken sich regelmäßig.

Teacher: Steht man unter Gruppendruck, Alkohol zu trinken?

Mia: Ja, manchmal. Gestern war ich auf einer Party und ich war die einzige, die keinen Alkohol getrunken hat. Leider haben viele das langweilig gefunden.

Teacher: Was ist das größte Gesundheitsproblem für Jugendliche?

Mia: Ich glaube, dass Übergewichtigkeit das größte Problem ist, weil viele übergewichtig sind. Sind Sie auch dieser Meinung?

Teacher: Ja, du hast recht. Was sollte man tun, wenn man übergewichtig ist?

Mia: Wenn ich übergewichtig wäre, würde ich gesunder essen und Sport treiben.

Teacher: Gibt es auch andere Gesundheitsprobleme unter Jugendlichen?

Mia: Jugendliche stehen oft unter Stress, was sehr gesundheitsschädlich ist.

Grade
8-9

Tick list:
✓ tenses: present, perfect, simple past
✓ good range of topical vocabulary
✓ correct use of the subjunctive

To improve:
+ use the future
+ use different phrases to express opinions

Now answer the questions yourself. You should speak for around two minutes. [15 marks]

Illnesses

Another joyous page. There's a mix of specific health problems and wider social health issues for you to enjoy.

Die Krankheit — *Illness*

krank	*ill*	das Krankenhaus	*hospital*
weh tun	*to hurt*	die Krankenversicherung	*health insurance*
verletzt sein	*to be injured*	der Kopf	*head*
der Schmerz	*pain*	der Hals	*neck / throat*
das Medikament	*medicine*	der Bauch	*stomach*
der Arzt / die Ärztin	*doctor*	der Rücken	*back*

Dr Ryan's artwork was great, but Klaus really just wanted to see his X-ray...

Ich habe Kopfschmerzen und eine Erkältung.

I have a headache and a cold.

> stomach ache — Bauchschmerzen
> hay fever — Heuschnupfen
> a fever — Fieber

Sie ist allergisch gegen Nüsse.

She's allergic to nuts.

> asthmatic — asthmatisch
> diabetic — zuckerkrank

Mein Rücken tut mir weh.

My back hurts.

Ich muss zur Apotheke gehen, weil ich ein Medikament brauche.

I need to go to the pharmacy because I need medicine.

> tablets — Tabletten
> antibiotics — Antibiotika

Grammar — reflexive verbs

Some reflexive verbs use reflexive pronouns in the dative case. 'Sich weh tun' *(to hurt oneself)* does this.

Ich habe mir weh getan.   I have hurt myself.

See p.73 for a list of dative reflexive pronouns.

Grammar — gegen

In German, you take medicine 'gegen' *(against)* an illness. The noun that follows is in the accusative.

Ich nehme Tabletten gegen meine Kopfschmerzen.

I'm taking tablets for my headache.

Das Gesundheitsproblem — *Health problem*

Psychische Probleme sind immer noch stigmatisiert.

Mental health problems are still stigmatised.

Es gibt viele Krankheiten, die noch nicht heilbar sind, zum Beispiel Asthma.

There are many illnesses that aren't yet curable, for example asthma.

> cancer — Krebs
> dementia — Demenz
> AIDS — Aids

In Deutschland muss man Krankenversicherung haben. Jedoch gibt es in Großbritannien einen nationalen Gesundheitsdienst.

In Germany, you have to have health insurance. However, in the UK, there is a national health service.

> to get good marks — gute Noten zu bekommen

Viele Jugendliche leiden an psychischen Problemen, da sie unter viel Druck stehen, ‚cool' zu sein.

Many young people suffer from mental health problems, as they are under a lot of pressure to be 'cool'.

> to conform to stereotypes — sich an Stereotypen anzupassen

READING

I always have a headache when it's time to do the ironing...

*Translate this passage into **English**. [9 marks]*

Letzte Woche war meine Schwester krank. Sie hatte Kopfschmerzen, ihr Hals tat weh und ihre Wangen waren sehr rot. Mein Vater dachte, dass sie Fieber hatte. Jetzt fühle ich mich krank und ich habe seit ungefähr einer Woche Bauchschmerzen. Ich muss zur Apotheke gehen. Ich werde Schmerztabletten kaufen.

Environmental Problems

Unfortunately, this isn't the most fun section, but you need to learn it if you want to make waves in your exam.

Die Umwelt — *The environment*

umweltfreundlich	*environmentally friendly*	der Brennstoff	*fuel*
umweltfeindlich	*bad for the environment*	das Kohlendioxid	*carbon dioxide*
schützen	*to protect*	die Sonnenenergie	*solar energy*
die Verschmutzung	*pollution*	die erneuerbare Energie	*renewable energy*
der Treibhauseffekt	*greenhouse effect*	zerstören	*to destroy*
der Klimawandel	*climate change*	die Abholzung	*deforestation*
der Verbrauch	*consumption*	das Hochwasser	*flood / flooding*
das Kraftwerk	*power station*	der Orkan	*hurricane*

Grammar — compound words

You can put two or more German words <u>together</u> to make <u>new</u> ones.

die Verschmutzung *pollution*

die <u>Luft</u>verschmutzung *<u>air</u> pollution*

die <u>Wasser</u>verschmutzung *<u>water</u> pollution*

The <u>gender</u> of the <u>new</u> word is determined by the <u>last</u> word in the <u>compound</u>. See p.61 for more.

Kraftwerke verschmutzen die Umwelt.
Power stations pollute the environment.

Fossile Brennstoffe sind umweltfeindlich.
Fossil fuels are bad for the environment.

Wir sollten die Umwelt schützen.
We should protect the environment.

Verschmutzen — *To pollute*

Es gibt zu viele Autos, die Kohlendioxid produzieren.
There are too many cars that produce carbon dioxide.

We use many vehicles — Wir benutzen viele Fahrzeuge

exhaust fumes — Abgase

Busse und Züge können umweltfreundlicher sein als Autos.
Buses and trains can be more environmentally friendly than cars.

Viele glauben, dass Abgase zum Treibhauseffekt beitragen.
Many think that exhaust fumes contribute to the greenhouse effect.

to the destruction of the ozone layer —zur Zerstörung der Ozonschicht

to climate change — zum Klimawandel

Manche Kraftwerke benutzen einen Brennstoff, der zu Luftverschmutzung führen kann.
Some power stations use fuel which can lead to air pollution.

coal — Kohle
oil — Öl

Die Erderwärmung — *Global warming*

Die Erderwärmung ist ein erhebliches Problem.
Global warming is a significant problem.

Einige befürchten, dass die Erderwärmung zu extremeren Wetterbedingungen führen könnte.
Some fear that global warming could lead to more extreme weather conditions.

Bäume können Kohlendioxid in Sauerstoff umwandeln, deswegen wirkt die Abholzung negativ auf den Klimawandel ein.
Trees can convert carbon dioxide to oxygen, so deforestation has a negative effect on climate change.

Alle Länder müssen zusammenarbeiten, um den Klimawandel zu bekämpfen.
All countries need to work together to fight climate change.

Environmental Problems

And more problems... Luckily, we've got some solutions on this page as well to cheer you up.

Die Naturkatastrophe — *Natural disaster*

Wegen der Erderwärmung könnte es mehr Naturkatastrophen geben.

Because of global warming, there could be more natural disasters.

Erdbeben können Tsunamis verursachen.

Earthquakes can cause tsunamis.

Wenn die Eisschichten schmelzen, könnte Hochwasser öfter auftreten.

If the ice caps melt, flooding could occur more often.

Orkane sind eine mögliche Folge des Klimawandels.

Hurricanes are one possible result of climate change.

droughts — Dürren

landslides — Erdrutsche
destruction — Zerstörung

Tornados — Wirbelstürme

Extreme temperatures — Extreme Temperaturen

Die Lösung — *Solution*

You can make your answers more sophisticated by talking about a problem and then giving a solution.

Statt Kohle und Öl zu verbrauchen, sollten wir erneuerbare Energiequellen nutzen.

Instead of consuming coal and oil, we should use renewable sources of energy.

Die Sonnenenergie ist eine mögliche Lösung.

Solar energy is a possible solution.

In Deutschland stammt ein hoher Anteil des Stroms aus erneuerbaren Energiequellen.

In Germany, a large percentage of power comes from renewable energy sources.

Die Windparks sind umstritten.

Wind farms are controversial.

alternative — alternative

Hydroelectric power — Die Wasserkraft
Geothermal energy — Die Erdwärme

Solar farms — Die Solarparks
Solar panels — Die Solarzellen

Die Zukunft — *The future*

Question

Denkst du, dass die Situation sich verbessern wird?

Do you think that the situation will improve?

Simple Answer

Ich glaube, dass wir eine Lösung für das Problem des Klimawandels finden werden. Man kann alles mit Technologie machen.

I believe we will find a solution to the problem of climate change. You can do anything with technology.

Extended Answer

Es gibt ziemlich viele Lösungen, zum Beispiel erneuerbare Energiequellen. Ich bin aber nicht sicher, ob wir den Treibhauseffekt verlangsamen können. Die Regierungen müssen zusammenarbeiten, aber oft streiten sie sich.

There are quite a few solutions, for example renewable energy sources. But I'm not sure if we can slow down the greenhouse effect. Governments need to work together, but they often argue.

 WRITING ## Wind turbines? I'm a big fan...

*Translate the following passage into **German**. [12 marks]*

I think that we have caused many environmental problems. Air pollution is very dangerous for people and animals. It can also lead to global warming. Renewable energy sources are a possible solution because they are more environmentally friendly than coal. If we do nothing, the problems will get worse in the future.

Problems in Society

From hurricanes to racism... This section isn't exactly a ray of sunshine. These are important topics though.

Soziale Probleme — *Social problems*

die Gesellschaft	*society*	die Gleichheit	*equality*
die Armut	*poverty*	die Menschenrechte	*human rights*
arbeitslos	*unemployed*	die Gleichberechtigung	*equal rights*
die Sozialhilfe	*income support*	die Diskriminierung	*discrimination*
die Verhältnisse	*(living) conditions*	der Rassismus	*racism*
die Einwanderung	*immigration*	das Verbrechen	*(a) crime*
der Einwanderer / die Einwanderin	*immigrant*	stehlen	*to steal*
der Flüchtling	*refugee*	die Gewalt	*violence*
die Eingliederung	*integration*	der Krieg	*war*

Ich mache mir Sorgen um den Rassismus.	*I'm worried about racism.*
Die Gleichheit ist mir wichtig.	*Equality is important to me.*
Für mich sind alle Menschen gleich.	*To me, all people are equal.*

Grammar — masculine, feminine and neuter

You can sometimes guess the gender of a word using its ending. Here are a few examples — for more see p.60.

Masculine	**-mus**	e.g. **der Sexismus**	*(sexism)*
Feminine	**-heit**	e.g. **die Freiheit**	*(freedom)*
	-ung	e.g. **die Eingliederung**	*(integration)*
Neuter	**-chen**	e.g. **das Kaninchen**	*(rabbit)*

In Armut leben — *To live in poverty*

In unserer Gesellschaft leben manche Leute in Armut.	*In our society, some people live in poverty.*
Es gibt viel Diskriminierung gegen Menschen, die arbeitslos sind.	*There's a lot of discrimination against people who are unemployed.*
Man hört oft in den Medien, dass Leute zu viel Sozialhilfe bekommen.	*You often hear in the media that people get too much in benefits.*
Die Kluft zwischen Arm und Reich nimmt zu.	*The gap between poor and rich is getting bigger.*
Die Arbeitslosigkeit ist ein großes Problem.	*Unemployment is a big problem.*

Die Kriminalität — *Crime*

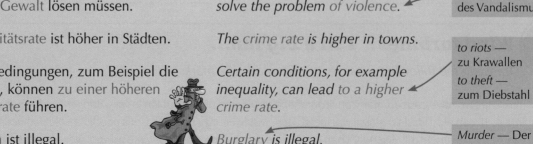

Ich bin davon überzeugt, dass wir das Problem der Gewalt lösen müssen.	*I am convinced that we must solve the problem of violence.*	of vandalism — des Vandalismus
Die Kriminalitätsrate ist höher in Städten.	*The crime rate is higher in towns.*	to riots — zu Krawallen
Bestimmte Bedingungen, zum Beispiel die Ungleichheit, können zu einer höheren Kriminalitätsrate führen.	*Certain conditions, for example inequality, can lead to a higher crime rate.*	to theft — zum Diebstahl
Der Einbruch ist illegal.	*Burglary is illegal.*	Murder — Der Mord

Problems in Society

Immigration is a complex topic, so it's important you're able to discuss the pros and cons.

Die Wanderung — *Migration*

Viele Ausländer ziehen nach Deutschland um, um dort zu arbeiten.

A lot of foreigners move to Germany in order to work there.

Wir müssen viel tun, um die Einwanderer zu integrieren.

We must do a lot to integrate immigrants.

Sie sprechen manchmal nur wenig Deutsch und haben Schwierigkeiten, eine Ausbildung zu bekommen.

They sometimes only speak a little German and have difficulty getting an education.

Die Einwanderer haben die Kultur in Deutschland bereichert.

Immigrants have enriched the culture in Germany.

migrants — Migranten	
refugees — Flüchtlinge	
must attend a German course — müssen einen Deutschkurs besuchen	
the European Union — der Europäischen Union	

Question	Simple Answer	Extended Answer
Sollte die Europäische Union mehr Flüchtlinge aufnehmen?	Idealerweise würde die EU jeder Person helfen, die Hilfe braucht. Es gibt aber so viele Flüchtlinge, deswegen ist es ganz schwierig.	Ja, weil die Flüchtlinge schon furchtbare Sachen erlebt haben. Es wäre menschlich, mehr Flüchtlinge aufzunehmen. Allerdings ist es schwierig, die Flüchtlinge zu integrieren, weil sie eine andere Sprache sprechen.
Should the European Union take in more refugees?	*Ideally, the EU would help every person that needs help. But there are so many refugees, so it's very hard.*	*Yes, because the refugees have already experienced horrible things. It would be humane to take in more refugees. However, it's hard to integrate the refugees because they speak another language.*

Der Konflikt — *Conflict*

Manchmal gibt es Konflikte zwischen verschiedenen Gemeinschaften.

Sometimes there are conflicts between different communities.

Wenn es Konflikt am Arbeitsplatz gibt, ist es oft wegen der Diskriminierung.

When there's conflict in the workplace, it's often because of discrimination.

Flüchtlinge fliehen aus Ländern, die im Krieg sind.

Refugees flee from countries that are at war.

Wie man den Flüchtlingen helfen sollte, ist immer noch ein umstrittenes Thema.

How we should help refugees is still a controversial topic.

ethnic groups — ethnischen Gruppen	
of sexism — des Sexismus	
in which human rights aren't protected — in denen Menschenrechte nicht geschützt sind	
in which there's a lot of violence — in denen es viel Gewalt gibt	

TRACK LISTENING 09

Hmmm — a page on fluffy animals would've been more fun...

Sofia, Peter und Lionel sprechen über soziale Probleme. Wähle das passende Thema für jede Person und schreib den richtigen Buchstaben neben den Namen.

A	der Diebstahl
B	die Einwanderung
C	die Gewalt

D	die Armut
E	die Gleichheit
F	der Vandalismus

1. Sofia [1]
2. Peter [1]
3. Lionel [1]

Contributing to Society

After all that doom and gloom, here's a more positive page on how you can make a difference.

Beitragen — *To contribute*

spenden	*to donate*	obdachlos	*homeless*	die Not	*need*
die Wohltätigkeit	*charity*	unterstützen	*to support*	der Müll	*rubbish*
ehrenamtlich	*voluntarily*	das Rote Kreuz	*the Red Cross*	wegwerfen	*to throw away*
die Suppenküche	*soup kitchen*	wiederverwerten	*to recycle*	verschwenden	*to waste*

Wenn ich älter bin, möchte ich für das Rote Kreuz arbeiten.

When I'm older, I would like to work for the Red Cross.

as a doctor — als Arzt (Ärztin)
as a police officer — als Polizist(in)

Ich habe an eine wohltätige Organisation für Obdachlose gespendet. Die Wohltätigkeit ist mir wichtig.

I donated to a charity for homeless people. Charity is important to me.

disabled people — Behinderte
cancer sufferers — Krebskranke

Ich arbeite ehrenamtlich bei einer Suppenküche. *I work voluntarily for a soup kitchen.*

Anderen helfen — *To help others*

Question

Was könnte man machen, um anderen zu helfen?

What could you do to help others?

Simple Answer

Man könnte einem Obdachlosen etwas zu essen geben. Man könnte auch Spenden für Behinderte sammeln.

You could give a homeless person something to eat. You could also collect money for disabled people.

Extended Answer

Es gibt viel, was man tun könnte, um anderen zu helfen. Meiner Meinung nach sollte jeder regelmäßig Freiwilligenarbeit machen. Wenn ich älter bin, möchte ich bei einem Sorgentelefon ehrenamtlich arbeiten. Das wäre eine sehr erfüllende Aufgabe.

There is a lot that you could do to help others. In my opinion, everyone should regularly do voluntary work. When I'm older, I would like to volunteer with a helpline. That would be a very rewarding task.

Despite all my good intentions, I rarely revise voluntarily...

SPEAKING

Chao is talking to his teacher about problems in society and how he tries to help.

Teacher: Welches Gesellschaftsproblem ist dir wichtig?

Chao: Die Obdachlosigkeit, da die Obdachlosen **keinen festen Wohnsitz**[1] haben.

Teacher: Was machst du, um zur Lösung dieses Problems beizutragen?

Chao: Ich gebe ihnen sehr oft etwas zu essen und ich habe ab und zu ehrenamtlich bei einer Suppenküche gearbeitet.

Teacher: Wirst du etwas anderes in der Zukunft machen?

Chao: Ich werde einen Marathon laufen, um Spenden zu sammeln.

Teacher: Ist dir die Umwelt wichtig?

Chao: Ja. Wir müssen alle etwas machen, um die Umwelt zu schützen.

Teacher: Was machst du zum Umweltschutz?

Chao: Früher habe ich alles im gleichen Mülleimer weggeworfen. Jetzt trenne ich den Müll, sodass ich ihn wiederverwerten kann.

Grade 8-9

[1] no fixed abode

Tick list:
✓ tenses: present, perfect, future
✓ good use of 'um... zu...' construction
✓ adverbs of time

To improve:
+ ask a question
+ justify opinions

Now answer the questions yourself. Aim to talk for around 2 minutes. [15 marks]

Where to Go

It might seem like an impossible dream right now, but one day you will be free to go on holiday again...

Wohin fahren wir? — *Where are we going?*

When you're <u>walking</u> somewhere, use '<u>gehen</u>'. When you're travelling in a <u>vehicle</u>, use '<u>fahren</u>'. '<u>Fliegen</u>' (*to fly*) and '<u>reisen</u>' (*to travel*) are handy words, too.

Mike and the gang just love Turkey...

Deutschland	*Germany*		Belgien	*Belgium*
Frankreich	*France*		Amerika	*America*
Spanien	*Spain*		Australien	*Australia*
Russland	*Russia*		China	*China*
Italien	*Italy*		Polen	*Poland*
Österreich	*Austria*		die Schweiz	*Switzerland*

Grammar — 'in' / 'nach' + country

To say you're <u>going</u> somewhere, you use '<u>in</u>' instead of '<u>nach</u>' for countries with an <u>article</u>.
Ich fahre <u>in die</u> Türkei. *I'm going to Turkey.*
Ich fahre <u>nach</u> China. *I'm going to China.*

Question

Wohin fährst du diesen Sommer?
Where are you going this summer?

Simple Answer

Ich reise mit meiner Familie nach Spanien und Portugal.
I'm going to Spain and Portugal with my family.

Extended Answer

Im Juli fliegen meine Eltern und ich nach Frankreich, weil es letzten Sommer jede Menge Spaß gemacht hat.
In July, my parents and I are flying to France because it was so much fun last summer.

Reiseziele — *Destinations*

der Schwarzwald	*the Black Forest*	der Rhein	*the Rhine*	Bayern	*Bavaria*
das Mittelmeer	*the Mediterranean*	die Donau	*the Danube*	Köln	*Cologne*
der Ärmelkanal	*the English Channel*	die Ostsee	*Baltic Sea*	München	*Munich*
die Alpen	*the Alps*	der Bodensee	*Lake Constance*	Wien	*Vienna*

Ich reise lieber in Europa, besonders in den Alpen.	*I prefer to travel in Europe, especially in the Alps.*	*in Asia* — in Asien *in the U.S.* — in den Vereinigten Staaten
Letzten Sommer bin ich ans Mittelmeer gefahren.	*Last summer, I went to the Mediterranean.*	*to the South of France* — nach Südfrankreich *to Lake Constance* — an den Bodensee

Abroad? Never heard of it. Sounds a bit foreign to me...

*Lies das Blog, das Ian über eine Reise geschrieben hat. Beantworte die Fragen auf **Deutsch**.*

Vor zehn Jahren war ich noch zu jung, um allein ins Ausland zu reisen. Ich musste also jeden Sommer mit meiner Stiefmutter und meinem Vater in Belgien zelten. Wir sind immer mit dem Auto dorthin gefahren — die Reise hat oft zwölf Stunden gedauert! Damals fand ich diese Urlaube todlangweilig und ich wollte einfach selbstständig sein.

Als ich mit den Prüfungen fertig war und nachdem ich achtzehn Jahre alt wurde, konnte ich endlich alleine fahren, deshalb bin ich mit Klamotten und Toilettensachen in einem Rucksack spontan nach Kanada geflogen! Das war zwar ganz stressig, ich fühlte mich aber befreit.

Und nächstes Jahr? Ich bin mit Nordamerika fertig. Ich will Belgien wieder besuchen, weil ich das Land eigentlich vermisse!

e.g. Warum konnte Ian vor zehn Jahren nicht allein in Urlaub fahren?
Er war zu jung.

1. Wie ist Ian nach Belgien gefahren? [1]

2. Wie beschreibt Ian die Urlaube in Belgien? [1]

3. Wie hat Ian seine Sachen nach Kanada transportiert? [1]

4. Wohin wird Ian nächstes Jahr fahren? [1]

Accommodation

Can't decide between a soggy tent and a five-star hotel? Here are some useful phrases to help you choose.

Die Unterkunft — *Accommodation*

der Aufenthalt	*stay*	das Hotel	*hotel*
übernachten	*to stay (overnight)*	die Pension	*small hotel*
wohnen	*to stay*	die Jugendherberge	*youth hostel*
reservieren	*to book*	der Campingplatz	*campsite*
der Wohnwagen	*caravan*	das Zelt	*tent*
das Gasthaus	*guesthouse*	zelten	*to camp*

Grammar — dative case

You use the <u>dative case</u> when saying <u>where</u> you stayed.
Wir wohnen in einem Hotel.
We are staying in a hotel.

Ich suche eine günstige Unterkunft.
I'm looking for cheap accommodation. ← a cheap hotel — ein günstiges Hotel

Gibt es ein Hotel in der Nähe?
Is there a hotel nearby? ← in the town centre — im Stadtzentrum

Kann man hier zelten?
Can you camp here? ← stay overnight — übernachten

Question	**Simple Answer**	**Extended Answer**
Wo haben Sie gewohnt? *Where did you stay?* 	Wir haben auf einem Campingplatz übernachtet. Es war unbequem, aber gesellig. Es gab sogar einen Jugendklub. *We stayed on a campsite. It was uncomfortable but sociable. There was even a youth club.*	Wir übernachteten in einem Gasthaus in Wolfsburg. Es war sehr bequem, aber teuer. Nächstes Mal werden wir in einer Jugendherberge wohnen, da es billiger ist. Da kann man selbst kochen und seine Wäsche waschen. *We stayed in a guesthouse in Wolfsburg. It was very comfortable, but expensive. Next time, we will stay in a youth hostel because it's cheaper. There, you can cook for yourself and do your washing.*

Wo werden Sie übernachten? — *Where will you stay?*

Describing your <u>holiday plans</u> is a good opportunity to use the <u>future</u> tense and <u>conditional</u> clauses.

In den Sommerferien wird meine Familie in einem Hotel in Wales wohnen.
In the summer holidays, my family will stay in a hotel in Wales. ← in the countryside — auf dem Land

Im August werde ich in einer altmodischen Pension in Devon übernachten.
In August, I will stay in an old-fashioned small hotel in Devon. ← in northern Scotland — in Nordschottland

Ich würde lieber in einem Hotel wohnen, da Zelten mir zu unbequem ist.
I would rather stay in a hotel because I find camping too uncomfortable. ← inconvenient — umständlich

Ich würde gern mit meinen Freunden in einer Jugendherberge am Meer wohnen.
I would like to stay with my friends in a youth hostel by the sea. ← in the mountains — in den Bergen

TRACK LISTENING 10

I'd love to go camping, but unfortunately I have a tent allergy...

*Drei Freunde reden über Unterkunft. Was meinen sie dazu? Sag welche Meinung **positiv** ist, welche Meinung **negativ** ist und welche Meinung **positiv und negativ** ist. [3 marks]*

1. Monika   **2.** Ben   **3.** Anton

Booking

This is the practical stuff you need for booking rooms... and for the exam role-plays...

Haben Sie Zimmer frei? — *Do you have any vacancies?*

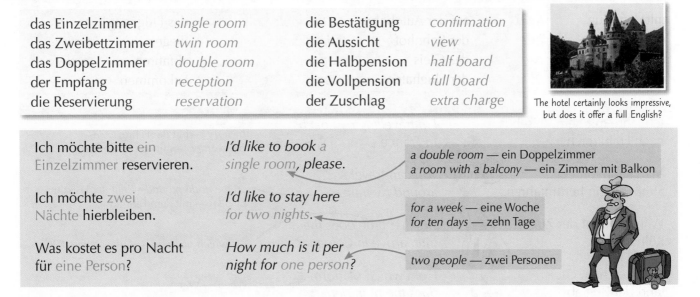

das Einzelzimmer	*single room*	die Bestätigung	*confirmation*
das Zweibettzimmer	*twin room*	die Aussicht	*view*
das Doppelzimmer	*double room*	die Halbpension	*half board*
der Empfang	*reception*	die Vollpension	*full board*
die Reservierung	*reservation*	der Zuschlag	*extra charge*

The hotel certainly looks impressive, but does it offer a full English?

Ich möchte bitte ein Einzelzimmer **reservieren**.

I'd like to book a single room, please.

> a double room — ein Doppelzimmer
> a room with a balcony — ein Zimmer mit Balkon

Ich möchte zwei Nächte **hierbleiben**.

I'd like to stay here for two nights.

> for a week — eine Woche
> for ten days — zehn Tage

Was kostet es pro Nacht für eine Person?

How much is it per night for one person?

> two people — zwei Personen

Bieten Sie Vollpension an? — *Do you offer full board?*

Gibt es einen Zuschlag fürs Frühstück?

Is there an extra charge for breakfast?

> for half board — für die Halbpension

Wenn möglich hätte ich gern ein Zimmer mit Klimaanlage.

If possible, I'd like a room with air-conditioning.

> with a view — mit Aussicht
> with a sea view — mit Meerblick
> with a bath — mit Badewanne

Wir sind vom achten bis zum fünfzehnten Mai da.

We'll be there from the 8th to the 15th May.

WRITING

Does the room come with a bouncy castle and a jacuzzi?

Read this conversation that Sam had with a hotel receptionist (HR).

Tick list:
✓ polite 'Sie' form

HR: Hotel Adler, wie kann ich Ihnen helfen?

Grade 4-5

Sam: Guten Morgen, ich möchte bitte ein Zimmer reservieren.

HR: Ja, sicher! Wann kommen Sie an?

Sam: Am siebzehnten Mai für eine Nacht. Ich besuche die Gegend, um **die Berliner Mauer**[1] zu besichtigen.

HR: Schön. Und was für ein Zimmer wollen Sie?

Sam: Einmal Einzelzimmer. Bieten Sie Halbpension an?

HR: Ja, aber dafür gibt es einen Zuschlag. Auf unserer Website gibt es ein **Formular**[2]. Füllen Sie bitte das Formular aus und schicken Sie es **so bald wie möglich**[3] per E-Mail an uns.

Sam: Danke schön. Auf Wiederhören!

[1] the Berlin Wall
[2] form
[3] as soon as possible

To improve:
+ use conjunctions, e.g. 'weil'
+ use the future tense with 'werden'
+ give more detail

*Du schreibst eine E-Mail, um ein Zimmer in einem Hotel zu reservieren. Schreib ungefähr **90 Wörter auf Deutsch** über die folgenden Punkte:*

- *was für ein Zimmer du willst*
- *Ankunftsdatum und Länge des Aufenthalts*
- *warum du die Gegend besuchst*
- *frag, ob das Hotel Halbpension anbietet*

[16 marks]

How to Get There

The bags are packed, the flip-flops are on, the comedy sombrero is ready to go and the plane is delayed...

Wie kommst du dahin? — *How are you getting there?*

mit dem Zug	*by train*	auf der Autobahn	*on the motorway*	das Flugzeug	*aeroplane*
mit dem Bus	*by bus*	der Bahnhof	*train station*	fliegen	*to fly*
mit dem Auto	*by car*	das Gleis	*platform*	abfahren	*to depart*
mit dem Boot	*by boat*	der Flughafen	*airport*	ankommen	*to arrive*

Ich fahre mit dem Reisebus nach Frankreich.

I'm travelling by coach to France.

> *by ferry* — mit der Fähre
> *by steamer* — mit dem Dampfer

Man kann mit der Straßenbahn herumfahren.

You can travel around by tram.

> *on the underground* — mit der U-Bahn
> *by bike* — mit dem Fahrrad

Wann kommt der Zug in Köln an?

At what time does the train arrive in Cologne?

> *On which platform* — Auf welchem Gleis

Von welchem Gleis fährt der Zug ab?

From which platform does the train depart?

> *When* — Wann

Man kann eine Fahrkarte am Fahrkartenautomaten kaufen.

You can by a ticket from the ticket machine.

> *at the ticket office* — am Fahrkartenschalter
> *at the bus station* — am Busbahnhof

Es gab Verspätungen — *There were delays*

unterwegs	*on the way*	die Verbindung	*connection*	der Platten	*flat tyre*
die Verspätung	*delay*	umsteigen	*to change (trains)*	der Stau	*traffic jam*
der Wartesaal	*waiting room*	verpasssen	*to miss (train / bus)*	seekrank	*seasick*

Question
Wie war die Reise?
How was the journey?

Simple Answer
Die Reise war sehr lang und langweilig. Sie hat vier Stunden gedauert.
The journey was very long and boring. It took four hours.

Extended Answer

Leider hatten wir viele Probleme unterwegs. Wir mussten umsteigen, aber der erste Zug hatte Verspätung, also haben wir die Verbindung verpasst. Wir mussten dann zwei Stunden auf den nächsten Zug warten und es war sehr kalt im Wartesaal. Am Ziel haben wir ein Auto vermietet und hatten bald einen Platten. Was für ein Albtraum!

Unfortunately, we had a lot of problems on the way. We had to change trains, but the first train was delayed, so we missed our connection. Then, we had to wait for two hours for the next train and it was very cold in the waiting room. At our destination, we rented a car and soon got a flat tyre. What a nightmare!

READING

On second thoughts, I'll just stay at home...

Translate the following passage into **English**. [9 marks]

Letzte Woche hat mein Vater ein Zelt gekauft. Morgen fliegt die ganze Familie in die Schweiz, wo wir auf einem Campingplatz am Bodensee wohnen werden. Ich finde das sehr spannend, aber meine Stiefschwester mag Flugzeuge nicht. Wir werden hoffentlich einen schönen Blick auf die Berge haben.

What to Do

So much to do, so much to learn... better get started then. This vocab sure isn't going to memorise itself.

Ausflüge — *Excursions*

Here's some vocab for saying what a town <u>has to offer</u> and what you like to <u>do on holiday</u>.

der Ausflug	*trip / excursion*
besichtigen	*to visit (an attraction)*
die Sehenswürdigkeit	*tourist attraction*
die Öffnungszeiten	*opening times*
das Museum	*museum*
das Schloss	*castle / palace*
die Burg	*castle*
der Stadtbummel	*stroll through town*
entdecken	*to discover*
die Führung	*guided tour*
der Strand	*beach*
das Erlebnis	*experience*
beliebt	*popular*

Grammar — comparatives

To <u>compare</u> one thing to another in German, you usually just add 'er' to the end of the <u>adjective</u>:

klein → klein<u>er</u>   *small → small<u>er</u>*

Provence ist <u>schöner</u> als das Ruhrgebiet.
Provence is <u>more beautiful</u> than the Ruhr District.

If the adjective is one syllable and its vowel is 'a', 'o' or 'u', you normally add an <u>umlaut</u> as well:

lang → l<u>ä</u>ng<u>er</u>   *long → long<u>er</u>*

Der Strand ist <u>näher</u> als das Museum.
The beach is <u>closer</u> than the museum.

A really common exception is '<u>gut</u>' (good):

gut → <u>besser</u>   *good → <u>better</u>*

> See p.68 for more info on comparing things.

Ich möchte in ein Museum gehen.	*I'd like to go to a museum.*
Ich würde gern etwas Neues erleben.	*I'd like to experience something new.*
Das Schloss ist sehenswert.	*The castle is worth seeing.*
Im Urlaub sonne ich mich gern am Strand.	*On holiday, I like to sunbathe on the beach.*

to visit a gallery — eine Galerie besuchen

to do a sightseeing tour of the town — eine Stadtrundfahrt machen

famous — berühmt

I like to hire a bicycle — miete ich gern ein Fahrrad

SPEAKING — *Sun, sea and speaking questions. Bliss...*

Here's a photo question. Have a look at the sample answer to get an idea of what to say.

Was machst du gern im Urlaub?

Grade 8-9

Für mich muss der Urlaub kulturell sein. Hauptsache ist, dass ich mehr über die Stadt oder das Land lerne; ich will mich den ganzen Tag nicht nur sonnen! Ich mache immer sehr gern eine Führung — das ist interessanter als am Strand zu liegen. Letztes Jahr bin ich mit meiner Familie in die Slowakei gefahren. Das war super, weil wir viele historische Orte besichtigt haben. Nächstes Jahr werde ich nach Belgien fahren, um viele Museen dort zu besuchen.

Tick list:
- ✓ tenses: present, perfect, simple past, future
- ✓ correct use of 'um...zu' construction
- ✓ correct use of modals

To improve:
- + give more detailed opinions
- + use the conditional to say what you would like to do in the future

Now try answering these questions out loud. Aim to talk for two minutes.

- Was kannst du auf dem Foto sehen?
- Was ist besser: am Strand liegen oder eine Stadtrundfahrt machen? Warum?
- Wie wäre dein idealer Urlaub?   *[10 marks]*

School Subjects

School subjects are a familiar topic, so you should have plenty to say about them by now.

Schulfächer — *School subjects*

das Schulfach	*school subject*	Fremdsprachen	*foreign languages*
das Wahlfach	*optional subject*	Deutsch	*German*
das Pflichtfach	*compulsory subject*	Spanisch	*Spanish*
die Stunde	*lesson*	Französisch	*French*
die Klasse	*class*	Geschichte	*history*
die Prüfung	*exam*	Geografie / Erdkunde	*geography*
Mathe	*maths*	Religion	*RE*
Englisch	*English*	Sport	*PE*
Naturwissenschaften	*science*	Werken	*design technology*
Biologie	*biology*	Theater	*drama*
Chemie	*chemistry*	Kunst	*art*
Physik	*physics*	Musik	*music*

Deutsch ist mein Lieblingsfach — *German is my favourite subject*

You might be asked about subjects you like and dislike, so make sure you can <u>justify</u> your <u>opinions</u>.

Sport gefällt mir immer, obwohl er sehr anstrengend ist.
I always enjoy PE, although it is very strenuous.
because I prefer being outdoors — weil ich lieber an der freien Luft bin

Werken mag ich nicht, weil ich nicht sehr praktisch bin.
I don't like design technology because I'm not very practical.
I find it boring — ich es langweilig finde

Ich lerne gern Fremdsprachen, weil sie nützlich sind.
I like learning foreign languages because they are useful.
I would like to work abroad — ich im Ausland arbeiten möchte

Ich mag Naturwissenschaften, weil ich verstehen will, wie alles funktioniert.
I like science because I want to understand how everything works.
the experiments are fun — die Experimente Spaß machen

 WRITING

It doesn't get much cooler than Schule...

Have a look at the text written by a student about the subjects offered at her school.

Hier müssen alle Schüler dreißig Stunden in der Woche lernen. Man muss einmal am Tag Spanisch oder Französisch lernen, weil eine Fremdsprache heutzutage sehr wichtig ist. Andere Pflichtfächer bei uns sind Deutsch, Mathe, Naturwissenschaften, entweder Geschichte oder Erdkunde, und Sport, weil unsere Schule eine Eliteschule des Sports ist. Wenn man kreativ ist, darf man Kunst, Musik oder Theater wählen. Die Schule bietet auch Religion und Werken an.

Grade 6-7

Tick list:
✓ relevant vocab
✓ 'weil' clauses
✓ time phrases

To improve:
+ use more adjectives
+ use more complex constructions, e.g. 'um...zu...'

*Dein Lehrer hat dich über deine Schulfächer gefragt. Schreib ungefähr **90** Wörter auf **Deutsch** über die folgenden Punkte:*

- *was dein Lieblingsfach ist, und warum*
- *welche Fächer du letzte Woche hattest*
- *welche Fächer du nächstes Jahr lernen wirst* [16 marks]

School Routine

DANGER! Now I've got your attention, here are some dull but useful sentences about the school routine.

Der Schulalltag — *School routine*

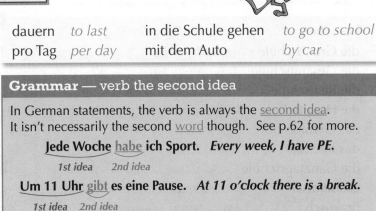

der Unterricht	*lessons / teaching*	dauern	*to last*
unterrichten	*to teach*	pro Tag	*per day*
der Stundenplan	*timetable*		
die (Mittags)pause	*(lunch) break*		
anfangen	*to start*		
aus sein	*to be over / finished*		
plaudern	*to chat / to talk*		
nachsitzen	*to have a detention*		
die Versammlung	*assembly*		
der Schultag	*school day*		

in die Schule gehen	*to go to school*
mit dem Auto	*by car*

Grammar — verb the second idea

In German statements, the verb is always the second idea. It isn't necessarily the second word though. See p.62 for more.

Jede Woche <u>habe</u> ich Sport. *Every week, I have PE.*

    1st idea   *2nd idea*

Um 11 Uhr <u>gibt</u> es eine Pause. *At 11 o'clock there is a break.*

    1st idea   *2nd idea*

Montags in der ersten Stunde habe ich Deutsch.

On Mondays, I have Geman in the first period.

in the second period — in der zweiten Stunde

Am Ende des Tages habe ich Geschichte.

At the end of the day, I have history.

Before the lunch break — Vor der Mittagspause

Zweimal pro Woche habe ich Chemie.

Twice a week, I have chemistry.

Every day — Jeden Tag
Once a week — Einmal pro Woche

Question

Kannst du mir deinen Schulalltag beschreiben?

Can you describe your school routine to me?

Simple Answer

Wir haben sechs Stunden pro Tag. Die Schule ist um 16 Uhr aus.

We have six lessons a day. School finishes at 4 o'clock.

Extended Answer

Die Schule fängt um Viertel vor neun an. Wir haben jeden Tag Mathe, aber es gibt nur eine Kunststunde pro Woche. Mittwochs nehme ich in der Mittagspause an der Chorprobe teil. Das gefällt mir sehr gut.

School starts at quarter to nine. We have maths every day, but there's only one art lesson a week.
On Wednesdays, I take part in choir practice during the lunch break. I really enjoy that.

Am Ende des Schultages — *At the end of the school day*

Oft schwatze ich im Schulhof.

Often, I chat in the schoolyard.

with my friends — mit meinen Freunden

Jeden Donnerstag habe ich Fußballtraining.

Every Thursday, I have football training.

a play rehearsal — eine Theaterprobe

Manchmal muss ich nachsitzen.

Sometimes, I have detention.

there's a class trip — gibt es eine Klassenfahrt

TRACK LISTENING 11

Eat. Sleep. Revise German. Repeat...

Tilly spricht über ihren Stundenplan.

1. *Schreib auf **Deutsch** einen **positiven** Aspekt ihres Stundenplans. Ein positiver Aspekt ist schon für dich als Beispiel gegeben.* [1]

   e.g. viermal in der Woche Geschichte

2. *Schreib auf **Deutsch** zwei **negative** Aspekte ihres Stundenplans.* [2]

Section 10 — Study and Employment

School Life

The German school system might seem baffling at first, so go through this page carefully.

Die Schulart — *Type of school*

besuchen	*to go to (a school)*
die Grundschule	*primary school*
die Gesamtschule	*comprehensive school*
die Realschule	*secondary school*
die Hauptschule	*(vocational) secondary school*
das Gymnasium	*grammar school*
das Internat	*boarding school*
die Ganztagsschule	*school that lasts all day*
akademisch	*academic*
praktisch	*vocational / practical*
gemischt	*mixed (sex)*

Question

Welche Schulart besuchst du?
What kind of school do you go to?

Simple Answer

Ich besuche eine gemischte Realschule.
I go to a mixed secondary school.

Extended Answer

Seit vier Jahren besuche ich eine Gesamtschule in meiner Heimatstadt. Sie ist ziemlich praktisch.

For four years, I've been going to a comprehensive school in my home town. It's quite vocational.

Das Schulleben — *School Life*

Ich besuche eine Ganztagsschule. Die Schule ist um 17 Uhr aus.

I go to a school that lasts all day. School finishes at 5 pm.

> a mixed private school — eine gemischte Privatschule

Ich finde Gesamtschulen besser, weil sie vielfältiger sind.

I think comprehensives are better because they are more diverse.

> they don't exclude anybody — sie niemanden ausschließen

Ich würde gern eine Hauptschule besuchen, weil ich sehr praktisch bin.

I'd like to go to a vocational secondary school because I'm very practical.

> I'm not so academic — ich nicht so akademisch bin

Ein Gymnasium wäre zu stressig.

A grammar school would be too stressful.

> very demanding — sehr anspruchsvoll

READING — Realschule? I'd rather go to a pretend one...

Read this email Anna wrote to her friend Nadine about German schools.

In deiner letzten E-Mail hast du über die Schularten hier gefragt. Wir haben in Deutschland mindestens drei Möglichkeiten nach der Grundschule!

Wenn man praktisch ist, ist eine Hauptschule vielleicht die beste Wahl. Schüler müssen fünf Jahre in dieser Schule bleiben. Eine Realschule ist auch eine gute Möglichkeit für praktische Jungen und Mädchen, aber sie dauert sechs Jahre. Wenn man akademischer ist und das Abitur machen will, muss man acht oder neun Jahre in einem Gymnasium lernen. Gesamtschulen, die eine Mischung von den drei Schularten sind, existieren in manchen Bundesländern auch.

According to the text, which **four** statements are true?

A   There are two different types of secondary school in Germany.

B   The Hauptschule is more vocational.

C   Pupils attend the Hauptschule for five years.

D   The Realschule is only suitable for academic students.

E   The Realschule is just for boys.

F   You can do your Abitur in the Gymnasium.

G   Gesamtschulen combine all the school types mentioned.

H   All German states offer Gesamtschulen.

[4 marks]

School Pressures

Feeling stressed? This soothing German will ease your pain. OK, I lied. But it'll all be worth it in the end.

Die Schulbelastungen — *School pressures*

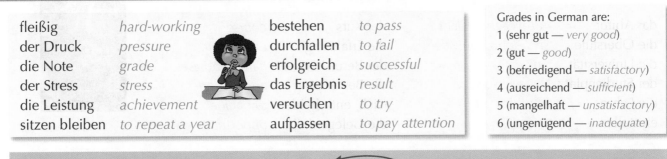

fleißig	*hard-working*	bestehen	*to pass*	
der Druck	*pressure*	durchfallen	*to fail*	
die Note	*grade*	erfolgreich	*successful*	
der Stress	*stress*	das Ergebnis	*result*	
die Leistung	*achievement*	versuchen	*to try*	
sitzen bleiben	*to repeat a year*	aufpassen	*to pay attention*	

Grades in German are:
1 (sehr gut — *very good*)
2 (gut — *good*)
3 (befriedigend — *satisfactory*)
4 (ausreichend — *sufficient*)
5 (mangelhaft — *unsatisfactory*)
6 (ungenügend — *inadequate*)

Ich stehe unter Druck, weil ich gute Noten haben will. → *I'm under pressure because I want to get good grades.*

Man sollte versuchen, alle Prüfungen zu bestehen. → *You should try to pass all your exams.*

I am very stressed — Ich bin sehr gestresst
I always work hard — Ich arbeite immer fleißig

be successful — erfolgreich zu sein
keep calm — ruhig zu bleiben

Es gibt strenge Regeln — *There are strict rules*

Man muss jeden Tag anwesend sein.

You must be present every day.

Man soll andere Schüler und die Lehrer respektieren.

You should respect other pupils and the teachers.

Man darf nicht schwänzen.

You are not allowed to play truant.

Man muss pünktlich sein.

You must be on time.

Grammar — modal verbs

Using '<u>man</u>' with a <u>modal verb</u> is a handy way to describe <u>rules</u>. You'll also need a <u>second verb</u> that's in the <u>infinitive</u> — this goes at the <u>end</u> of the clause. See p.87 for more info.

<u>Man darf nicht</u> rauchen.
<u>You're not allowed</u> to smoke.

SPEAKING ***I'd be less stressed if it weren't for all these exam questions...***

Here's a photo question. Read the example to get an idea of what to say.

Stehst du unter Druck im Schulleben?

Ja, ich stehe unter Druck und fühle mich die ganze Zeit äußerst gestresst. Ich will unbedingt erfolgreich sein, deswegen muss ich immer fleißig arbeiten. Letzte Woche hatten wir viele schwierige Prüfungen und ich weiß nicht, ob ich gute Noten haben werde.

In unserer Schule gibt es auch viele Regeln. Man muss eine Uniform tragen. Man darf nicht schwänzen und man muss andere respektieren. Ich finde die Schulregeln ziemlich wichtig — ohne Regeln würde das Schulleben ganz chaotisch werden. Jedoch hätte ich gern weniger Stress im Schulleben. Mehr Freizeit wäre auch schön.

Grade 8-9

Tick list:
✓ tenses: present, simple past, future, conditional, subjunctive
✓ correct use of modal verbs with 'man'

To improve:
+ use 'weil' clauses to justify statements

Now try answering these questions. Aim to talk for about 2 minutes.
- Was kannst du auf dem Foto sehen?
- Wie findest du die Regeln in deiner Schule? Warum?
- Fühlst du dich gestresst in der Schule? Warum?
- Wie kann man Schuldruck vermeiden?   *[10 marks]*

© iStock.com/shironosov

Education Post-16

It's time to start thinking about what you're going to do once all those GCSEs are in the bag.

Die Weiterbildung — *Further education*

das Abitur	*A-Level equivalent*	der Kurs	*course*
die Oberstufe	*sixth-form equivalent*	die Erfahrung	*experience*
die Universität	*university*	der Berufsberater	*careers adviser*
der Studienplatz	*university place*	die Bewerbung	*application*
die Lehre	*apprenticeship*	(sich) entscheiden	*to decide*
einstellen	*to employ*	die Gelegenheit	*opportunity*

Alan's art school application was strong, and he knew it...

Nach dem Abitur werde ich auf die Uni gehen, um Biologie zu studieren.

After my A-levels, I will go to uni to study biology.

study abroad — im Ausland studieren

Vor der Uni werde ich ein Jahr freinehmen, um Geld zu verdienen.

Before uni, I will take a year out in order to earn money.

to travel the world — um durch die Welt zu reisen

Der Berufsberater in der Schule denkt, dass ich etwas Praktisches machen sollte.

The school careers adviser thinks that I should do something vocational.

attend a course — einen Kurs besuchen

Die Berufserfahrung — *Work experience*

Ich möchte an einer Fachschule lernen, um praktische Erfahrung zu sammeln.

I'd like to study at a technical college to gain practical experience.

do voluntary work — ehrenamtlich arbeiten

Ich möchte eine Lehre machen, weil sie zu einer festen Anstellung führen kann.

I'd like to do an apprenticeship because it can lead to a permanent job.

a work placement — ein Praktikum

Berufserfahrung ist oft sehr wichtig, wenn man sich um einen Job bewirbt.

Work experience is often very important when you're applying for a job.

useful — nützlich

Question

Was wirst du nach den Prüfungen machen?

What will you do after your exams?

Simple Answer

Ich möchte ein Praktikum bei einer Bank machen.

I would like to do a work placement at a bank.

Extended Answer

Zuerst habe ich vor, ein Jahr freizunehmen, weil ich unbedingt auf Reisen gehen will. Danach werde ich wahrscheinlich auf die Uni gehen, aber ich habe mich noch nicht entschieden, was ich studieren möchte.

Firstly, I'm planning to take a year out because I really want to go travelling. After that, I will probably go to university, but I haven't yet decided what I would like to study.

WRITING *I think I'm edumacated enough, thanks...*

Translate the following passage into **German**. [12 marks]

Sechs mal vier gibt...

Last year, I learned English, maths and geography. I enjoyed geography, but my maths teacher was very strict. After the exams, I will take a year out. I will find a job because I want to earn money. After that, I want to go to university to study English. I think it will be an interesting experience.

Career Choices and Ambitions

If you've got detailed future plans, great — if you haven't, make something up. Job's a good 'un.

Bei der Arbeit — *At work*

arbeiten	*to work*
das Gehalt	*salary*
der Lohn	*wage*
der Lebenslauf	*CV*
der / die Angestellte	*employee*
berufstätig (sein)	*(to be) in work*
das Büro	*office*
die Karriere	*career*
der / die Beamte	*civil servant*
der Arzt / die Ärztin	*doctor*
der Tischler	*carpenter*

Grammar — jobs and genders

With German job titles, you have to show whether the person is a <u>man</u> or a <u>woman</u>.

For '<u>Friseur</u>' (*hairdresser*), '<u>Polizist</u>' (*police officer*) and roles ending in '<u>er</u>', you add '<u>-in</u>' for females.

der Verkäufer — **die** Verkäufer**in**
sales assistant (m) — *sales assistant (f)*

For roles ending in '<u>mann</u>', you change the word to '<u>frau</u>' if you're talking about a woman.

der Feuerwehr<u>mann</u> — **die** Feuerwehr<u>frau</u>
firefighter (m) — *firefighter (f)*

Question	**Simple Answer**	**Extended Answer**
Was willst du als Beruf machen?	In der Zukunft will ich in einer Bäckerei arbeiten, denn Schichtarbeit stört mich nicht.	Im Moment habe ich einen Teilzeitjob als Verkäuferin, aber ich werde bald Vollzeitarbeit als Klempnerin beginnen, um einen besseren Lohn zu verdienen.
What do you want to do for a living?	*In the future, I'd like to work in a bakery, as I don't mind shift work.*	*At the moment, I have a part-time job as a sales assistant, but I will soon start full-time work as a plumber, in order to earn a better wage.*

Warum willst du das machen? — *Why do you want to do that?*

Whether your plans are real or not, you need to be able to give <u>reasons</u> for them.

Ich suche eine Stelle als Gärtner, weil ich im Freien arbeiten will.	*I'm looking for a position as a gardener because I want to work in the open air.*	postman / woman — Briefträger / in
Ich möchte Maler werden, weil ich sehr kreativ bin.	*I'd like to be a painter / decorator because I'm very creative.*	actor / actress — Schauspieler / in
Es wäre toll, selbstständig zu sein, da man keinen Chef hat.	*It would be great to be self-employed because you have no boss.*	no fixed working hours — keine festen Arbeitsstunden
Ich möchte Krankenpfleger werden, weil der Beruf erfüllend ist.	*I'd like to be a (male) nurse because the profession is rewarding.*	(female) nurse — Krankenschwester

READING

In the future, I'd like a promotion and more pay (hint hint)...

*Translate the following passage into **English**. [9 marks]*

Im Moment weiß ich nicht, was ich in der Zukunft machen will. Ich habe meine Prüfungen in der Schule nicht bestanden und ich muss einen Job finden. Mein Vater ist Polizist und ich machte im Juni mit ihm mein Arbeitspraktikum, aber das möchte ich nicht als Beruf machen. Ich würde lieber selbstständig arbeiten.

Nigel's new job made him feel like a bit of a clown...

Cases	# Cases — Nominative and Accusative

Cases are a tricky business — but if you can get to grips with the four cases, the rest of German grammar will seem much easier, and you'll be on your way to getting a good mark.

Cases mean that you have to change words to fit

1) In German, words are <u>written differently</u> depending on which <u>case</u> they're in.

> Der kleine Hund **grüßt** den kleinen Hund.   *The small dog **greets** the small dog.*

> Both these bits mean 'the small dog', but they're written differently. This is because the second bit is in a different case from the first bit.

Marvin wasn't convinced by all this socialising malarkey...

2) This page and the next page are all about <u>when</u> you use the different cases.

3) Often, you have to <u>change the words</u> to fit the case — see p.60 for <u>nouns</u>, p.65 for <u>articles</u> and p.66-67 for <u>adjectives</u>.

The nominative and accusative cases

1) The <u>nominative case</u> and the <u>accusative case</u> are the cases you'll need to use <u>the most</u>.

2) The <u>case</u> of a word <u>depends</u> on what the word's <u>doing</u> in the sentence.

> Der Lehrer **liest** den Brief.   *The teacher **reads** the letter.*

> The teacher is doing the action. This makes him the 'subject' of the sentence. The 'subject' is always in the nominative case.

> This bit of the sentence is the verb. It tells you what's going on.

> This last bit is what the verb is done to. It's in the accusative case.

> When you look a word up in a dictionary, it'll always tell you what it is in the nominative case.

So remember the golden rules...

> Better hang on to these golden rules — just in case!

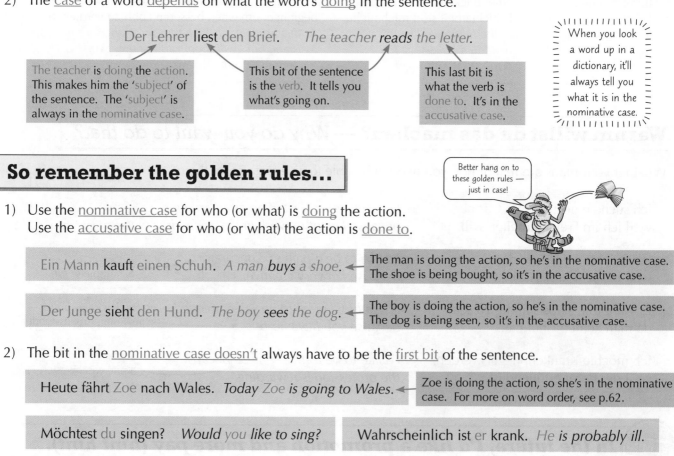

1) Use the <u>nominative case</u> for who (or what) is <u>doing</u> the action. Use the <u>accusative case</u> for who (or what) the action is <u>done to</u>.

> Ein Mann **kauft** einen Schuh.   *A man **buys** a shoe.*
>
> The man is doing the action, so he's in the nominative case. The shoe is being bought, so it's in the accusative case.

> Der Junge **sieht** den Hund.   *The boy **sees** the dog.*
>
> The boy is doing the action, so he's in the nominative case. The dog is being seen, so it's in the accusative case.

2) The bit in the <u>nominative case doesn't</u> always have to be the <u>first bit</u> of the sentence.

> Heute **fährt** Zoe nach Wales.   *Today Zoe **is going** to Wales.*
>
> Zoe is doing the action, so she's in the nominative case. For more on word order, see p.62.

> Möchtest du singen?   *Would you like to sing?*   Wahrscheinlich ist er krank.   *He is probably ill.*

Cases are quite tricky — get this stuff sorted and you'll be flying...

Read the sentences. Say which words are in the nominative case and which words are in the accusative case.

1. Der Mann spricht Deutsch.   **3.** Ich habe eine Schwester.   **5.** Meine Mutter hat ein neues Auto.

2. Die Stadt hat eine Bibliothek.   **4.** Er kauft Schokolade.   **6.** Morgen werde ich einen Rock kaufen.

Cases — Genitive and Dative

Here are some more cases — their names might sound a bit odd, but they're not as terrifying as they seem.

Use the genitive case to talk about belongings

1) When you want to say things like 'Sarah's' or 'Otto's' or 'my dad's', you need the genitive case.

Der Wagen meines Vaters.   *My father's car.* ◄ Literally, 'the car of my father'.

Hermann isst die Suppe des Mädchens.   *Hermann eats the girl's soup.* ◄ Literally, 'the soup of the girl'.

2) Watch out — you don't need the genitive case for phrases like 'my dad's a doctor'. This is short for 'my dad is a doctor', which is very different to saying that a doctor belongs to your dad.

Use the dative case to say 'to someone', 'from someone'...

1) Before you get going on the dative case, make sure you understand the accusative case (p.58) really well. Then have a look at these two sentences:

Accusative case	Dative case
Eva schreibt einen Brief. *Eva writes a letter.*	Eva schreibt einem Freund. *Eva writes to a friend.*

2) In the first one, Eva is writing a letter. Eva is in the nominative case because she's writing, and the letter is in the accusative case because it's being written.

3) In the second one, Eva is writing to a friend. The friend isn't being written — he's being written to. This means he can't be in the accusative case. Instead, he's in the dative case.

4) You normally need to use the dative case when you're translating these words: ⇨ **on, at, from, of, in, by, with, to**

5) There are some exceptions though — have a look at page 76 for situations when you need the accusative case with some of these words.

6) Sometimes you need the dative case even though you don't have one of these words. See page 78 for more.

Nouns sometimes get endings to fit the case

1) Nouns (see p.60) sometimes change depending on what case they're in.

2) Masculine and neuter nouns add 's' in the genitive case.

Das Haus meines Onkels.   *My uncle's house.*

> There are some words where you have to add 'es' rather than just 's'. They usually end in '-s', '-ß', '-x' or '-z'.

3) Plural nouns add 'n' in the dative.

Ich schreibe den Kindern.   *I write to the children.*

> Normally, 'children' = 'Kinder', but in the dative, it becomes 'Kindern'. If the noun already ends in '-n', you don't need to add another 'n'. 'Streets' = 'Straßen', so in the plural dative, it's still 'Straßen'.

Get to grips with German grammar — just in case...

Read these sentences. Say which words are in the genitive case and which words are in the dative case.

1. Sie ist die Schwester meiner Mutter.
2. Wir wohnen auf dem Land.
3. Ich gebe meinem Bruder das Buch.
4. Er ist der Bruder meines Vaters.
5. Wir fahren mit dem Zug.
6. Er steht in der Küche.

Nouns	# Words for People, Places and Objects

Nouns (words for people, places and objects) crop up loads — so it's important to use them properly.

German nouns start with capital letters

1) In English, some <u>nouns</u> like '<u>Leeds</u>' or '<u>December</u>' always start with a capital letter.

2) In German, <u>absolutely every noun</u>, whether it's a <u>person</u>, <u>place</u> or <u>object</u>, starts with a <u>capital letter</u>.

der Elefant	*the elephant*		das Baby	*the baby*

German nouns are either masculine, feminine or neuter

1) Every German noun has a gender. If a noun has '<u>der</u>' in front, it's <u>masculine</u> (in the nominative case). If it has '<u>die</u>' in front, it's <u>feminine</u> or <u>plural</u>, and if it has '<u>das</u>' in front, it's <u>neuter</u>.

2) The <u>gender of a noun</u> affects lots of things — the words for '<u>the</u>' and '<u>a</u>' change, and so do any <u>adjectives</u> (words like big, green and smelly).

eine große Kuh	*a big cow*

When you learn a new noun, learn whether it needs 'der', 'die' or 'das'.

Use these rules to help you recognise what gender a noun is

You can use these rules to help you recognise whether a noun is <u>masculine</u>, <u>feminine</u> or <u>neuter</u>.

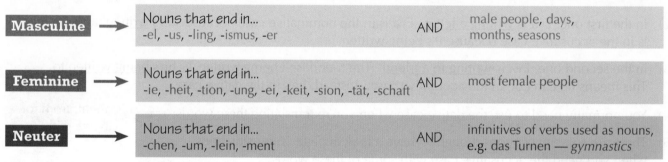

Masculine →	Nouns that end in... -el, -us, -ling, -ismus, -er	AND	male people, days, months, seasons
Feminine →	Nouns that end in... -ie, -heit, -tion, -ung, -ei, -keit, -sion, -tät, -schaft	AND	most female people
Neuter →	Nouns that end in... -chen, -um, -lein, -ment	AND	infinitives of verbs used as nouns, e.g. das Turnen — *gymnastics*

Weak nouns have strange endings

Some <u>masculine</u> nouns are called <u>weak nouns</u>, and they are mostly words for <u>people</u> and <u>animals</u>. They stay the <u>same</u> in the <u>nominative singular</u> case, but in <u>all other cases</u>, they <u>add</u> either '<u>-n</u>' (if the noun ends in '-e') or '<u>-en</u>' (for all others).

Masculine he could deal with, but weak — never.

'Der Herr' is tricky. Even though it doesn't end in '-e', it only adds '-n' in the singular.

	Accusative	Genitive	Dative
der Junge (boy)	-n	-n	-n
der Mensch (person)	-en	-en	-en
der Name (name)	-n	-ns	-n
der Herr (sir / Mr)	-n	-n	-n

'der Name' is sneaky — it adds '-ns' in the genitive singular rather than just '-n'. The same happens with 'der Glaube' (*belief*), 'der Gedanke' (*thought*) and 'der Buchstabe' (*letter of the alphabet*).

Gib dem Jungen ein Hemd.	*Give the boy a shirt.*		die Ohren des Elefanten	*the ears of the elephant*

This gender thing's all neuter me...

Have a look at these German nouns and use the rules on this page to fill in the gaps with 'der', 'die' or 'das'.

1. ...... Gesellschaft
2. ...... Mittwoch
3. ...... Frühling
4. ...... Mädchen
5. ...... Meinung
6. ...... Polizei
7. ...... Katrin
8. ...... Schwimmen

Words for People, Places and Objects | Nouns

Life would be boring if there were just one of everything — you need to know how to make nouns plural too.

Making nouns plural

1) When you want to make nouns plural in English, you normally just add an 's'. German is a bit harder — there are lots of different ways to make nouns plural.

How to make the word plural	Example
No change	der Metzger (the butcher) → die Metzger (the butchers)
Add an umlaut to the stressed syllable	der Apfel (the apple) → die Äpfel (the apples)
Add an 'e'	der Tag (the day) → die Tage (the days)
Add an umlaut and an 'e'	die Hand (the hand) → die Hände (the hands)
Add 'er'	das Lied (the song) → die Lieder (the songs)
Add an umlaut and 'er'	das Haus (the house) → die Häuser (the houses)
Add an 's'	das Sofa (the sofa) → die Sofas (the sofas)
Add an 'n'	die Straße (the street) → die Straßen (the streets)
Add 'en'	die Frau (the woman) → die Frauen (the women)

When nouns are plural and are in the dative case, they add an 'n' on the end. See p.59.

Feminine nouns usually do one of these things.

2) A compound noun is a noun made of two or more words stuck together. The last word in the compound 'decides' what the noun's gender is and how the plural will be formed.

die Haustür *front door* → die Haustüren *front doors*

der Bildschirm *screen* → die Bildschirme *screens*

3) When you learn a new German noun, you should learn its plural form too. When you look for a noun in the dictionary, you'll see its plural in brackets like this... 'Bett(en)', which means 'Betten'.

You can also use adjectives as nouns

When an adjective is working as a noun in German, it needs a capital letter.

1) Sometimes in English we use adjectives as nouns — e.g. the homeless. You can do the same with lots of adjectives in German too:

Der Deutsche ist sehr freundlich.   *The German (man) is very friendly.*

The old man — Der Alte
The helpful woman — Die Hilfreiche

2) In German, you don't always need to say whether you're talking about a man or a woman. If you use 'der', it's clear you're talking about a man, and if you use 'die', it's clear you're talking about a woman.

der Deutsche   *the German man*   die Deutsche   *the German woman*

3) You can also use an adjective as a noun with 'ein' for males and 'eine' for females.

ein Angestellter   *a male employee*   eine Angestellte   *a female employee*

When an adjective is working as a noun, it has the same ending that it would have if it were still an adjective. Have a look at page 66 for the tables of endings.

Eyes down, everyone — make it look like you're working hard...

Get comfortable with all these German nouns and plurals...

Translate these sentences into German. You might need to look some of the plurals up in a dictionary first.
1. There are many cars.
2. The children are small.
3. The tables are expensive.
4. The doctors are nice.
5. The old woman is called Renate.
6. The youth (male) is called Ali.

| Word Order | **Word Order** |

You need to write proper sentences — so I'm going to tell you where to stick your words...

The five commandments for German word order

The word order for questions and instructions is different. See p.4 and p.85 for more details.

1) Put the verb second

The verb is almost always the second idea in a German sentence.

| Ich spiele Fußball. | *I play football.* |

The word order for simple sentences like this is the same as in English. The person or thing doing the action goes first, and the verb comes second.

2) Keep the verb second

1) As long as you keep the verb second, German word order can be fairly flexible.

2) You can swap the information around as long as the verb is still the second idea in the sentence (although it might not be the second word).

3) So, if you want to say 'I play football on Mondays', you can say:

| Ich spiele montags Fußball. *(I play on Mondays football.)* | **OR** | Montags spiele ich Fußball. *(On Mondays, I play football.)* |

Ida often has second thoughts about keeping the verb second...

3) If there are two verbs, send one to the end

If you've got two verbs, treat the first one as normal and send the second one to the end of the clause.

| Ich werde nach China fahren. *(I will to China go).* | Ich werde viel machen. *(I will a lot do).* |

4) Remember — *When, How, Where*

At school, you might have heard the phrase 'Time, Manner, Place' — it just means that if you want to describe when, how and where you do something, that's exactly the order you have to say it in.

Ich gehe heute mit meinen Freunden ins Kino. *(I am going today with my friends to the cinema).*

WHEN (Time)   HOW (Manner)   WHERE (Place)

5) Watch out for 'joining words' — *they can change the word order*

Some conjunctions (joining words) can mess up the word order by sending the verb to the end of the clause. Watch out though — they don't all do this. See p.63-64 for more info.

Ich schwimme, weil ich sportlich bin. *(I swim because I sporty am.)*

'Weil' ('because') is a joining word which sends the verb ('bin') to the end of the clause.

Thou shalt not forget German word order...

Tick the sentences that use word order correctly and cross the ones that don't.

1. Ich Basketball spiele.
2. Am Montag gehe ich ins Kino.
3. Ich werde in die Disco gehen.
4. Er lacht, weil er ist glücklich.
5. Ich esse mit meiner Familie heute.
6. Wir fahren am Freitag nach Berlin.

Coordinating Conjunctions

These words help you join phrases and clauses together to make interesting sentences — examiners love this.

Link sentences using coordinating conjunctions

Coordinating conjunctions join phrases and clauses. They don't affect word order — the verb comes second.

Und — And

Ich habe eine Katze. **und** Er hat einen Hund. → Ich habe eine Katze und er hat einen Hund.

I have a cat. **and** He has a dog. → I have a cat and he has a dog.

Christiane spielt gern Tennis und Rugby. *Christiane likes playing tennis and rugby.*

Open your eyes, Joel, open your eyes!

Oder — Or

Ich treffe mich mit Alex. **oder** Ich spiele mit Ayesha Golf. → Ich treffe mich mit Alex oder ich spiele mit Ayesha Golf.

I meet up with Alex. **or** I play golf with Ayesha. → I meet up with Alex or I play golf with Ayesha.

Rainer spielt jeden Tag Fußball oder Rugby. *Rainer plays football or rugby every day.*

Aber — But

You need to use a comma before 'aber'.

Ich möchte backen. **aber** Ich habe kein Mehl. → Ich möchte backen, aber ich habe kein Mehl.

I would like to bake. **but** I don't have any flour. → I would like to bake, but I don't have any flour.

Otto will Fußball spielen, aber es regnet. *Otto wants to play football, but it's raining.*

Extend your answers using coordinating conjunctions

Using coordinating conjunctions to join phrases together will help you get the best marks. Here's an example using denn (*because, since*), which is another coordinating conjunction.

Question	Simple Answer	Extended Answer
Was ist dein Lieblingsfach?	Kunst ist mein Lieblingsfach.	Mein Lieblingsfach ist Kunst, denn ich male gern.
What's your favourite subject?	*Art is my favourite subject.*	*My favourite subject is art because I like painting.*

Joined-up sentences?! I've only just learned joined-up writing...

Translate these sentences into German.

1. I go by bus and you go by train.
2. We'll go to a museum or we'll play tennis.
3. I want to listen to music or watch TV.
4. He's a vegetarian, but she eats meat.
5. I love German, but hate English.

Subordinating Conjunctions

Use a subordinating conjunction and get one fab German sentence. Just watch the word order.

Subordinating conjunctions send the verb to the end

A subordinating conjunction sends the <u>verb</u> to the <u>end</u> of the clause. Here are some <u>common</u> ones:

wenn	*if / when*	bevor	*before*	ob	*whether / if*	während	*while*
nachdem	*after*	bis	*until*	obwohl	*although*	weil	*because*
damit	*so that*	als	*when*	dass	*that*	da	*as, because*

Ich weiß nicht, ob er hungrig ist.
I don't know if he is hungry.

Ich frühstücke, bevor ich in die Schule gehe.
I eat breakfast before I go to school.

'Bevor' has sent 'gehe' to the end.

Make sure you can use 'weil', 'wenn', 'als' and 'obwohl'

Weil — *Because*

Ich tanze.	**weil**	Ich bin froh.	→	Ich tanze, weil ich froh bin.
I am dancing.	*because*	*I am happy.*		*I am dancing because I am happy.*

All these conjunctions need a comma before them.

Wenn — *If / When*

Ich werde kommen.	**wenn**	Ich will.	→	Ich werde kommen, wenn ich will.
I will come.	*if*	*I want to.*		*I will come if I want to.*

Ich spreche mit Faye.	**wenn**	Wir spielen Tennis.	→	Ich spreche mit Faye, wenn wir Tennis spielen.
I speak to Faye.	*when*	*We play tennis.*		*I speak to Faye when we play tennis.*

Als — *When*

'<u>Als</u>' also means '<u>when</u>', but you only use it to refer to the <u>past</u>.

Ich habe oft geweint.	**als**	Ich war jünger.	→	Ich habe oft geweint, als ich jünger war.
I often cried.	*when*	*I was younger.*		*I often cried when I was younger.*

Obwohl — *Although*

Ich werde mitspielen.	**obwohl**	Ich bin müde.	→	Ich werde mitspielen, obwohl ich müde bin.
I will play.	*although*	*I'm tired.*		*I will play although I'm tired.*

No 'ifs' and 'buts' — learn your German conjunctions...

Write these sentences in German — remember to put the verb in the right place.

1. I like reading because it's relaxing.
2. Come to my party if you have time (inf. sing.).
3. We were best friends when we were children.
4. I want to be a teacher although it's hard work.

'The', 'A' and 'No'

'The' and 'a' are really tricky in German because they change to match the gender of the noun (masculine, feminine or neuter — see p.60) and the case (nominative, accusative, genitive or dative — see p.58-59).

'The' — start by learning der, die, das, die

1) In English, there's just <u>one</u> word for 'the' — simple.

2) In German, you need to know whether to use the <u>masculine</u>, <u>feminine</u> or <u>neuter</u> word for '<u>the</u>' and what <u>case</u> to use (<u>nominative</u>, <u>accusative</u>, <u>genitive</u> or <u>dative</u>).

3) Start by learning the <u>first line</u> of the grid — <u>der</u>, <u>die</u>, <u>das</u>, <u>die</u>. You <u>absolutely</u> have to know those ones.

	Masculine	Feminine	Neuter	Plural
Nominative	der	die	das	die
Accusative	den	die	das	die
Genitive	des	der	des	der
Dative	dem	der	dem	den

Masculine, nominative →	Der Apfel ist rot. *The apple is red.*
Plural, dative →	Ich singe den Äpfeln. *I sing to the apples.*

To find out why there's an '-n' at the end of 'Äpfeln', see p.59.

'A' — start by learning ein, eine, ein

1) Like the German for 'the', the word for 'a' is different for <u>masculine</u>, <u>feminine</u> or <u>neuter</u> nouns, and for different <u>cases</u>.

2) Start by learning the <u>first line</u> of the grid — <u>ein</u>, <u>eine</u>, <u>ein</u>. Then, move on to the other ones.

	Masculine	Feminine	Neuter
Nominative	ein	eine	ein
Accusative	einen	eine	ein
Genitive	eines	einer	eines
Dative	einem	einer	einem

Masculine, nominative →	Ein Hund bellt. *A dog barks.*
Feminine, accusative →	Ich habe eine Katze. *I have a cat.*

'No' — kein

1) '<u>Kein</u>' means '<u>no</u>' — as in '<u>I have no potatoes</u>'.

2) It <u>changes</u> a bit like '<u>ein</u>' changes.

Plural, nominative →	Keine Hunde sind lila. *No dogs are purple.*

	Masculine	Feminine	Neuter	Plural
Nominative	kein	keine	kein	keine
Accusative	keinen	keine	kein	keine
Genitive	keines	keiner	keines	keiner
Dative	keinem	keiner	keinem	keinen

Singular, neuter, accusative	Ich habe kein Buch. *I have no book.*

Der-die-das — sounds like German trainers...

Fill in the gaps with the German for the word in brackets.

1. Ich mag ...... Film. *(the)*
2. Ich gebe es ...... Frau. *(the)*
3. Ich habe ...... Birne. *(a)*
4. Wer hat ...... Onkel? *(a)*
5. Ich habe ...... Bleistift. *(no)*
6. Sie wird dir ...... Geld geben. *(no)*

| Adjectives | # Words to Describe Things |

Make your sentences more interesting (which means more marks) with some adjectives.

Adjectives that go after the noun don't change

When the adjective is somewhere <u>after</u> the word it's describing (e.g. apple), it <u>doesn't change</u> at all. You just use the <u>basic</u> adjective, <u>without</u> any <u>endings</u>.

| Der Apfel ist rot. | *The apple is red.* | Das Haus ist rot. | *The house is red.* |

Sarah was determined to make her investment in paint worthwhile...

Endings for when the adjective comes before the noun

1) If the adjective comes <u>before</u> the noun, you have to give it the right <u>ending</u> from the table.

	Masculine	Feminine	Neuter	Plural
Nominative	rot<u>er</u>	rot<u>e</u>	rot<u>es</u>	rot<u>e</u>
Accusative	rot<u>en</u>	rot<u>e</u>	rot<u>es</u>	rot<u>e</u>
Genitive	rot<u>en</u>	rot<u>er</u>	rot<u>en</u>	rot<u>er</u>
Dative	rot<u>em</u>	rot<u>er</u>	rot<u>em</u>	rot<u>en</u>

Plural accusative

Ich habe rot<u>e</u> Äpfel.
I have red apples.

2) You also use these endings if the adjective comes <u>after</u> a <u>number</u> bigger than one, or after <u>viele</u> (*many*), <u>wenige</u> (*few*), <u>einige</u> (*some*), <u>etwas</u> (*something*) or <u>nichts</u> (*nothing*).

After 'etwas' and 'nichts', you need the neuter endings and a capital.

| Ich habe viele groß<u>e</u> Äpfel. | *I have many big apples.* | etwas Neu<u>es</u> | *something new* |

There are special endings after 'the'

You've got to add these endings if the adjective comes <u>after the</u> (<u>der</u>, <u>die</u>, <u>das</u> etc.), <u>dieser</u> (*this*), <u>jeder</u> (*each / every*), <u>beide</u> (*both*), <u>welcher</u> (*which*) and <u>alle</u> (*all*).

	Masculine	Feminine	Neuter	Plural
Nominative	rot<u>e</u>	rot<u>e</u>	rot<u>e</u>	rot<u>en</u>
Accusative	rot<u>en</u>	rot<u>e</u>	rot<u>e</u>	rot<u>en</u>
Genitive	rot<u>en</u>	rot<u>en</u>	rot<u>en</u>	rot<u>en</u>
Dative	rot<u>en</u>	rot<u>en</u>	rot<u>en</u>	rot<u>en</u>

Masculine nominative

Der rot<u>e</u> Apfel.   *The red apple.*
Dieser klein<u>e</u> Apfel ist gut.
This small apple is good.

There are special endings after 'a' and belonging words

You need these endings when the adjective comes <u>after ein</u> (*a*, or *one*) or <u>kein</u> (*no*, or *none*), or after pronouns like <u>mein</u>, <u>dein</u>, <u>sein</u>, <u>ihr</u>...

	Masculine	Feminine	Neuter	Plural
Nominative	rot<u>er</u>	rot<u>e</u>	rot<u>es</u>	rot<u>en</u>
Accusative	rot<u>en</u>	rot<u>e</u>	rot<u>es</u>	rot<u>en</u>
Genitive	rot<u>en</u>	rot<u>en</u>	rot<u>en</u>	rot<u>en</u>
Dative	rot<u>en</u>	rot<u>en</u>	rot<u>en</u>	rot<u>en</u>

Masculine nominative

Mein rot<u>er</u> Apfel ist gut.
My red apple is good.

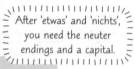

This is a roten way to spend an evening...

Translate these sentences into German.

1. The horse is grey.
2. I see three grey horses.
3. He has two grey horses.
4. She likes the grey horse.
5. Which grey horse?
6. The grey horse is big.
7. I have a grey horse.
8. This grey horse is old.

Words to Describe Things

Here are some adjectives to whet your appetite. You need to know how to say my, his, your... too.

Learn these adjectives

groß	*big / tall*	einfach	*easy*	neu	*new*	interessant	*interesting*
klein	*small / short*	schwierig	*difficult*	schnell	*fast*	spannend	*exciting*
lang	*long*	schön	*beautiful*	langsam	*slow*	lustig	*funny*
breit	*wide*	hässlich	*ugly*	doof	*stupid*	gut	*good*
glücklich	*happy*	alt	*old*	langweilig	*boring*	schlecht	*bad*
traurig	*sad*	jung	*young*	seltsam	*strange*	schlimm	*bad*

My, your, our — *words for who it belongs to*

1) You have to be able to use these words to say that something belongs to you ('mein') or to someone else.

2) But watch out — they need the right ending to go with the object you're talking about
(they're the same as the kein / keine / kein / keine table — see p.65).

	Masculine	Feminine	Neuter	Plural
Nominative	mein	meine	mein	meine
Accusative	meinen	meine	mein	meine
Genitive	meines	meiner	meines	meiner
Dative	meinem	meiner	meinem	meinen

Meine Tasche ist blau.
My bag is blue.

Ich mag mein Fahrrad.
I like my bike.

3) The other possessive words are pretty neat — all of them use the same endings as 'mein' does.

The Possessive Adjectives

mein	my	unser	our
dein	your (informal singular)	euer	your (informal plural)
sein	his	Ihr	your (formal singular & plural)
ihr	her		
sein	its	ihr	their

Dein Onkel heißt Mark. *Your uncle is called Mark.*

Seine Tasche ist blau. *His bag is blue.*

Unsere Lehrer sind streng. *Our teachers are strict.*

Welcher, dieser and jeder — *Which, this and every*

The endings for these words follow the same pattern as 'der'. Look at the last letter for each
word in the first table on p.65 — the last line would be diesem, dieser, diesem, diesen.

You use 'welcher' here because 'Bus' is masculine. 'Welche' is for feminine words and 'welches' is for neuter words.

Question
Welcher Bus fährt in die Stadt?
Which bus goes into town?

Simple Answer
Dieser Bus fährt direkt in die Stadt.
This bus goes directly into town.

Extended Answer
Dieser Bus fährt direkt in die Stadt, aber jeder Bus fährt in diese Richtung.
This bus goes directly into town, but every bus goes in that direction.

The happy student revised the interesting German...

Rewrite these sentences in German — check the tables on this page and p.65-66 to get all the right endings.

1. My house is big.
2. Her baby is happy.
3. Every job is boring.
4. Who has my new pen?
5. This music is great.
6. I bought this fast car
7. Which coat does he want?
8. My sister's dog is funny.

Words to Compare Things

Sometimes, something isn't just big, or red, or whatever — it's the biggest, or bigger than something else...

How to say smaller, smallest, etc.

Check the top of p.67 for more adjectives.

1) In English, you say small, small**er**, small**est**. It's almost the same in German:

Anna ist klein.
Anna is small.

Omar ist kleiner.
Omar is smaller.

Tina ist die Kleinste.
Tina is the smallest.

Here the adjective acts as a noun, just like in English — and of course all German nouns get a capital letter.

Stem	Stem + '-er'	'der', 'die', 'das' + stem + '-(e)ste'
billig *cheap*	billig**er** *cheaper*	der / die / das Billig**ste** *the cheapest*
interessant *interesting*	interessant**er** *more interesting*	der / die / das Interessant**este** *the most interesting*

2) Comparative adjectives are made up of a normal adjective and the ending '-er'.
In German, you can't add 'mehr' (*more*) before the adjective like you can in English.

die wichtigeren Tage   *the more important days*

Comparatives work like adjectives, so you've got to use the right adjective endings — see p.66.

3) To form a superlative, you normally add '-ste' to the stem of the adjective. Sometimes you add '-este' instead, to make it easier to pronounce.

Maria ist die Klugste.   *Maria is the cleverest.*
Das Auto ist das Lauteste.   *The car is the loudest.*

4) You can add '-er' and '-(e)ste' to almost any adjective. A lot of short ones add an umlaut.

Jay ist älter als Mike, aber Gavin ist der Älteste.   *Jay is older than Mike, but Gavin is the oldest.*

There are some odd ones

Just like in English, there are exceptions — for example, you don't say good, gooder, goodest...

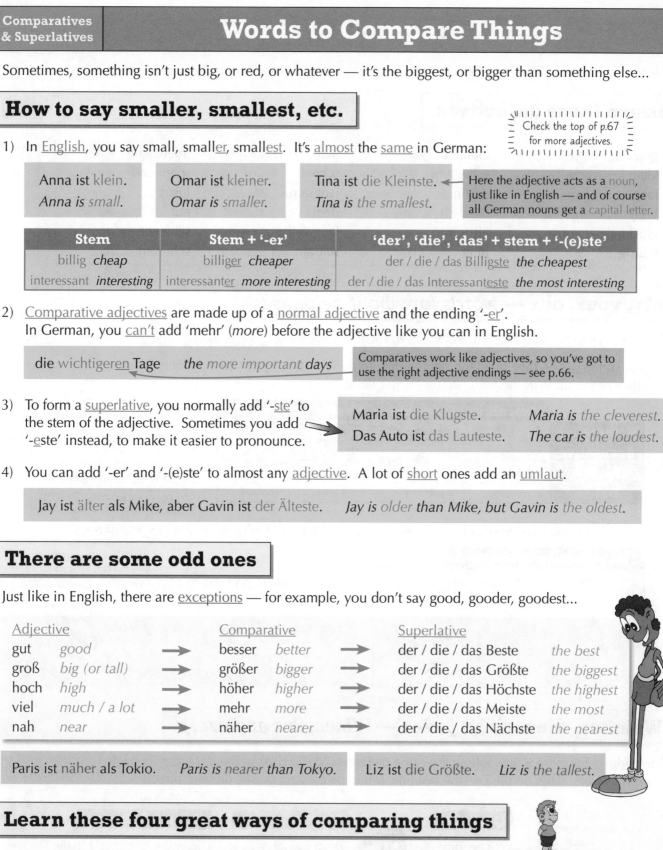

Adjective		Comparative		Superlative	
gut	*good*	besser	*better*	der / die / das Beste	*the best*
groß	*big (or tall)*	größer	*bigger*	der / die / das Größte	*the biggest*
hoch	*high*	höher	*higher*	der / die / das Höchste	*the highest*
viel	*much / a lot*	mehr	*more*	der / die / das Meiste	*the most*
nah	*near*	näher	*nearer*	der / die / das Nächste	*the nearest*

Paris ist näher als Tokio.   *Paris is nearer than Tokyo.*

Liz ist die Größte.   *Liz is the tallest.*

Learn these four great ways of comparing things

① Jo ist älter als Li.
Jo is older than Li.

② Jo ist weniger alt als Li.
Jo is less old than Li.

③ Jo ist so alt wie Li.
Jo is as old as Li.

④ Jo ist genauso alt wie Li.
Jo is just as old as Li.

Never compare yourself to others — except in German...

Translate these words, phrases and sentences into German.

1. happy, happier, the happiest
2. slow, slower, the slowest
3. pretty, prettier, the prettiest
4. sad, more sad, the most sad
5. That's the bigger house.
6. Katrin is just as lazy as Klaus.

Words to Describe Actions

This page is about describing things you do, e.g. 'I speak German perfectly', and about adding more info, e.g. 'I speak German almost perfectly'. I'll tell you how — make yourself a nice cuppa, sit down and read on.

Make your sentences better by saying how you do things

1) In <u>English</u>, you don't say 'We speak strange' — you <u>add 'ly'</u> onto the end to say 'We speak strange<u>ly</u>'.

2) In <u>German</u>, you <u>don't</u> have to do anything — you just stick the describing word in <u>as it is</u>.

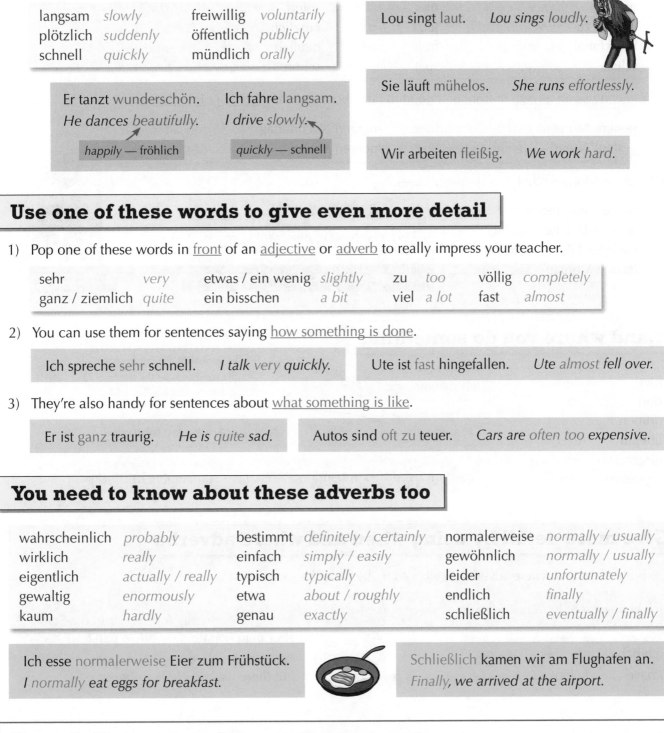

langsam	*slowly*	freiwillig	*voluntarily*
plötzlich	*suddenly*	öffentlich	*publicly*
schnell	*quickly*	mündlich	*orally*

Lou singt laut.   *Lou sings loudly.*

Er tanzt wunderschön.   Ich fahre langsam.
He dances beautifully.   *I drive slowly.*

happily — fröhlich   quickly — schnell

Sie läuft mühelos.   *She runs effortlessly.*

Wir arbeiten fleißig.   *We work hard.*

Use one of these words to give even more detail

1) Pop one of these words in <u>front</u> of an <u>adjective</u> or <u>adverb</u> to really impress your teacher.

sehr	*very*	etwas / ein wenig	*slightly*	zu	*too*	völlig	*completely*
ganz / ziemlich	*quite*	ein bisschen	*a bit*	viel	*a lot*	fast	*almost*

2) You can use them for sentences saying <u>how something is done</u>.

Ich spreche sehr schnell.   *I talk very quickly.*   Ute ist fast hingefallen.   *Ute almost fell over.*

3) They're also handy for sentences about <u>what something is like</u>.

Er ist ganz traurig.   *He is quite sad.*   Autos sind oft zu teuer.   *Cars are often too expensive.*

You need to know about these adverbs too

wahrscheinlich	*probably*	bestimmt	*definitely / certainly*	normalerweise	*normally / usually*
wirklich	*really*	einfach	*simply / easily*	gewöhnlich	*normally / usually*
eigentlich	*actually / really*	typisch	*typically*	leider	*unfortunately*
gewaltig	*enormously*	etwa	*about / roughly*	endlich	*finally*
kaum	*hardly*	genau	*exactly*	schließlich	*eventually / finally*

Ich esse normalerweise Eier zum Frühstück.
I normally eat eggs for breakfast.

Schließlich kamen wir am Flughafen an.
Finally, we arrived at the airport.

I speak German good (but English less good)...

Rewrite each of these sentences, adding an adverb. Use more than one adverb where you can for a prize*.

1. Ich gehe.   **3.** Er hat gesprochen.   **5.** Das Auto hält.   **7.** Stephan kam spät.

2. Sie laufen.   **4.** Ich helfe Lukas.   **6.** Wir werden gewinnen.   **8.** Es kostet zwei Euro.

---

*Prize to be revealed...um...never...

Adverbs	**Words to Describe Actions**

Adverbs can also give details about time and place — when and where you'll be doing your German homework, for example, or something like that. Add a few to your sentences to bag loads of marks.

Use adverbs to say when you do something...

1) Adverbs can tell you <u>when</u> or <u>how often</u> something happens.

immer	*always*	täglich	*daily*	gleich	*immediately / in a minute*
oft	*often*	nie	*never*	sofort	*immediately / straightaway*
ab und zu	*now and again*	jetzt	*now*	kürzlich	*recently / lately*
manchmal	*sometimes*	früh	*early*	neulich	*recently / the other day*
selten	*seldom / rarely*	spät	*late*	schon	*already*

2) You can use an <u>adverb</u> in front of a <u>noun</u> to talk about a more <u>specific point in time</u>.

gestern Morgen	*yesterday morning*	morgen Nachmittag	*tomorrow afternoon*
gestern Abend	*yesterday evening*	morgen Abend	*tomorrow evening*

3) There are lots of other useful time phrases.

heute Vormittag	*this morning*
nächste Woche	*next week*
nächstes Jahr	*next year*
letzten Montag	*last Monday*

Wir feiern am kommenden Freitag.
We're celebrating this coming Friday.

'Nächste' and 'letzten' are adjectives, so you have to give them the right ending — see p.66.

Derek knew he was going to have a smashing time at the party...

...and where you do something

hier	*here*
dort	*there*
drüben	*over there*
überall	*everywhere*
nirgendwo	*nowhere*
irgendwo	*somewhere*

Ich wohne hier. *I live here.*

The word order changes because the verb has to be the second idea in the sentence. See p.62.

Drüben spielen wir Fußball. *Over there, we play football.*

Er wohnt irgendwo in London. *He lives somewhere in London.*

Give more detail by using when and where adverbs

Use <u>both</u> when and where adverbs <u>together</u> to really wow the examiners.

Ich gehe gleich dorthin. *I'm going there immediately.*

Ich habe schon überall gesucht.
I have already looked everywhere.

Letzten Donnerstag fuhren wir in die Stadt, aber man konnte nirgendwo parken.

Last Thursday, we went into town, but there was nowhere to park.

Time, place — and space? I was on Mars visiting the aliens...

Write these sentences in German. The adverbs are all from the boxes above.

1. I brush my teeth daily.
2. Andrea often tells jokes.
3. I never play tennis there.
4. There are birds everywhere.
5. They sometimes meet over there.
6. I'll see you here this coming Monday.

Words to Compare Actions

If you do something, and then someone else does it differently — or maybe even better (annoying, isn't it) — you can talk about it using comparisons. It's a lot of the same stuff from p.68, but here it's comparing actions.

You can compare how people do things

1) To say someone is doing something '<u>more... than</u>' someone else, add '<u>er</u>' to the adverb and use '<u>als</u>'.

> Ida fährt langsam<u>er</u> als ich.   *Ida drives more slowly than me.*
> Neil singt süß<u>er</u> als Leo.   *Neil sings more sweetly than Leo.*

2) You can say someone is doing something '<u>less... than</u>' someone else by using '<u>nicht so... wie</u>'.

> Grace arbeitet nicht so hart wie Ruth.   *Grace works less hard than Ruth.*

3) If you want to say someone is doing something '<u>just as...</u>' or '<u>just as much as...</u>' someone else, use '<u>genauso... wie</u>' and '<u>genauso viel wie</u>'.

> Aaron läuft genauso langsam wie Ethel.   *Aaron walks just as slowly as Ethel.*

> Mädchen mögen Tennis genauso viel wie Jungen.   *Girls like tennis just as much as boys.*

You can say who does something the quickest, slowest...

If you want to say something's the <u>quickest</u>, the <u>slowest</u> or the <u>craziest</u>, you use '<u>am</u>' and then add '<u>-(e)sten</u>' to the end of the adverb.

This is the superlative.

> Dani tanzt am schnell<u>sten</u>.   *Dani dances the fastest.*
> Der Vogel kräht am lau<u>testen</u>.   *The bird crows the loudest.*

If the adverb ends in '-d' or '-t', you need to add '-esten'.

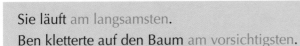

> Sie läuft am langsamsten.   *She runs the slowest.*
> Ben kletterte auf den Baum am vorsichtigsten.   *Ben climbed up the tree the most carefully.*

Watch out for these odd ones

'<u>Gern</u>', '<u>gut</u>' and '<u>viele</u>' are three strange ones that <u>don't</u> follow the rules.

gern	*willingly*
lieber	*preferably*
am liebsten	*best of all*

gut	*good*
besser	*better*
am besten	*best*

viele	*lots*
mehr	*more*
am meisten	*the most*

> Ich spreche lieber Deutsch.   *I prefer speaking German.*

> Berlin gefällt mir am besten.   *I like Berlin the best.*

> Er mag die Schuhe am meisten.   *He likes the shoes the most.*

I missed my alarm today — never have I run to school schneller...

Translate these phrases from English into German.

1. I run faster than her.
2. They play football the best.
3. We will eat more slowly.
4. He jumps the farthest.
5. The man sings the most beautifully.
6. Albert paints better than Liesl.

Subject Pronouns	# I, You, He, She, We, They

Pronouns are useful little words like 'I' and 'them'. They crop up everywhere, so it's worth learning them.

You use subject pronouns in the nominative case

Check p.58 for more on the nominative case.

Words like 'I', 'you', 'he', etc. are <u>subject pronouns</u>. They replace the <u>subject</u> of a sentence.

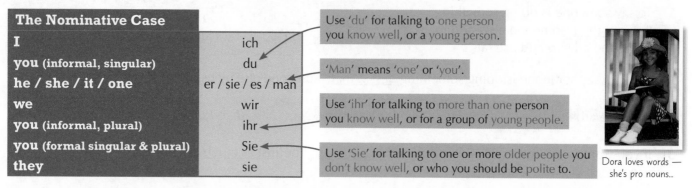

The Nominative Case	
I	ich
you (informal, singular)	du
he / she / it / one	er / sie / es / man
we	wir
you (informal, plural)	ihr
you (formal singular & plural)	Sie
they	sie

Use 'du' for talking to one person you know well, or a young person.

'Man' means 'one' or 'you'.

Use 'ihr' for talking to more than one person you know well, or for a group of young people.

Use 'Sie' for talking to one or more older people you don't know well, or who you should be polite to.

Dora loves words — she's pro nouns...

Der Hund beißt den Kamm. Er beißt den Kamm.   *The dog bites the comb. He bites the comb.*

There are pronouns for the accusative case...

Words like 'me', 'you' and 'him' are for the person / thing that's <u>having the action done to it</u> (the direct object).

The Accusative Case						
me	**you** (inf. sing.)	**him / her / it**	**us**	**you** (inf. pl.)	**you** (frml. sing. & plu.)	**them**
mich	dich	ihn / sie / es	uns	euch	Sie	sie

'Anrufen' is a separable verb. See p.86.

Er ruft mich an.
He calls me.

... and for the dative case

For things like writing <u>to someone</u>, you use the <u>dative</u> case (see p.59).

The Dative Case						
to me	**to you** (inf. sing.)	**to him / her / it**	**to us**	**to you** (inf. pl.)	**to you** (frml. sing. & plu.)	**to them**
mir	dir	ihm / ihr / ihm	uns	euch	Ihnen	ihnen

Ich schreibe ihr.
I write to her.

Jemand, niemand — *someone, no one*

'<u>Jemand</u>' means '<u>someone</u>' or '<u>anyone</u>'. To say '<u>no one</u>', use '<u>niemand</u>'.

Ist jemand da?   *Is someone / anyone there?*   Niemand hat mich gesehen.   *No one has seen me.*

These examiners are really taking the mich now...

Write these sentences in German, using the right case for each pronoun.

1. He sees her.
2. They see us.
3. I speak to you (inf. plu.).
4. You (frml. sing.) speak to me.
5. I know you (inf. sing.).
6. She knows them.

There are two verbs for 'to know' in German — make sure you use the right one.

Reflexive Pronouns

Some verbs don't make sense if you don't add 'myself', 'yourself', etc., so you've got to learn this stuff.

Talking about yourself — 'sich'

'Sich' means 'oneself'. It changes depending on who's doing the action.

> You can tell which verbs need 'self' by checking in the dictionary. E.g. if you look up 'to get dressed', it'll say 'sich anziehen'.

Reflexive Pronouns

mich	*myself*	uns	*ourselves*
dich	*yourself (inf. sing.)*	euch	*yourselves (inf. plu.)*
sich	*himself / herself /*	sich	*yourself / yourselves (frml. sing. & plu.)*
	itself	sich	*themselves / each other*

Ich wasche mich — *I wash myself*

1) <u>Reflexive pronouns</u> help you talk about your daily routine. They normally go <u>after</u> the <u>verb</u>.

ich wasche mich	*I wash myself*	wir waschen uns	*we wash ourselves*
du wäschst dich	*you wash yourself*	ihr wascht euch	*you wash yourselves*
er wäscht sich	*he washes himself*	Sie waschen sich	*you wash yourself / yourselves*
sie wäscht sich	*she washes herself*	sie waschen sich	*they wash themselves*
es wäscht sich	*it washes itself*		

2) Here are some examples of verbs that need <u>reflexive pronouns</u>. They're called <u>reflexive verbs</u>. See p.79.

sich anziehen	*to get dressed*	sich entschuldigen	*to excuse oneself*
sich fühlen	*to feel*	sich setzen	*to sit down*
sich umziehen	*to get changed*	sich sonnen	*to sun oneself*

Ich ziehe mich an. *I get dressed.*

With separable verbs (p.86), the 'sich' bit goes straight after the main verb.

Ich putze mir die Zähne — *I clean my teeth*

Some verbs need you to add '<u>to myself</u>' and '<u>to yourself</u>'. This is the dative case.

sich die Zähne putzen	*to clean one's teeth*
sich ... wünschen	*to want / wish for...*
sich ... vorstellen	*to imagine...*

Reflexive Pronouns in the Dative Case

mir	*to myself*	uns	*to ourselves*
dir	*to yourself (inf. sing.)*	euch	*to yourselves (inf. plu.)*
sich	*to himself /*	sich	*to yourself / yourselves (frml. sing. & plu.)*
	herself / itself	sich	*to themselves / each other*

Ich wünsche mir ein Pferd. *I want a horse.*

Ich habe mich gewaschen — *I have washed myself*

The <u>perfect tense</u> of these verbs is pretty much the same as normal (see p.80) except they <u>all go with 'haben'</u>, not 'sein'.

Er hat sich schlecht gefühlt. *He felt bad (ill).*

Put the 'sich' straight after 'haben'.

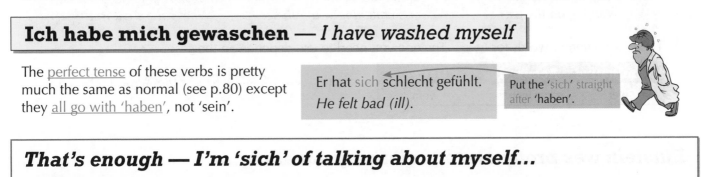

That's enough — I'm 'sich' of talking about myself...

Turn these English sentences into glittery German ones.

1. They wash themselves.   3. He excuses himself.   5. You (inf. sing.) clean your teeth.   7. We get changed.
2. I feel happy.   4. She suns herself.   6. You (frml. plu.) want a dog.   8. I got changed.

| Relative Pronouns | # Relative and Interrogative Pronouns |

Tricky stuff this, but learn it and you'll nab yourself loads of juicy marks.

Relative pronouns — 'that', 'which', 'whom', 'whose'

1) Words like 'that', 'which', 'whom' and 'whose' are relative pronouns — they relate back to the things you're talking about.

2) In German, relative pronouns send the verb to the end of the relative clause.

> The pronoun refers back to 'der Mann'.

Der Mann, der in der Ecke sitzt, ist klein.
The man who sits in the corner is small.

> The verb goes to the end of the clause.

> The relative clause (the bit with the relative pronoun in) is introduced by a comma.

You've got to use the right one

The relative pronoun you need depends on the noun's case (p.58-59) and its gender (p.60).

	Masculine	Feminine	Neuter	Plural
nominative	der	die	das	die
accusative	den	die	das	die
genitive	dessen	deren	dessen	deren
dative	dem	der	dem	denen

Die Katze, die mich kratzte, war weiß.
The cat which scratched me was white.

Die Hunde, denen er folgt, sind groß.
The dogs that he follows are big.

Der Mann, den ich sah, war witzig.
The man whom I saw was funny.

Das Pferd, dessen Bein gebrochen ist, ist traurig.
The horse whose leg is broken is sad.

'Was' can be used as a relative pronoun too

1) 'Was' can also be used as a relative pronoun.

2) It can be used after 'alles', 'nichts', 'etwas', 'vieles' and 'weniges'.

Alles, was der Lehrer sagte, war interessant.
Everything that the teacher said was interesting.

Wer? Was? Was für? — Who? What? What sort of?

> See p.4-5 for more about questions.

1) Some pronouns can be used as question words. These are called interrogative pronouns.

Wer sitzt auf der Katze?
Who is sitting on the cat?

Was kratzt dich, Albert?
What is scratching you, Albert?

Was für eine Katze ist sie?
What sort of cat is it?

2) There are different words for 'wer'. The one you need to use depends on the case.

Nominative	Accusative	Dative
wer	wen	wem

Mit wem spreche ich?   *Whom am I talking to?*

Einstein was pretty clever, relatively speaking...

Translate these sentences into German. Make sure you use the right gender/case and remember the commas.

1. The woman who wears a hat is pretty.
2. The people to whom I write are nice.
3. The child whose coat is red laughs.
4. Whom did he see?
5. Nothing that she does is easy.

Prepositions

Prepositions are tiny little words that help make it clear what's happening in a sentence.

To — *zu or nach*

1) Where we use 'to', German speakers often use '<u>zu</u>'.

When you want to say 'to go' or 'to do', you need the infinitive, not a preposition. E.g. gehen = to go, machen = to make.

| Komm zu mir. *Come to me.* | zum Bahnhof gehen *to go (by foot) to the station* | zum = zu dem — see p.76. |

2) For travelling to somewhere in a <u>vehicle</u>, it's usually '<u>nach</u>', but '<u>an</u>' and '<u>in</u>' are sometimes used too.

| nach Berlin *to Berlin* | in die USA *to the USA* | ans Meer *to the sea* | ans = an das — see p.76. |

At — *an, bei, um or zu*

1) Where we use 'at', in German it's usually '<u>an</u>', but sometimes '<u>bei</u>' is used:

| Ich studiere an der Universität. *I study at university.* | Er ist bei einer Party. *He is at a party.* |

2) For 'at home', it's '<u>zu</u>', and for times, it's '<u>um</u>'.

| zu Hause *at home* | um acht Uhr *at 8 o'clock* |

On — *an or auf*

1) Where we use 'on', in German it tends to be '<u>an</u>'.

| an der Wand *on the wall* | am Montag *on Monday* | am = an dem — see p.76. |

2) For 'on foot', it's '<u>zu</u>' and for on top of something, it's '<u>auf</u>'.

| Es ist auf dem Tisch. *It is on the table.* | zu Fuß *on foot* |

From — *von or aus*

1) When we use 'from' in English, they usually use '<u>von</u>' in German, including for where someone / something has come from <u>recently</u>.

| Der Zug ist von Paris gekommen. *The train has come from Paris.* |

To say what something is 'made from', use 'aus'.

2) For where someone/thing is from <u>originally</u>, it's '<u>aus</u>'.

| Ich komme aus Wales. *I come from Wales.* |

In — *in or an*

1) Where we use 'in', German speakers also tend to use '<u>in</u>'.

| Sina wohnt in Wien. *Sina lives in Vienna.* | Nico ist im Bett. *Nico is in bed.* | im = in dem — see p.76. |

2) For 'in the morning / evening', it's '<u>an</u>'.

| am Morgen *in the morning* |

This page is a gift to you, from me...

Say which German preposition should be used in each sentence. Check above for help.

1. We walk to the park.   **3.** I'll find it at home.   **5.** The cat is on top of the sofa.   **7.** It's in the fridge.

2. The bus to Bath is slow.   **4.** She goes on foot.   **6.** I originally come from York.   **8.** It's in the evening.

Prepositions	**Prepositions**

Yep, more prepositions. Learn which words to use where — it's not always obvious from the English.

Of — 'von', 'aus' or left out

Where we use 'of', the German is usually '<u>von</u>', but you <u>leave it out</u> of dates and it's often <u>left out</u> in <u>genitive</u> sentences too.

ein Freund von mir	*a friend of mine*

aus Holz	*made of wood*	der erste Mai	*the first of May*	einer der Besten	*one of the best*

For — für or seit

To say 'for', German speakers usually use '<u>für</u>', but for time amounts in the past, it's '<u>seit</u>'.

ein Geschenk für mich	Ich habe sie seit zwei Jahren nicht gesehen.
a present for me	*I haven't seen her for two years.*

Zum, am, im — short forms

Some of the words on page 75 and above get <u>shortened</u> when they go with 'dem', 'das' or 'der'.

am ersten Januar	*on the first of January*

Short forms

an dem	→	am	bei dem	→	beim
an das	→	ans	von dem	→	vom
in dem	→	im	zu der	→	zur
in das	→	ins	zu dem	→	zum

Valerie reckoned that being tall was overrated...

To be 100% right, you have to use the right case

1) These words <u>change the case</u> (p.58-59) of the stuff <u>after</u> them. To know <u>what case</u> to use, <u>learn</u> these lists.

Accusative
bis *till, by*
durch *through*
entlang *along*
für *for*
gegen *against, about*
ohne *without*
um *round, around, at*

You might also see 'entlang' with the genitive case.

Dative
aus *from, out of*
bei *at, near*
gegenüber *opposite*
mit *with*
nach *to, after*
seit *since, for*
von *from, by, of*
zu *to, at, for*

Genitive
außerhalb *outside of*
statt *instead of*
trotz *despite*
während *during*
wegen *because of*

Dative or Accusative
an *to, on, in, at*
auf *on, to, at*
hinter *after, behind*
in *in, into, to*
neben *next to, beside*
über *via, above, over*
unter *under, among*
vor *before, ago, in front of*

2) For prepositions which use <u>either</u> the dative or accusative case, use the <u>accusative</u> when what you're talking about is <u>moving</u> and the <u>dative</u> if there's <u>no movement</u>.

Die Katze schläft hinter dem Sofa.	*The cat sleeps behind the (dative) sofa.*	The cat <u>isn't</u> moving.

Die Katze läuft hinter das Sofa.	*The cat runs behind the (accusative) sofa.*	The cat <u>is</u> moving.

In, out, shake it all about...

Write out these phrases and sentences in German.

1. through the wood   **3.** from her father   **5.** despite the rain   **7.** I ran along the road.

2. without his pen   **4.** after the film   **6.** during the party   **8.** He stands under the bridge.

Verbs in the Present Tense

Verbs are pretty darn important — and the present tense is a useful place to start.

Use the present tense for what's happening now

1) Verbs in the <u>present tense</u> describe something that's occurring <u>now</u>.

2) The present tense is used to say '<u>I do</u>' and '<u>I am doing</u>' — German doesn't have a separate '<u>-ing</u>' form.

3) You have to <u>change the verb</u> for <u>different people</u>. Normally, you just change the <u>ending</u> of the word.

4) The <u>endings are the same</u> for all <u>regular verbs</u>. '<u>Machen</u>' is regular, so here it is with its endings:

The first bit ('mach') doesn't change.

machen — to do or make			
ich mache	*I make*	wir machen	*we make*
du machst	*you (inf. sing.) make*	ihr macht	*you (inf. plu.) make*
er macht	*he makes*	Sie machen	*you (frml. sing.*
sie macht	*she makes*		*& plu.) make*
es macht	*it makes*	sie machen	*they make*

For the different forms of 'you' and when to use them, see p.72.

But there's a catch — see sub 2 below.

Watch out — *there's a catch*

Some regular verbs don't end in '-en' — they end in '<u>-rn</u>' or '<u>-ln</u>'.

For '-rn' verbs, you can miss out the 'e' before the 'r' for ich.

feiern — to celebrate			
ich	feire	wir	feiern
du	feierst	ihr	feiert
er / sie / es	feiert	Sie / sie	feiern

For '-ln' verbs, miss out the 'e' before the 'l' for ich.

segeln — to sail			
ich	segle	wir	segeln
du	segelst	ihr	segelt
er / sie / es	segelt	Sie / sie	segeln

Add '-n' not '-en' for wir, Sie and sie.

Instead of 'I go swimming', say 'I go to swim'

1) You sometimes need to say '<u>I go swimming</u>' rather than just 'I swim' — so you need <u>two</u> verbs.

2) You need to put the <u>first verb</u> in the <u>right form</u> for the <u>person</u>.
The <u>second verb</u> needs to be in the <u>infinitive</u> (the form ending in '<u>-en</u>' e.g 'sehen').

The infinitive is the form you'll find in a dictionary.

Ich gehe + schwimmen = Ich gehe schwimmen.   *I go swimming.*

Use 'seit' to say how long you've been doing something

To say things like 'I have been learning German <u>for</u> three years', use '<u>seit</u>' and the <u>present tense</u>.

Ich lerne seit drei Jahren Deutsch.   *I have been learning German for three years.*

Use the dative case after 'seit' (see p.59).

Great, I love presents...

Write these sentences in German. Use the endings for 'machen' unless the verb ends in '-rn' or '-ln'.

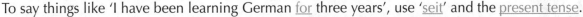

1. I play.
2. We believe.
3. You (inf. sing.) ask.
4. You (frml. plu.) dance.
5. I celebrate.
6. They sail.
7. I go running.
8. Jan goes camping.
9. I have been playing the piano for a year.

Present Tense	**More About the Present Tense**

You could be conned into thinking nearly all verbs are regular (see p.77). But in fact, loads aren't.

'Sein' and 'haben' are irregular

1) Verbs that <u>don't</u> follow the <u>same pattern</u> as regular verbs are called '<u>irregular verbs</u>'. Here are the <u>two</u> that you'll need most...

'Sein' means 'to be' — it's probably the most important verb... ever.

sein — to be

ich bin	*I am*	wir sind	*we are*
du bist	*you are*	ihr seid	*you are*
er / sie / es ist	*he / she / it is*	Sie / sie sind	*you / they are*

haben — to have

ich habe	*I have*	wir haben	*we have*
du hast	*you have*	ihr habt	*you have*
er / sie / es hat	*he / she / it has*	Sie / sie haben	*you / they have*

'Haben' means 'to have' — you'll need this verb loads.

2) All of these verbs are irregular too, so <u>watch out</u> for them:

lesen (er liest)	*to read (he reads)*	fahren (er fährt)	*to go (he goes)*
wissen (er weiß)	*to know (he knows)*	finden (er findet)	*to find (he finds)*
geben (er gibt)	*to give (he gives)*	tragen (er trägt)	*to wear, carry (he wears, carries)*

Er weiß viel über Sport. *He knows a lot about sport.*

Sie fährt nach Berlin. *She goes to Berlin.*

Some verbs make you use the dative case

1) You normally only need the <u>dative case</u> when you're saying '<u>to</u> something or someone'. See p.59.

2) But some German verbs <u>always</u> need the <u>dative</u> case, like '<u>helfen</u>' ('to help').

Ich helfe den Kindern. *I help the children.*

You use 'den' because 'Kinder' is plural and 'helfen' needs the dative.

3) These verbs all need the <u>dative case</u> — make sure you learn them:

danken	*to thank*	antworten	*to answer*	schreiben	*to write to*	gratulieren	*to congratulate*
folgen	*to follow*	weh tun	*to hurt*	glauben	*to believe*	empfehlen	*to recommend*

Ich gratuliere meinem Onkel. *I congratulate my uncle.*

Kannst du mir ein Café empfehlen? *Can you recommend a café to me?*

Irregular verbs make life that little bit more exciting — honestly...

Translate these sentences into German. Watch out for any irregular verbs.

1. She has a cat.
2. We are teachers.
3. I thank my aunt.
4. You (inf. sing.) follow the man.
5. Do you (frml. plu.) believe me?
6. She wears a tie.

More About the Present Tense

The present tense just keeps getting more and more exciting — here are some different ways of using verbs.

Use negative forms to say what's not happening now

To say what <u>doesn't happen</u>, you can add a <u>negative phrase</u> to the sentence.

nicht	*not*
gar nicht	*not at all*
nicht mehr	*no longer*
noch nicht	*not yet*
nichts	*nothing*
nirgendwo	*nowhere*

Der Vogel singt nicht.   *The bird doesn't sing.*

Es ist noch nicht fertig.   *It's not ready yet.*

Der Mann sieht nichts.   *The man sees nothing.*

Use reflexive verbs to talk about 'myself', 'yourself'…

Use <u>reflexive verbs</u> when you want to talk about what people do to themselves.
See p.73 for how to say '<u>myself</u>', '<u>yourself</u>' etc. in German in the accusative and dative cases.

Er zieht sich um.
He gets changed.

Ich fühle mich krank.
I feel sick.

Wir waschen uns die Hände.
We wash our hands.

This one's in the dative case. See p.73.

Impersonal forms with 'es'

Some German phrases have 'es' as the subject. Learn these common examples:

Wie geht es dir?   *How are you?*   Es tut weh.   *It hurts.*   Es regnet.   *It's raining.*

Es gefällt mir.   *I like it.*   Es gibt viel zu tun.   *There is lots to do.*   Es tut mir Leid.   *I'm sorry.*

Using the infinitive

1) You can use the <u>infinitive</u> to say things like '<u>in order to</u>' and '<u>without</u>'.

Ich habe es gemacht, um Geld zu sparen.
I did it in order to save money.

Sie fährt nie nach Italien ohne Pizza zu essen.
She never travels to Italy without eating pizza.

2) If you want to <u>link verbs</u> in a sentence, you need to add '<u>zu</u>'.

Ich versuche ein Buch zu schreiben.   *I'm trying to write a book.*

3) <u>Leave</u> the 'zu' out if the first verb is a <u>modal verb</u>. See p.87.

Ich muss nach Hause gehen.   *I must go home.*

'Müssen' is a modal verb, so you don't need a 'zu'.

The present — the gift that just keeps on giving…

Translate these sentences into German.

1. She does nothing.   **3.** I should say something.   **5.** I want to be famous in order to earn lots of money.

2. It's snowing.   **4.** He gives it back to me.   **6.** I can't go away without saying something.

Perfect Tense	# Talking About the Past

It's good to be able to talk about what's already happened. To say what you 'have done', use the perfect tense.

Use the perfect tense for things that have finished

See p.78 for all the endings for 'haben'.

1) The <u>perfect tense</u> usually starts with '<u>haben</u>' ('to have') and ends with a <u>past participle</u>.

Ich habe einen Sessel gekauft.	Er hat zwei Bücher gelesen.	Sie haben viel gegessen.
I have bought an armchair.	*He has read two books.*	*They have eaten a lot.*

2) To form the <u>past participle</u> (the past tense bit) of regular verbs, follow these steps:

kaufen *to buy*	→	kaufen - en = kauf	→	gekauft *bought*
Begin with the verb in the infinitive.		Remove '-en' from the end of the infinitive.		Add 'ge' to the start and add 't' to the end.

3) Here are some <u>more examples</u> — they all work the same way.

to do / make	machen	→	gemacht	*done / made*		to book	buchen	→	gebucht	*booked*
to ask	fragen	→	gefragt	*asked*		to clean	putzen	→	geputzt	*cleaned*

4) You don't always need the 'have' part in English.

Ich habe mein Haus geputzt.	Sie hat ihren Flug gebucht.	Wir haben es gemacht.
I (have) cleaned my house.	*She (has) booked her flight.*	*We have done / did it.*

Irregular verbs don't follow the pattern

<u>Irregular</u> verbs <u>work differently</u>. These are the <u>most important</u> ones:

to sleep	schlafen	→	geschlafen		to see	sehen	→	gesehen
to take	nehmen	→	genommen		to sing	singen	→	gesungen
to eat	essen	→	gegessen		to break	brechen	→	gebrochen
to drink	trinken	→	getrunken		to receive	bekommen	→	bekommen
to give	geben	→	gegeben		to forget	vergessen	→	vergessen
to bring	bringen	→	gebracht		to understand	verstehen	→	verstanden

Watch out — there's no 'ge' on the front.

Ist sie gegangen? — *Has she gone?*

See p.78 for the different forms of 'sein'.

1) Some verbs need '<u>sein</u>' ('to be') instead of '<u>haben</u>' in the <u>perfect tense</u>. Ich bin gegangen. *I have gone.*

2) It's mostly <u>movement verbs</u> that need '<u>sein</u>'. Here's a list of some common ones:

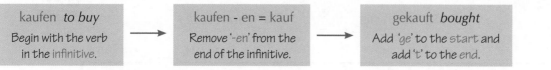

to go / drive	fahren	→	gefahren		to come	kommen	→	gekommen
to run	laufen	→	gelaufen		to stay	bleiben	→	geblieben
to climb	steigen	→	gestiegen		to be	sein	→	gewesen
to follow	folgen	→	gefolgt		to happen	passieren	→	passiert

That's all perfectly clear...

Write these sentences in German. Remember to check whether you need 'haben' or 'sein'.

1. I have drunk tea.
2. We have stayed at home.
3. He has seen me.
4. You (inf. sing.) have received a letter.
5. They have asked him.
6. You (frml. plu.) have come here.

Talking About the Past

It's your lucky day — time for another form of the past tense. But this one's used for saying things like 'I saw'.

Regular verbs in the simple past

You might hear the simple past referred to as the 'imperfect', too.

1) You use the simple past to say what happened in the past without using 'haben' or 'sein'.

2) The simple past is used more in written German, though some forms are common in speech too.

3) This is how you form the simple past form of a regular verb:

kaufen *to buy*	kaufen - en = kauf	ich kaufte *I bought*
Begin with the verb in the infinitive.	Remove '-en' from the end of the infinitive.	Add the correct simple past ending for the person.

machen — to make

ich machte	*I made*	wir machten	*we made*
du machtest	*you made*	ihr machtet	*you made*
er / sie / es machte	*he / she / it made*	Sie / sie machten	*you / they made*

spielen — to play

ich spielte	*I played*	wir spielten	*we played*
du spieltest	*you played*	ihr spieltet	*you played*
er / sie / es spielte	*he / she / it played*	Sie / sie spielten	*you / they played*

Er hasste **mich**.	Wir lernten **Deutsch**.	Ihr kochtet **zusammen**.	Ich spielte **Saxofon**.
*He hated **me**.*	*We learned **German**.*	*You cooked **together**.*	*I played **the saxophone**.*

Ich hatte — *I had* / Ich war — *I was*

1) You'll use the simple past forms of 'haben' and 'sein' loads in writing and in speech, so it's well worth learning them.

2) You need to know the simple past forms of the verb for each person.

Ich hatte — *I had*

ich hatte	wir hatten
du hattest	ihr hattet
er / sie / es hatte	Sie / sie hatten

Sie hatten vier Brüder.	Sie hatte ein blaues Kleid.
They had four brothers.	*She had a blue dress.*

Ich war — *I was*

ich war	wir waren
du warst	ihr wart
er / sie / es war	Sie / sie waren

Wir waren sehr müde.	Ich war ein komisches Kind.
We were very tired.	*I was a strange child.*

The Mad Hatter hatte a very strange tea party...

Try translating these sentences into German.

1. I had a dog.
2. We were very sad.
3. I played tennis.
4. They were there.
5. You (inf. sing.) had a good idea.
6. You (frml. sing.) bought a dog.
7. He used to cook.
8. She was young.

Simple Past	# Talking About the Past

You can use the simple past to say all kinds of things. Use it yourself to gain some juicy extra marks.

Irregular verbs in the simple past

1) Some verbs are <u>irregular</u> in the <u>simple past</u>. Here are some examples you need to learn.

gehen — to go

I went	ich ging
you (inf. sing.) went	du gingst
he / she / it went	er / sie / es ging
we went	wir gingen
you (inf. plu.) went	ihr gingt
they went	sie gingen
you (frml. sing. & plu.) went	Sie gingen

fahren — to go / drive

I went / drove	ich fuhr
you (inf. sing.) went / drove	du fuhrst
he / she / it went / drove	er / sie / es fuhr
we went / drove	wir fuhren
you (inf. plu.) went / drove	ihr fuhrt
they went / drove	sie fuhren
you (frml. sing. & plu.) went / drove	Sie fuhren

Er ging nach Hause.
He went home.

Use 'gehen' when you mean 'to go by foot'.

Wir fuhren nach Bonn.
We went / drove to Bonn.

Use 'fahren' for going somewhere in a vehicle, even if you're not the one doing the driving.

laufen — to run

I ran	ich lief
you (inf. sing.) ran	du liefst
he / she / it ran	er / sie / es lief
we ran	wir liefen
you (inf. plu.) ran	ihr lieft
they ran	sie liefen
you (frml. sing. & plu.) ran	Sie liefen

kommen — to come

I came	ich kam
you (inf. sing.) came	du kamst
he / she / it came	er / sie / es kam
we came	wir kamen
you (inf. plu.) came	ihr kamt
they came	sie kamen
you (frml. sing. & plu.) came	Sie kamen

2) Here are some other verbs which are also <u>irregular</u> in the <u>simple past</u>.

denken	ich dachte	*I thought*	trinken	ich trank	*I drank*	essen	ich aß	*I ate*
helfen	ich half	*I helped*	sehen	ich sah	*I saw*	singen	ich sang	*I sang*
schreiben	ich schrieb	*I wrote*	werden	ich wurde	*I became*	ziehen	ich zog	*I pulled*
nehmen	ich nahm	*I took*	bringen	ich brachte	*I brought*	geben	ich gab	*I gave*

Using 'seit' with the simple past

You can see more about 'seit' on p.77.

Use the <u>simple past</u> with 'seit' to say that something '<u>had been</u>' happening 'for' or 'since' a <u>certain time</u>.

Ich wartete seit zwei Stunden. *I had been waiting for two hours.*

You need the dative case after 'seit' (see p.59), so 'hours' needs to be 'Stunden'.

Seit 2003 brachte er Kuchen zur Schule. *Since 2003, he had been bringing cakes to school.*

Not so simple after all, then...

These sentences need translating — into German, not Latin, that is.

1. I drank a cup of tea.
2. I took the pen.
3. Maria wrote a book.
4. We saw him.
5. They had been helping for a year.
6. I had been eating for an hour.

Talking About the Past

Just one more form of the past tense to go — this one's called the pluperfect.

I had seen / I had bought etc...

1) The <u>pluperfect tense</u> is used to talk about things that happened <u>further back in the past</u>. You use it to say what you <u>had done</u>.

2) For the pluperfect tense, you need the <u>simple past form</u> of '<u>haben</u>' (see p.81) and the <u>past participle</u>.

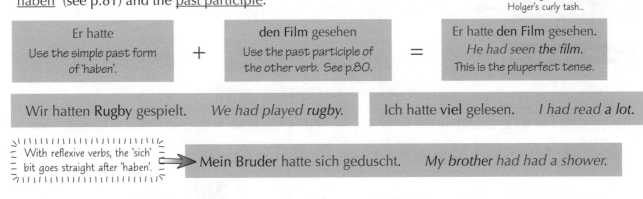

Kathi had grown fond of
Holger's curly tash...

| Er hatte
Use the simple past form
of 'haben'. | **+** | den Film gesehen
Use the past participle of
the other verb. See p.80. | **=** | Er hatte den Film gesehen.
He had seen the film.
This is the pluperfect tense. |

| Wir hatten Rugby gespielt. | *We had played rugby.* | | Ich hatte viel gelesen. | *I had read a lot.* |

With reflexive verbs, the 'sich' bit goes straight after 'haben'. ⟹ Mein Bruder hatte sich geduscht. *My brother had had a shower.*

Some verbs need 'sein' (*to be*) instead of 'haben' (*to have*)

1) In the <u>perfect</u> tense, some <u>verbs</u> need '<u>sein</u>' instead of '<u>haben</u>'. It's the same in the <u>pluperfect tense</u>.

2) You need the <u>simple past form</u> of '<u>sein</u>' (see p.81) and the <u>past participle</u>.

| Ich war
Use the simple past form
of 'sein'. | **+** | nach Ungarn gereist
Use the past participle of
the other verb. | **=** | Ich war nach Ungarn gereist.
I had travelled to Hungary.
This is the pluperfect tense. |

| Er war hier geblieben. | *He had stayed here.* | | Du warst schon gelandet. | *You had already landed.* |

3) You often need the pluperfect tense after <u>prepositions</u>.

Ich sprach mit ihnen, nachdem ich angekommen war.   *I spoke to them after I had arrived.*

I had been playing / I had been singing etc...

You can use the <u>pluperfect</u> tense to say things like '<u>I had been playing</u>' in German.

| Es war nass. Es hatte viel geregnet.
It was wet. It had been raining a lot. | → | This can also be translated
like the examples above: | → | Es war nass. Es hatte viel geregnet.
It was wet. It had rained a lot. |

After I had bought a German revision guide, revising was a doddle...

Write these pluperfect sentences in German.

1. I had learnt music.
2. He had eaten an ice cream.
3. She had got dressed.
4. They had gone to the park.
5. Tim had stayed at home.
6. We had been doing our homework.

Future Tense	**Talking About the Future**

You'll need to talk about things that are going to happen at some point in the future. There are two ways you can do it — and the first one's a piece of cake, so I'd learn that first if I were you.

1) You can use the present tense to talk about the future

1) Wahey — an easy bit. All you need to do to say something is <u>going</u> to happen in the <u>future</u> is to say it <u>does happen</u> and then say <u>when</u> it's going to happen. Brilliant.

Happening now	→	Ich fahre nach Wales.	*I am going to Wales.*

See p.77-79 for more on the present tense.

Going to happen	→	Ich fahre nächstes Jahr nach Wales.	*I am going to Wales next year.*

This tells you when it's going to happen.

2) The <u>time bit</u> can go <u>anywhere</u> in the sentence, as long as you keep to the rules of <u>word order</u> — see p.62.

Nächstes Jahr fahre ich nach Wales.   *Next year, I'm going to Wales.*

nächste Woche	*next week*	am Montag	*on Monday*	im Mai	*in May*
morgen	*tomorrow*	diesen Sommer	*this summer*	in der Zukunft	*in the future*

2) You can use 'werden' to say 'will' or 'to be going to do...'

1) This part's slightly trickier. '<u>Ich werde</u>' means '<u>I will</u>' or '<u>I am going to</u>'. To form the future tense with '<u>werden</u>', you need the right form of '<u>werden</u>' and the <u>infinitive</u> of the other verb.

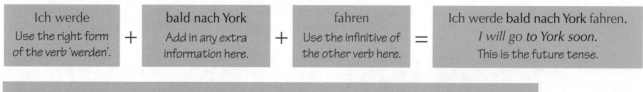

Ich werde		bald nach York		fahren		Ich werde bald nach York fahren.
Use the right form of the verb 'werden'.	+	Add in any extra information here.	+	Use the infinitive of the other verb here.	=	*I will go to York soon.* This is the future tense.

Ich werde mehr für die Umwelt tun.   *I am going to do more for the environment.*

2) '<u>Werden</u>' is an <u>irregular verb</u>, so you'll have to learn its <u>endings</u>.

Werden — will / to be going to do			
ich werde	*I will*	wir werden	*we will*
du wirst	*you (inf. sing.) will*	ihr werdet	*you (inf. plu.) will*
er / sie / es wird	*he / she / it will*	Sie / sie werden	*you (frml. sing. & plu.) / they will*

Wir werden unsere Hausaufgaben machen.   *We will do our homework.*

Eines Tages wirst du in die Schule gehen.   *One day, you will go to school.*

To infinitive and beyond...

Write these sentences in German using both the easy and the hard way of making the future tense.

1. I will go to the cinema on Monday.
2. He will explain it soon.
3. Angela will meet us next week.
4. They will visit us next year.
5. I'll eat pizza tomorrow.
6. Next time, we'll buy the car.

Giving Orders

	Imperatives

You're almost at the end — hurrah. Now it's your chance to boss someone about by using imperatives.

Use the imperative to give orders

1) Imperatives are used to give instructions. They tell people what to do, e.g. 'sit still' or 'let's eat'.

2) To form the imperative, use the present tense of the verb for 'du', 'ihr', 'Sie' and 'wir'. The only form that ends differently from the normal present tense is the 'du' form. It loses its ending (the '-st').

3) Here's how to turn a verb into an imperative:

Ivan wasn't sure how long he could stay like this...

> *The form you need depends on the person you're talking to. See p.72 for the different ways to say 'you'.*

Example — telling people to go		
Verb	Imperative	English
du gehst	Geh!	Go! (inf. sing.)
ihr geht	Geht!	Go! (inf. plu.)
Sie gehen	Gehen Sie!	Go! (frml. sing. & plu.)
wir gehen	Gehen wir!	Let's go!

Bleib hier!	*Stay here! (inf. sing.)*
Esst mehr!	*Eat more! (inf. plu.)*

4) Lots of verbs have an optional 'e' on the 'du' form of the imperative, like 'fragen' (to ask): Frag(e)! (Ask!).

There are some irregular imperatives

1) Some imperatives don't follow the rules in the 'du' form, e.g. 'lesen' only loses the 't' from 'du liest'.

Lies die Zeitung!	*Read the newspaper! (inf. sing.)*

2) 'Haben' and 'werden' also have a different stem in the 'du' form.

Verb	Imperative	English		Verb	Imperative	English
du hast	Hab!	*Have! (inf. sing.)*		du wirst	Werde!	*Become! (inf. sing.)*

3) The stem of 'sein' is 'sei' in all the imperative forms.

Verb	Imperative	English
du bist	Sei!	*Be! (inf. sing.)*

Imperatives can be used with negatives and reflexive verbs

1) To form negative imperatives, use 'nicht'.

Sei nicht traurig!	*Don't be sad! (inf. sing.)*		Weint nicht!	*Don't cry! (inf. plu.)*

2) For reflexive verbs with 'du' or 'ihr', the reflexive pronoun ('dich' or 'euch') goes after the verb.

Zieh dich an!	*Get yourself dressed! (inf. sing.)*		Bedient euch!	*Help yourselves! (inf. plu.)*

3) For reflexive verbs with 'wir' or 'Sie', the reflexive pronoun ('uns' or 'sich') goes after the 'wir' or 'Sie'.

Benehmen wir uns!	*Let's behave!*		Entscheiden Sie sich!	*Decide! (frml. sing. & plu.)*

Revise! That's an order.

Translate these sentences into German. The bit in brackets tells you who you're talking to.

1. Dance! (inf. sing.) **3.** Sit down! (frml. sing.) **5.** Don't help us! (inf. plu.) **7.** Let's go shopping!

2. Be polite! (inf. plu.) **4.** Work! (inf. sing.) **6.** Follow me! (frml. plu.) **8.** Relax! (inf. sing.)

Separable Verbs

Dealing with separable verbs sounds like a messy business, but just follow these steps towards GCSE glory.

Separable verbs can be split up in the present tense...

1) <u>Separable verbs</u> are made up of two bits: the <u>main verb</u> and a <u>bit on the front</u> that can be taken off.

> abwaschen (*to wash up*) = ab + waschen

2) In the <u>present tense</u>, change the verb for the <u>right person</u> and send the '<u>ab</u>' bit to the <u>end of the clause</u>.

> Ich wasche gern ab.   *I like washing up.*

3) Here are some examples of <u>separable verbs</u>. The bits that can be taken off are underlined.

<u>ab</u>waschen	*to wash up*	<u>heraus</u>kommen	*to come out*
<u>an</u>kommen	*to arrive*	<u>mit</u>nehmen	*to take with you*
<u>auf</u>hören	*to stop*	<u>weg</u>gehen	*to go out / away*
<u>aus</u>gehen	*to go out*	<u>zu</u>sehen	*to watch*
<u>ein</u>treten	*to enter*	<u>zurück</u>geben	*to give back*

It'd be a lot easier if they could just stay apart!

> Sie nimmt ihre Katze mit.
> *She takes her cat with her.*

> Ich gehe jetzt aus.
> *I'm going out now.*

> Ich trete ins Zimmer ein.
> *I enter the room.*

4) You might want to use separable verbs as <u>imperatives</u> — but you'll need to <u>split them up</u> first.

> Ruf mich an, Bernhard!   *Call me, Bernhard!*

> Passen Sie auf, bitte!   *Pay attention, please!*

...and in other tenses too

1) To use a separable verb in the <u>perfect tense</u> (see p.80), keep the <u>front bit</u> the same, but put the <u>main verb</u> in the <u>perfect tense</u>.

> Don't forget to use the correct form of 'haben' or 'sein' as well.

> aufhören (*to stop*) = auf + hören → aufgehört (*stopped*) → Er hat endlich aufgehört.
> *He has finally stopped.*

2) For the <u>simple past</u> (see p.81), send the <u>front bit</u> to the <u>end</u> and put the <u>main verb</u> in the <u>simple past</u>.

> ankommen (*to arrive*) = an + kommen → kam...an (*arrived*) → Ich kam spät an.
> *I arrived late.*

3) When you use separable verbs in the <u>future tense</u> with '<u>werden</u>' (see p.84), you use them in their <u>infinitive</u> form.

> Ich werde morgen ausgehen.   *I will go out tomorrow.*

> Er wird aufräumen.   *He will tidy up.*

zu sehen   zurück geben   mit nehmen   weg gehen   heraus kommen

We're not just splitting hairs — this separating stuff's important...

Translate these sentences into German using separable verbs.

1. I arrive tomorrow.
2. She goes out.
3. He took his brother with him.
4. You (inf. sing.) have washed up.
5. I have given it back.
6. Go away, Eric!
7. Let's go out.
8. I will stop.

Modal Verbs

Modal verbs are words like 'should' and 'could'. They're really good for giving opinions.

Ich muss diese Verben lernen... — *I must learn these verbs...*

1) Here are <u>six really handy</u> modal verbs:

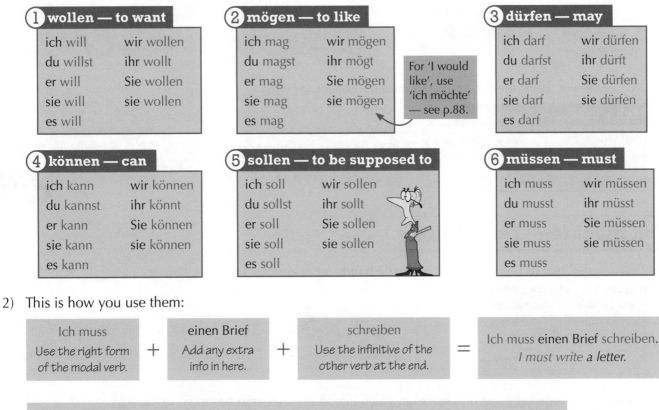

① wollen — to want

ich will	wir wollen
du willst	ihr wollt
er will	Sie wollen
sie will	sie wollen
es will	

② mögen — to like

ich mag	wir mögen
du magst	ihr mögt
er mag	Sie mögen
sie mag	sie mögen
es mag	

For 'I would like', use 'ich möchte' — see p.88.

③ dürfen — may

ich darf	wir dürfen
du darfst	ihr dürft
er darf	Sie dürfen
sie darf	sie dürfen
es darf	

④ können — can

ich kann	wir können
du kannst	ihr könnt
er kann	Sie können
sie kann	sie können
es kann	

⑤ sollen — to be supposed to

ich soll	wir sollen
du sollst	ihr sollt
er soll	Sie sollen
sie soll	sie sollen
es soll	

⑥ müssen — must

ich muss	wir müssen
du musst	ihr müsst
er muss	Sie müssen
sie muss	sie müssen
es muss	

2) This is how you use them:

Ich muss
Use the right form of the modal verb.

+

einen Brief
Add any extra info in here.

+

schreiben
Use the infinitive of the other verb at the end.

=

Ich muss einen Brief schreiben.
I must write a letter.

Du sollst deine Hausaufgaben machen. *You are supposed to do your homework.*

You can use modal verbs in the past tense too

1) To say something like 'I wanted to wash the car', you have to use the <u>past tense</u> of the <u>modal verb</u>.

2) For the simple past, <u>take off</u> the '<u>-en</u>' and the <u>umlaut</u> if there is one, and then <u>add the endings</u> in bold.

können — can

ich konn**te**	wir konn**ten**
du konn**test**	ihr konn**tet**
er / sie / es konn**te**	Sie / sie konn**ten**

Follow the same pattern for 'wollen', 'dürfen', 'sollen' and 'müssen' too.

WATCH OUT
'Mögen' is a bit different. It changes to 'mochten' in the past tense. It takes the same endings as all the others though.

Ich konnte meine Tasche nicht finden.
I couldn't find my bag.

Wir mochten in der Band spielen.
We liked playing in the band.

I prefer modal aeroplanes really...

Write these sentences in German.

1. I want a new guitar.
2. We like playing rugby.
3. You (inf. plu.) may sit down.
4. He can ski very well.
5. I'm supposed to go.
6. She must stay.
7. Jane had to play.
8. They wanted to fly.

Conditional	# Would, Could and Should

Use the conditional tense to say what you would, could and should do. You could pick up some marks too.

Ich würde Deutsch sprechen — *I would speak German*

1) You can say '<u>I would</u>...' in German by using the conditional form of '<u>werden</u>' and an <u>infinitive</u>.

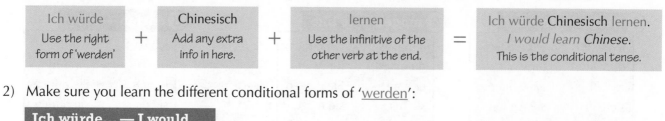

| Ich würde
Use the right
form of 'werden' | **+** | Chinesisch
Add any extra
info in here. | **+** | lernen
Use the infinitive of the
other verb at the end. | **=** | Ich würde **Chinesisch** lernen.
I would learn Chinese.
This is the conditional tense. |

2) Make sure you learn the different conditional forms of '<u>werden</u>':

Ich würde... — I would...

ich würde	wir würden
du würdest	ihr würdet
er / sie / es würde	Sie / sie würden

Was würdest du ihm sagen?
What would you say to him?

Wir würden es erlauben.
We would allow it.

Ich möchte — *I would like*

1) '<u>Ich möchte</u>' means '<u>I would like</u>'. It's really handy for asking for things.

> You can also use 'Ich hätte gern' to say what you'd like. See p.6.

Ich möchte — I would like

ich möchte	wir möchten
du möchtest	ihr möchtet
er / sie / es möchte	Sie / sie möchten

Was möchten Sie?
What would you like?

Ich möchte **eine Tasse Tee**, bitte.
I would like a cup of tea, please.

2) If you're adding <u>another verb</u> to say what you'd like to do, that verb has to go to the <u>end</u>.

Ich möchte das Hemd anprobieren, bitte.
I would like to try on the shirt, please.

Wir möchten in die Stadtmitte fahren, bitte.
We would like to go into the city centre, please.

Ich könnte — *I could*   Ich sollte — *I should*

1) You need to know how to use '<u>könnten</u>' (*could*) and '<u>sollten</u>' (*should*) too.

2) Be careful, though — 'ich <u>könnte</u>' means 'I could' as in 'I <u>would be</u> able', as opposed to 'ich <u>konnte</u>', which means 'I <u>was</u> able' (see p.87).

Ich könnte — I could

ich könnte	wir könnten
du könntest	ihr könntet
er / sie / es könnte	Sie / sie könnten

Ich sollte — I should

ich sollte	wir sollten
du solltest	ihr solltet
er / sie / es sollte	Sie / sie sollten

Monika wondered whether she should quit while she was ahead...

Es könnte schlimmer sein.   *It could be worse.*

Ich sollte mehr essen.   *I should eat more.*

What's the conditional — I würde know...

Translate these sentences into German using the conditional tense.

1. They would not visit me.
2. Selma would like to sing.
3. We could run to the park.
4. We could ask our teacher.
5. You (inf. sing.) should wait.
6. I should eat a sandwich.

I would be / I would have | Subjunctive

You can use the subjunctive to say what you would be or what you would have if you were rich and famous. It's a tricky bit of grammar, but examiners will love it if you can use it — and that means more marks.

The subjunctive

1) The <u>subjunctive</u> in German is used to talk about things that <u>could be true</u>, but <u>aren't</u>.

2) Subjunctive phrases in <u>English</u> are things like 'if I <u>were</u> you'. 'Were' is in the <u>subjunctive</u> because it's talking about something that <u>isn't true</u>.

3) For your exams, you need to know the forms '<u>ich wäre</u>' (*I would be*) and '<u>ich hätte</u>' (*I would have*).

Ich wäre — *I would be*

To say '<u>I would be</u>', you use '<u>ich wäre</u>'. Here's how you say it for <u>different people</u>:

Ich wäre — I would be	
ich wäre	wir wären
du wärst	ihr wärt
er / sie / es wäre	Sie / sie wären

Du wärst **gut im Ballett.**
*You would be **good at ballet.***

Ich wäre **ein guter Pilot.**
*I would be **a good pilot.***

Ich hätte — *I would have*

To say '<u>I would have</u>', use '<u>ich hätte</u>'. Here's how you say it for <u>different people</u>:

Ich hätte — I would have	
ich hätte	wir hätten
du hättest	ihr hättet
er / sie / es hätte	Sie / sie hätten

Er hätte **ein besseres Auto.**
*He would have **a better car.***

Wir hätten **mehr Zeit.**
*We would have **more time.***

Angela hoped that one day she would have the ability to fly...

Using 'wäre' and 'hätte' together

If you want to be really fancy, you can combine '<u>wäre</u>' and '<u>hätte</u>' together in one sentence.

Wenn ich fünf Millionen Euro hätte, wäre ich reich.   *If I had five million euros, I would be rich.*

Question	Simple Answer	Extended Answer
Wie wäre dein ideales Haus?	Mein ideales Haus wäre modern und es hätte viele Zimmer.	Mein ideales Haus hätte einen großen Garten. Wenn es auch einen Balkon hätte, wäre ich sehr glücklich.
What would your ideal house be like?	*My ideal house would be modern and it would have lots of rooms.*	*My ideal house would have a big garden. If it also had a balcony, I would be very happy.*

If only I had a shiny leotard, I'd be an Olympic gymnast...

Translate the following sentences into German.

1. I would be a good actor.
2. He would have a dog.
3. Niklas would have a brother.
4. They would be very sad.
5. If I had a car, it would be red.
6. If I were hungry, I would eat potatoes.

The Listening Exam

Ah. Your reward for conquering all that grammar is a section about those pesky exams... Sorry about that. But there is some good news — these pages are crammed full of advice to help you tackle them head-on.

There are four exams for GCSE German

1) Your AQA German GCSE is assessed by four separate exams — Listening, Speaking, Reading and Writing.

2) Each exam is worth 25% of your final mark. You'll get a grade between 1 and 9 (with 9 being the highest).

3) You won't sit all of the papers at the same time — you'll probably have your speaking exam a couple of weeks before the rest of your exams.

The Listening Exam has two sections

If you're sitting foundation tier papers, the format of your exams will be slightly different, but this advice will still be useful.

1) For the listening paper, you'll listen to various recordings of people speaking in German and answer questions on what you've heard.

2) The paper is 45 minutes long (including 5 minutes' reading time) and is split into Section A and Section B.

3) Section A is the longer section — the questions are in English, and you'll write your answers in English. Section B is shorter, but the questions are in German and your answers need to be, too.

Read through the paper carefully at the start of the test

1) Before the recordings begin, you'll be given five minutes to read through the paper.

It was plain sailing once Ray had read the instructions...

2) Use this time to read each question carefully. Some are multiple-choice, and others require you to write some short answers — make sure you know what each one is asking you to do.

3) In particular, look at the questions in Section B, which are written in German. Try to work out what the questions mean. There's a list of exam-style German question words and phrases on the inside front cover of this book to help you prepare for this.

4) Reading the question titles, and the questions themselves, will give you a good idea of the topics you'll be asked about. This should help you predict what to listen out for.

5) You can write on the exam paper, so scribble down anything that might be useful.

Make notes while listening to the recordings

1) You'll hear each audio track twice, and then there'll be a pause for you to write down your answer.

2) While you're listening, it's a good idea to jot down a few details — e.g. dates, times, names or key words. But make sure you keep listening while you're writing down any notes.

Listen to the speaker's tone, too — this will hint at their mood, e.g. angry or excited.

3) Listen right to the end, even if you think you've got the answer — sometimes the person will change their mind or add an important detail at the end.

4) Don't worry if you can't understand every word that's being said — just listen carefully both times and try to pick out the vocabulary you need to answer the question.

Listen up — it's time to put your German to the test...

If you've heard a track twice, and you're still not sure of the answer, scribble one down anyway — you never know, it might be the right one. You may as well write something sensible just in case — it's worth a shot.

The Speaking Exam

The Speaking Exam can seem daunting, but remember — no one is trying to catch you out, so try to stay calm.

There are three parts to the Speaking Exam

> During your preparation time, you can make notes to take in with you for the first two tasks. You can't keep the notes for the general conversation.

1) Your speaking exam will be conducted and recorded by your teacher.

2) The exam is in three parts. Before you start, you'll get 12 minutes to prepare for the first two sections:

① Role-play (2 min.)	② Photo Card (3 min.)	③ Conversation (5-7 min.)
You'll get a card with a scenario on it. It'll have five bullet points — three will be notes on what to say, in German. The '!' means you'll be asked an unknown question, and '?' shows you have to ask a question about the words next to it. See p.5 for an example.	Before the exam, you'll receive a photo and three questions relating to it (look at the example on p.51). Your teacher will ask you the three questions that are on the photo card, as well as two questions you haven't seen.	You and your teacher will have a conversation. The conversation will be based on the theme that you've chosen, and the other theme that hasn't been covered on the photo card. You'll have to ask your teacher at least one question.

3) The role-play card will tell you if you should use 'du', but otherwise, use 'Sie' to talk to your teacher.

Try to be imaginative with your answers

You need to find ways to show off the full extent of your German knowledge. You should try to:

1) Use a range of tenses — e.g. for a question on daily routine, think of when something different happens.

> Morgen wird es anders sein, weil ich nach der Schule schwimmen gehen werde.
> *Tomorrow, it will be different because I will go swimming after school.*

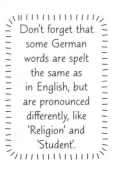

> Don't forget that some German words are spelt the same as in English, but are pronounced differently, like 'Religion' and 'Student'.

2) Talk about other people, not just yourself — it's fine to make people up if that helps.

> Meine Schwester liebt Eislaufen.   *My sister loves ice-skating.*

3) Give loads of opinions and reasons for your opinions.

> Meiner Meinung nach sollte man nicht rauchen, weil es sehr ungesund ist.
> *In my opinion, you shouldn't smoke because it is very unhealthy.*

If you're really struggling, ask for help in German

1) If you get really stuck trying to think of a word or phrase, you can ask for help — as long as it's in German.

2) For example, if you can't remember how to say 'homework' in German, ask your teacher. You won't get any marks for vocabulary your teacher's given you though.

> Wie sagt man 'homework' auf Deutsch?   *How do you say 'homework' in German?*

3) If you don't hear something clearly, just ask:

> Könnten Sie das bitte wiederholen?   *Could you repeat that, please?*

> You could also ask this if you're desperately in need of time to think of an answer.

Mein Deutsch ist gut, aber mein Denglisch ist noch besser...

Given that you're only human, you're bound to have a few slip-ups in the speaking exam. Don't panic, it's completely natural. What's important is how you deal with a mistake — just correct yourself and move on.

Section 12 — Exam Advice

The Reading Exam

After all that listening and speaking, the reading exam offers some nice peace and quiet. Apart from the voice inside your head that screams "WHAT ON EARTH DOES THAT WORD MEAN?!" (Or maybe that's just me...)

Read the questions and texts carefully

1) The higher tier reading paper is 1 hour long, and has three sections.

2) In Sections A and B, you'll be given a variety of German texts and then asked questions about them. The texts could include blog posts, emails, newspaper reports, adverts and literary texts. Section A has questions and answers in English, and Section B has questions and answers in German.

3) Section C is a translation question — you'll have to translate a short passage of text from German into English. See p.94 for more tips on tackling translation questions.

4) In Sections A and B, scan through the text first to get an idea of what it's about. Then read the questions that go with it carefully, making sure you understand what information you should be looking out for.

5) Next, go back through the text. You're not expected to understand every word, so don't get distracted by trying to work out what everything means — focus on finding the information you need.

> The inside front cover of this book has a list of common German question words, phrases and instructions.

Don't give up if you don't understand something

1) Use the context of the text to help you understand what it might be saying. You might be able to find some clues in the title of the text or the type of text.

2) Knowing how to spot different word types (e.g. nouns, verbs) can help you work out what's happening in a sentence. See the grammar section (p.58-89) for more.

3) You can guess some German words that look or sound the same as English words, e.g. die Schule — *school*, die Musik — *music*, der Markt — *market*.

> Look out for compound nouns: long words which contain several smaller words. E.g. 'Reisetasche' (travel bag) is made up of 'Reise' (journey, travel) and 'Tasche' (bag).

4) Be careful though — you might come across some 'false friends'. These are German words that look like an English word, but have a completely different meaning:

bald	*soon*	also	*so / therefore*	der Chef	boss	der Rock	*skirt*	bekommen	*to get*
fast	*almost*	sensibel	*sensitive*	die Fabrik	factory	die Note	*grade / mark*	das Gymnasium	*grammar school*
still	*quiet*	das Handy	*mobile phone*	das Boot	boat	spenden	*to donate*	der Rat	*advice*

Keep an eye on the time

1) There are quite a few questions to get through in the reading exam, so you need to work at a good speed.

2) If you're having trouble with a particular question, you might want to move on and come back to it later.

Ben couldn't work out why rodents kept cropping up in the exam passages.

3) Don't forget that the last question in the paper (Section C) is a translation — this is worth more marks than any other question, so you should leave plenty of time to tackle it.

4) Make sure you put an answer down for every question — lots of the questions are multiple-choice, so even if you can't work out the answer, it's always worth putting down one of the options.

Don't use your phone, no matter how Handy it might be...

Don't forget, the questions in Section B will be in German. Don't panic if you don't understand them — search for any familiar vocabulary and use any answer lines or boxes to help you guess what you have to do.

The Writing Exam

The Writing Exam is a great way of showing off what you can do — try to use varied vocabulary, include a range of tenses, and pack in any clever expressions that you've learnt over the years.

There'll be three tasks in the Writing Exam

1) The higher tier writing paper is 1 hour and 15 minutes long and has three tasks.

2) Each task is worth a different number of marks, so you should spend more time on the higher-mark tasks.

① Structured Task (16 marks)

There will be two tasks to choose from. You'll be asked to write about 90 words in German, based on four bullet points. Make sure you write about each bullet point and give some opinions.

② Open-ended Task (32 marks)

There will also be two tasks to choose from. You'll need to write about 150 words in German, based on two bullet points. This task is more creative — make sure you include some opinions with reasons.

③ Translation (12 marks)

You'll be given an English passage to translate into German. The passage could be on any topic you've studied. There's more advice for doing translations on p.94.

Read the instructions carefully, and spend some time planning

1) Read the instructions for questions 1 and 2 carefully — you'll need to make sure you cover all of the bullet points. You can often use words from the question in your answer too.

2) Spend a few minutes for each question planning out your answer. Decide how you're going to cover everything that's required and in what order you're going to write things.

Try to use varied vocab and a range of tenses.

3) Write the best answer you can, using the German that you know — it doesn't matter if it's not true.

Check through your work thoroughly

Checking your work is really important — even small mistakes can cost marks. Take a look at this checklist:

- Are all the verbs in the right tense?
  Morgen ging ich in die Stadt. ✘   Morgen werde ich in die Stadt gehen. ✓

- Does the verb match the subject?
  Du hat einen Bruder. ✘   Du hast einen Bruder. ✓

- Are the adjective endings correct?
  Das blaues Hemd. ✘   Das blaue Hemd. ✓

All of the points on this checklist are covered in the grammar section — see p.58-89.

- Is the word order correct?
  Ich mag ihn, weil er ist nett. ✘   Ich mag ihn, weil er nett ist. ✓

- Have you used the right case with prepositions?
  Ich esse mit meinen Freund. ✘   Ich esse mit meinem Freund. ✓

- Have you spelt everything correctly, including using the right umlauts?
  Eine gesunde Ernahrung ist wishtig. ✘   Eine gesunde Ernährung ist wichtig. ✓

Trying to use the dative gives me a serious case of the blues...

When you're nervous and stressed, it's dead easy to miss out something the question has asked you to do. For tasks one and two, try to write about the bullet points in order, and tick them off as you go along.

Section 12 — Exam Advice

The Translation Tasks

When you're studying German, you do little bits of translation in your head all the time. For the translation questions, you just need to apply those skills — one sentence at a time — to a couple of short passages.

In the Reading Exam, you'll translate from German to English

1) The final question of the reading paper will ask you to translate a <u>short German passage</u> (about 50 words) <u>into English</u>. The passage will be on a <u>topic you've studied</u>, so most of the vocabulary should be familiar.

2) Here are some <u>top tips</u> for doing your translation:

- Read the whole text <u>before you start</u>. Make some <u>notes in English</u> to remind you of the main ideas.

- Translate the text <u>one sentence at a time</u>, rather than word by word —
  this will avoid any of the German word order being carried into the English.

Er hat Fußball gespielt.	*He has football played.*	✖	*He has played football.*	✔
Ich denke, dass es prima ist.	*I think, that it great is.*	✖	*I think that it is great.*	✔

- Keep an eye out for <u>different tenses</u> — there will definitely be a variety in the passage.

- <u>Read through</u> your translation to make sure it sounds <u>natural</u>.
  Some words and phrases don't translate literally, so you'll need
  to make sure that your sentences sound like <u>normal English</u>:

Watch out for adverbs that might suggest a change in tense, e.g. gestern — yesterday, morgen — tomorrow.

Dienstags fahre ich immer mit dem Bus.	*Tuesdays I always go with the bus.*	✖	*On Tuesdays, I always go by bus.*	✔

3) Make sure you've translated <u>everything</u> from the original text — you'll lose marks if you miss something.

In the Writing Exam, you'll translate from English to German

1) In the writing paper, you will have to translate <u>a short English passage</u> (about 50 words) <u>into German</u>.

2) Here are <u>some ideas</u> for how you could approach the translation:

- <u>Read</u> through the <u>whole text</u> before you get started so you know exactly what the text is about.

- Tackle the passage <u>one sentence at a time</u> — work carefully through each one.

Don't try to write a perfect translation first time — do it roughly first, and then write it up properly, crossing out any old drafts.

- <u>Don't</u> translate things <u>literally</u> — think about what each English sentence means and try to write it in the <u>most German way</u> you know. Don't worry — the translation is likely to include similar sentences to the ones you've learnt.

- Work on the <u>word order</u> — remember that some conjunctions, such as 'weil' (*because*) and 'obwohl' (*although*) send the verb to the end.

3) Once you've got something that you're happy with, go back through and <u>check that you've covered everything</u> that was in the English.

4) Now <u>check</u> your German text thoroughly using the <u>list from p.93</u>.

Deutsch — schwer? Nein, es ist ganz leicht...

Thankfully, none of that got lost in translation...

Congratulations — you've made it to the end of the book. Getting through 94 pages is no mean feat, so give yourself a pat on the back. Make sure you read this page properly though, and take the advice on board.

Vocabulary

Section 1 — General Stuff

Coordinating Conjunctions (p.63)

aber	*but*
denn	*because*
oder	*or*
und	*and*

Subordinating Conjunctions (p.64)

als	*when*
als ob	*as if / as though*
bevor	*before*
bis	*until*
damit	*so that*
dass	*that*
nachdem	*after*
ob	*whether*
obwohl	*although*
während	*while*
weil	*because*
wenn	*if / when*

Connectives

außerdem	*besides / furthermore*
danach	*afterwards*
dennoch	*nevertheless*
deshalb	*therefore*
doch	*after all / on the contrary*
eigentlich	*actually / really*
entweder... oder...	*either... or...*
erstens, zweitens, drittens	*firstly, secondly, thirdly*
jedoch	*however*
leider	*unfortunately*
natürlich	*of course*
nicht nur... sondern auch...	*not only... but also...*
ohne Zweifel	*without a doubt*
schließlich	*eventually / finally*
sowohl... als auch...	*both... and...*
trotzdem	*nevertheless*
weder... noch...	*neither... nor...*

Comparisons (p.68)

ähnlich	*similar*
anders	*different(ly)*
Gegenteil n (-e)	*opposite*
groß / größer / (der, die, das) Größte	*big / bigger / the biggest*
im Großen und Ganzen	*by and large*
gut / besser / (der, die, das) Beste	*good / better / the best*
hoch / höher / (der, die, das) Höchste	*high / higher / the highest*

nah / näher / (der, die, das) Nächste	*near / nearer / the nearest*
so... wie	*as... as*
so viel(e)... wie	*as much / many... as*
Unterschied m (-e)	*difference*
unterschiedlich	*different*
Vergleich m (-e)	*comparison*
vergleichen	*to compare*
viel / mehr / (der, die, das) Meiste	*much / more / the most*

Prepositions (p.75-76)

ab	*from*
an	*at / in / on / to*
auf	*on / onto / on top of / upon*
aus	*from / of / out of*
bei	*near / at*
durch	*through*
entlang	*along*
gegen	*against / at about*
gegenüber	*opposite*
hinter	*after / behind*
nach	*after / to / according to*
neben	*beside / next to*
ohne	*without*
über	*above / over / via*
um	*around / at*
unter	*among / under*
von	*from / by / of*
vor	*in front of / before / ago*
vorbei	*over / past / by*
während	*during*
wegen	*because of*
zu	*to / at / for*
zwischen	*between*

Negatives (p.79)

gar nicht	*not at all*
nicht einmal	*not even*
nicht mehr	*no longer*
nichts	*nothing*
nie	*never*
niemals	*never*
niemand	*nobody*
nirgendwo	*nowhere*
noch nicht	*not yet*
überhaupt nicht	*not at all*

Numbers (p.1)

null	*zero*
eins	*one*
zwei	*two*
drei	*three*
vier	*four*
fünf	*five*

sechs	*six*
sieben	*seven*
acht	*eight*
neun	*nine*
zehn	*ten*
elf	*eleven*
zwölf	*twelve*
dreizehn	*thirteen*
vierzehn	*fourteen*
fünfzehn	*fifteen*
sechzehn	*sixteen*
siebzehn	*seventeen*
achtzehn	*eighteen*
neunzehn	*nineteen*
zwanzig	*twenty*
einundzwanzig	*twenty-one*
zweiundzwanzig	*twenty-two*
dreiundzwanzig	*twenty-three*
dreißig	*thirty*
vierzig	*forty*
fünfzig	*fifty*
sechzig	*sixty*
siebzig	*seventy*
achtzig	*eighty*
neunzig	*ninety*
hundert	*hundred*
tausend	*thousand*
zweitausend	*two thousand*
eine Million	*one million*
zweitausendfünf	*two thousand and five*

das erste	*first*
das zweite	*second*
das dritte	*third*
das vierte	*fourth*
das fünfte	*fifth*
das sechste	*sixth*
das siebte	*seventh*
das achte	*eighth*
das neunte	*ninth*
das zehnte	*tenth*
das zwanzigste	*twentieth*
das einundzwanzigste	*twenty-first*
das siebzigste	*seventieth*
das hundertste	*hundredth*
Dutzend n (-e)	*dozen*
einige	*some / a few*
genug	*enough*
mehrere	*several*
eine Menge	*a lot of / lots of*
Nummer f (-n)	*number*
Paar n (-e)	*pair*
viele	*many*
Zahl f (-en)	*number / figure / digit*

Times and Dates (p.2-3)

Montag	*Monday*
Dienstag	*Tuesday*
Mittwoch	*Wednesday*
Donnerstag	*Thursday*
Freitag	*Friday*
Samstag	*Saturday*
Sonntag	*Sunday*
Januar	*January*
Februar	*February*
März	*March*
April	*April*
Mai	*May*
Juni	*June*
Juli	*July*
August	*August*
September	*September*
Oktober	*October*
November	*November*
Dezember	*December*
Jahreszeit f (-en)	*season*
Frühling m (-e)	*spring*
Sommer m (-)	*summer*
Herbst m (-e)	*autumn*
Winter m (-)	*winter*
ab und zu	*now and again*
Abend m (-e)	*evening*
abends	*in the evenings*
alle zwei Wochen	*every two weeks*
Anfang m (-¨e)	*beginning / start*
Augenblick m (-e)	*moment / instant*
bald	*soon*
Datum n (Daten)	*date*
dauern	*to last*
ehemalig	*former*
einmal	*once*
endlich	*finally*
erst	*at first / only*
fast	*almost / nearly*
früh	*early*
Gegenwart f	*present (time, tense)*
genau	*exactly*
gerade	*just*
gestern	*yesterday*
gewöhnlich	*usually / normally*
gleich	*in a minute / immediately*
halb	*half past*
heute	*today*
heute Morgen	*this morning*
heute Nacht	*tonight*
heutzutage	*nowadays / these days*
immer	*always*
immer wieder	*again and again*
inzwischen	*in the meantime*
Jahr n (-e)	*year*
Jahrhundert n (-e)	*century*
jetzt	*now*
kürzlich	*recently / lately*
langsam	*slow(ly)*

Mal n (-e)	*time*
manchmal	*sometimes*
Mittag m (-e)	*midday*
Mitternacht f	*midnight*
Monat m (-e)	*month*
montags	*on Mondays*
morgen	*tomorrow*
morgen früh	*tomorrow morning*
morgens	*in the morning*
nachgehen	*to be slow*
nachher	*afterwards*
Nachmittag m (-e)	*afternoon*
Nacht f (-¨e)	*night*
neulich	*recently*
noch einmal	*once again*
normalerweise	*normally / usually*
oft	*often*
plötzlich	*suddenly*
pünktlich	*punctual / on time*
regelmäßig	*regularly*
schnell	*quick(ly)*
schon	*already*
seit	*since / for (time)*
selten	*rarely / seldom*
sofort	*immediately*
spät	*late*
Stunde f (-n)	*hour (length)*
Tag m (-e)	*day*
jeden Tag	*every day*
täglich	*daily*
übermorgen	*the day after tomorrow*
Uhr f (-en)	*clock / watch / o'clock*
Vergangenheit f	*past (time, tense)*
Viertel nach	*quarter past*
Viertel vor	*quarter to*
im Voraus	*in advance*
vorgestern	*the day before yesterday*
Vormittag m (-e)	*morning*
wieder	*again*
Woche f (-n)	*week*
diese Woche	*this week*
letze Woche	*last week*
Wochenende n (-n)	*weekend*
am Wochenende	*at the weekend*
Zeit f (-en)	*time*
Zukunft f	*future (time, tense)*

Colours and Shapes

blau	*blue*
braun	*brown*
bunt	*colourful*
dunkel	*dark*
grau	*grey*
grün	*green*
hell	*bright / light*
Farbe f (-n)	*colour*
Kreis m (-e)	*circle*
lila	*purple*
rosa	*pink*

rot	*red / ginger*
rund	*round*
schwarz	*black*
viereckig	*square*
weiß	*white*

Weights and Measures

alle (-r, -s)	*all / all the*
alle sein	*to be all gone / to have run out of*
alles	*everything*
anderer / andere / anderes	*other / different*
beide	*both*
breit	*broad / wide*
Ding n (-e)	*thing*
Dose f (-n)	*can / tin*
ein bisschen	*a little*
ein paar	*a few / a couple*
einzeln	*single*
etwa	*about / roughly*
Flasche f (-n)	*bottle*
ganz	*whole / complete / quite*
gewaltig	*enormously*
Gewicht n (-e)	*weight*
Größe f (-n)	*size*
irgend...	*some...*
Karton m (-s)	*cardboard box*
Kasten m (-¨)	*box / case / crate*
kaum	*hardly*
leer	*empty*
leicht	*light*
Maß n (-e)	*measure*
messen	*to measure*
mindestens	*at least*
mittelgroß	*medium-sized*
noch	*still*
Packung f (-en)	*packet / pack*
Paket n (-e)	*parcel*
Pfund n (-)	*pound*
pro	*per*
Schachtel f (-n)	*box / packet*
Scheibe f (-n)	*slice*
schwer	*heavy*
Stück n (-e)	*piece*
Tüte f (-n)	*bag*
ungefähr	*about*
voll	*full*
wenig	*little / not much*
wiegen	*to weigh*

Materials

Baumwolle f	cotton
bestehen aus	to consist of / to be made of
Eisen n	iron
Holz n	wood
Leder n	leather
Pappe f	cardboard
Seide f	silk
Stoff m (-e)	material
Wolle f	wool

Access

auf sein	to be open
aufmachen	to open
Ausfahrt f (-en)	exit (motorway)
Ausgang m (-¨e)	exit (building)
besetzt	occupied / engaged
Einfahrt f (-en)	entry / entrance
Eingang m (-¨e)	entrance (building)
Eintritt m (-e)	admission
frei	free
geschlossen	closed
offen	open
öffnen	to open
schließen	to close
verboten	forbidden
zu sein	to be closed
zumachen	to close

Questions (p.4-5)

Wann?	When?
Warum?	Why?
Was für...?	What sort / type of...?
Was?	What?
Welcher/e/s	Which?
Wer / Wen / Wem?	Who / Whom?
Wie lang(e)?	How long?
Wie viel(e)?	How much / many?
Wie?	How?
Wieso?	Why? / How come...?
Wo?	Where?
Woher?	Where from?
Wohin?	Where to?
Womit?	What with?
Um wie viel Uhr?	At what time? / When?
Wie viel Uhr ist es?	What's the time?
Wie spät ist es?	What's the time?

Being Polite (p.6-7)

Alles Gute!	All the best!
Auf Wiederhören!	Goodbye (on the phone)
Auf Wiedersehen!	Goodbye
Bis bald!	See you later
bitte	please
bitte schön	you're welcome
danke (schön)	thank you
Darf ich?	May I?

Darf ich Petra vorstellen?	May I introduce Petra?
Entschuldigung!	Excuse me
Es freut mich, dich kennen zu lernen	Pleased to meet you (inf.)
Es freut mich, Sie kennen zu lernen	Pleased to meet you (frml.)
Es tut mir Leid	I'm sorry
Gern geschehen!	Don't mention it
Grüß dich!	Hello (inf.)
Guten Abend!	Good evening
Guten Morgen!	Good morning
Guten Tag!	Good day
Herzlich willkommen!	Welcome!
Herzlichen Glückwunsch!	Congratulations!
Ich hätte gern...	I would like...
Ich würde gern...	I would like to...
Mir geht's gut	I'm well
nichts zu danken	it was nothing
Prost!	Cheers!
Setzen Sie sich!	Please sit down! (frml.)
Tschüss!	Bye (inf.)
Wie geht's?	How are you?
Wie geht es dir?	How are you? (inf.)
Wie geht es euch?	How are you? (inf. plu.)
Wie geht es Ihnen?	How are you? (frml.)
Viel Glück!	Good luck!

Opinions (p.8-10)

Ahnung f (-en)	idea / suspicion
im Allgemeinen	generally
amüsant	amusing / funny
angenehm	pleasant / agreeable
Angst haben	to be afraid / scared
ängstlich	anxious / apprehensive
anstrengend	strenuous
ausgezeichnet	excellent
bequem	comfortable
bestimmt	definitely / certainly
billig	cheap
blöd	stupid
Blödsinn m	nonsense / rubbish
böse	naughty / evil / angry
dafür sein	to be in favour of something
dagegen sein	to be opposed to something
das ist mir egal	it doesn't matter / it's all the same to me
das stimmt (nicht)	that's (not) right
denken	to think
Denkst du das auch?	Do you agree?

deprimiert	depressed
die Nase voll haben	to be fed up with something
doof	stupid
eindrucksvoll	impressive
entsetzlich	terrible
entspannend	relaxing
es gefällt mir	I like it
es geht	it's OK
es ist mir egal	I don't mind
es kommt darauf an, ob...	it depends whether...
es satt haben	to be fed up with something
fabelhaft	fabulous
fantastisch	fantastic
freundlich	friendly
froh	happy / glad
furchtbar	terrible
gemütlich	cosy / comfortable
genießen	to enjoy
glauben	to believe
hassen	to hate
herrlich	marvellous
hervorragend	excellent
interessant	interesting
keine Ahnung haben	to have no idea
klasse	brilliant / great
kompliziert	complicated
sich langweilen	to be bored
langweilig	boring
leicht	easy
lieb	kind / lovely / dear
lieben	to love
etwas lieber machen	to prefer to do something
lustig	amusing / funny
meinen	to think
Meiner Meinung nach...	In my opinion...
Meinung f (-en)	opinion
mies	rotten / lousy
mögen	to like
möglich	possible
mühelos	effortless
mühsam	arduous / laborious
Nachteil m (-e)	disadvantage
nett	nice (person)
nützlich	useful
nutzlos	useless
prima	great
sauer sein	to be cross / annoyed
schade	it's a shame / pity
schlecht	bad

schlimm	bad / terrible
schön	lovely
schrecklich	awful
schwierig	difficult
sensibel	sensitive
sich für etwas interessieren	to be interested in something
sicher	sure / safe
sogar	even
spannend	exciting
Spitze!	Great!
sympathisch	nice (person)
teuer	expensive
toll	great
typisch	typical(ly)
überrascht	surprised
unglaublich	unbelievable
unmöglich	impossible
unsicher	unsure
vielleicht	perhaps
völlig	completely
Vorteil m (-e)	advantage
vorziehen	to prefer
wahrscheinlich	probably

Was denkst du über...?	What do you think of...?
Was hältst du von...?	What do you think of...?
Was meinst du?	What do you think?
wichtig	important
Wie findest du...?	How do you find...?
wirklich	real(ly)
wunderbar	wonderful
wunderschön	beautiful
sich wünschen	to wish
zufrieden	happy / content
zustimmen	to agree

Correctness

falsch	false / wrong / incorrect
Fehler m (-)	mistake / error
Recht haben	to be right
richtig	right / correct
Unrecht haben	to be wrong
verbessern	to correct / to improve
Verbesserung f (-en)	correction / improvement

Abbreviations

AG (Arbeitsgruppe / Arbeits- gemeinschaft)	work group (extra- curricular / school)
DB (Deutsche Bahn)	German Railways
d.h. (das heißt)	i.e. (that is)
Dr (Doktor)	doctor
gem. (gemischt)	mixed
ICE (Inter-City- Express) m	fast long-distance train
inkl. (inklusive)	included
LKW (Lastkraftwagen) m (-)	HGV / lorry
PLZ (Postleitzahl) f	postcode
usw. (und so weiter)	etc. / and so on
z.B. (zum Beispiel)	e.g. (for example)

Section 2 — Me, My Family and Friends

You and Your Family (p.11-12)

Alleinerziehende m/f (-n)	single parent
Alter n (-)	age
aufpassen auf	to look after
Bruder m (-¨)	brother
Buchstabe m (-n)	letter of the alphabet
buchstabieren	to spell
Cousin/e m/f (-s/-n)	cousin
Einzelkind n (-er)	only child
Eltern	parents
Enkel/in m/f (-/-nen)	grandson / granddaughter
Erwachsene m/f (-n)	adult / grown-up
Familienmitglied n (-er)	family member
Familienname m (-n)	last name
Freund/in m/f (-e/-nen)	boy/girlfriend or male / female friend
geboren (am)	born (on)
Geburtsdatum n (Geburtsdaten)	date of birth
Geburtsort m (-e)	place of birth
Geburtstag m (-e)	birthday
Geschlecht n (-er)	sex / gender
Geschwister (-)	siblings
Großeltern	grandparents
Großmutter f (-¨)	grandmother
Großvater m (-¨)	grandfather
Halb...	half...

heißen	to be called
Jugendliche m/f (-n)	youth
Junge m (-n)	boy
Mädchen n (-)	girl
Mutter f (-¨)	mother
Neffe m (-n)	nephew
nennen	to name / call
Nichte f (-n)	niece
Onkel m (-)	uncle
Schwester f (-n)	sister
Schwieger...	...in-law
Sohn m (-¨e)	son
Spielzeug n (-e)	toy
Spitzname m (-n)	nickname
Stief...	step...
Tante f (-n)	aunt
Tochter f (-¨)	daughter
Vater m (-¨)	father
Verwandte m/f (-n)	relative
Vorname m (-n)	first name
sich vorstellen	to introduce oneself
wohnen	to live
Zwillinge	twins

Describing People (p.13-14)

Angeber/in m/f (-/-nen)	show-off / poser
Augen	eyes
aussehen	to look like
Ausweis m (-e)	identity card
Bart m (-¨e)	beard
berühmt	famous
blond	blonde

Brille f (-n)	glasses
dick	fat
dünn	thin
egoistisch	selfish
ehrlich	honest
eifersüchtig	jealous
eingebildet	conceited
ernst	serious
faul	lazy
fleißig	hard-working
frech	cheeky
geduldig	patient
gemein	mean
glatt	straight (hair)
glücklich	happy
groß	big / tall
großzügig	generous
gut gelaunt	good-tempered
gute Laune haben	to be in a good mood
Haare (pl.)	hair
hässlich	ugly
hilfsbereit	helpful
höflich	polite
hübsch	pretty
humorlos	humourless
humorvoll	humorous / witty
jung	young
klein	small / short
komisch	strange / comical
kurz	short
lang	long
lästig	annoying

lebhaft	*lively*	Braut f (-¨e)	*bride*	küssen	*to kiss*
lockig	*curly*	Bräutigam m (-e)	*groom*	lachen	*to laugh*
Mensch m (-en)	*person*	Brieffreund/in m/f	*penfriend*	ledig	*single*
Ohr n (-en)	*ear*	(-e/-nen)		leiden	*to suffer*
ordentlich	*neat*	Ehe f (-n)	*marriage*	Leute f	*people*
Persönlichkeit f	*personality*	Elternschaft f	*parenting*	minderjährig	*minor / underage*
(-en)		sich entschuldigen	*to apologise*	miteinander	*with one another*
ruhig	*quiet*	entspannt	*relaxed*	nerven	*to get on someone's*
Schnurrbart m (-¨e)	*moustache*	erlauben	*to allow*		*nerves*
schüchtern	*shy*	Freundschaft f (-en)	*friendship*	Partnerschaft f (-en)	*partnership*
selbstbewusst	*confident*	sich fühlen	*to feel*	sich schämen	*to feel ashamed*
selbstständig	*independent*	Gefühl n (-e)	*feeling*	sich scheiden	*to get divorced*
Sinn für Humor m	*sense of humour*	geschieden	*divorced*	lassen	
Sommersprossen	*freckles*	getrennt	*separated*	Scheidung f (-en)	*divorce*
streng	*strict*	gleichgeschlechtlich	*same-sex (marriage*	sorgen für	*to care for*
Tätowierung f (-en)	*tattoo*		*/ partnership)*	Streit m (-e)	*argument*
traurig	*sad*	Grund m (-¨e)	*reason*	sich streiten mit	*to argue with*
unternehmungs-	*adventurous / likes*	heiraten	*to marry*	Traum m (-¨e)	*dream*
lustig	*doing lots of things*	Hochzeit f (-en)	*marriage*	Trauung f (-en)	*wedding ceremony*
verrückt	*crazy*	homosexuell	*homosexual*	sich trennen	*to separate*
witzig	*funny*	ich kann... gut	*I like... (very much)*	treu	*faithful*
Zahn m (-¨e)	*tooth*	leiden		unterstützen	*to support*
zuverlässig	*reliable*	ich kann... nicht	*I can't stand / I don't*	vergeben	*to forgive*
		leiden	*like...*	Verhältnis n (-se)	*relationship*
		Junggeselle m (-n)	*bachelor*	in einem Verhältnis	*to be in a*
		kennen	*to know (a person)*	sein	*relationship*

Relationships (p.15-16)

		kennen lernen	*to get to know*	verheiratet	*married*
allein	*alone*	sich kümmern um	*to look after*	sich verloben	*to get engaged*
alleinstehend	*single*			Verlobte m/f (-n)	*fiancé(e)*
ärgerlich	*annoying*			sich verstehen mit	*to get on with*
sich ärgern über	*to be annoyed about*			verzeihen	*to forgive*
auf die Nerven	*to get on one's*			weinen	*to cry*
gehen	*nerves*			Witz m (-e)	*joke*
auskommen mit	*to get on with*			wohl	*good / comfortable*
Bekannte m/f	*acquaintance /*			zivile Partnerschaft	*civil partnership*
(-n/-nen)	*friend*			f (-en)	
Besuch m (-e)	*visit*			zurechtkommen mit	*to cope with*
besuchen	*to visit (person)*			zusammen	*together*
Beziehung f (-en)	*relationship*				
bitten	*to ask for / beg*				

Section 3 — Free-Time Activities

Music, Cinema and TV (p.17-19)

		beeindruckend	*impressive*	gruselig	*scary*
Abenteuerfilm m	*adventure film*	bewegend	*moving*	Handlung f (-en)	*plot*
(-e)		Bildschirm m (-e)	*screen (TV)*	hören	*to listen to*
abonnieren	*to subscribe to*	Blaskapelle f (-n)	*brass band*	Horrorfilm m (-e)	*horror film*
Actionfilm m (-e)	*action film*	Blockflöte f (-n)	*recorder*	Instrument n (-e)	*instrument*
sich amüsieren	*to have fun*	Chor m (-¨e)	*choir*	Interesse haben an	*to be interested in*
anschauen	*to watch*	Dirigent/in m/f	*conductor*	Kino n (-s)	*cinema*
aufnehmen	*to record*	(-en/-nen)		Klarinette f (-n)	*clarinet*
aufregend	*exciting*	Dokumentarfilm m	*documentary*	klassische Musik f	*classical music*
ausschalten	*to turn off (TV)*	(-e)		Klavier n (-e)	*piano*
Band f (-s)	*band*	Eintrittsgeld n	*admission fee*	Komödie f (-n)	*comedy*
		Eintrittskarte f (-n)	*ticket*	Konzert n (-e)	*concert*
		essen	*to eat*	Krimi m (-s)	*crime film*
		faszinierend	*fascinating*	langweilig	*boring*
		fernsehen	*to watch television*	Leinwand f (-¨e)	*screen (in cinema)*
		Flachbildschirm m	*flat-screen TV*	Liebesfilm m (-e)	*romantic film*
		(-e)		Lied n (-er)	*song*
		Flimmerkiste f (-n)	*TV / box / telly*	Musiker/in m/f	*musician*
		Geige f (-n)	*violin*	(-/-nen)	
				Musikgeschmack m	*taste in music*

Nachrichten (pl.)	news
Orchester n (-)	orchestra
Popmusik f	pop music
Promi m/f (-s)	celebrity
Querflöte f (-n)	flute
Quizsendung f (-en)	quiz show
Rapmusik f	rap music
Reality-Show f (-s)	reality show
Rockmusik f	rock music
sammeln	to collect
Sänger/in m/f (-/-nen)	singer
Schauspieler/in m/f (-/-nen)	actor / actress
Schlagzeug n	percussion / drums
Science-Fiction-Film m (-e)	sci-fi film
Seifenoper f (-n)	soap opera
senden	to broadcast
Sender m (-)	TV channel
Sendung f (-en)	TV programme
Serie f (-n)	series
singen	to sing
Sitzplatz m (-¨e)	seat
Spaß machen	to be fun
Stimme f (-n)	voice
teilnehmen an	to take part in
Trailer m (-)	trailer
Trickeffekte	special effects
Trompete f (-n)	trumpet
übertragen	to stream
umschalten	to switch channels
unterhaltsam	entertaining
Unterhaltung f (-en)	entertainment
Untertitel m (-n)	subtitle
Vergnügen n	fun / enjoyment
Volksmusik f	folk music
Vorstellung f (-en)	showing / performance
Werbung f	advert(s)
Zeichentrickfilm m (-e)	cartoon
Zeitschrift f (-en)	magazine
Zeitung f (-en)	newspaper
Zuschauer/in m/f (-/-nen)	spectator / member of the audience

Food and Eating Out (p.20-21)

Ananas f (-se)	pineapple
Apfel m (-¨)	apple
Apfelsine f (-n)	orange
Aprikose f (-n)	apricot
Banane f (-n)	banana
bedienen	to serve
Bedienung inbegriffen	service included
sich beschweren	to complain
bestellen	to order
bezahlen	to pay
Bier n (-e)	beer
Birne f (-n)	pear
Blumenkohl m (-e)	cauliflower
Bratwurst f (-¨e)	fried sausage

Brot n (-e)	bread
Brötchen n (-)	bread roll
Butter f	butter
Café n (-s)	café
Durst haben	to be thirsty
durstig	thirsty
Ei n (-er)	egg
Eisdiele f (-n)	ice cream parlour
ekelhaft	disgusting
empfehlen	to recommend
Ente f (-n)	duck
Erbsen	peas
Erdbeere f (-n)	strawberry
Essig m (-e)	vinegar
fettig	fatty
Fisch m (-e)	fish
Fleisch n	meat
Forelle f (-n)	trout
fremd	foreign
Fruchtsaft m (-¨e)	fruit juice
Gabel f (-n)	fork
Gasthaus n (-¨er)	pub
Gemüse n	vegetables
geräuchert	smoked
Gericht n (-e)	dish (food)
Geschmack m (-¨e)	taste
Gurke f (-n)	cucumber
Haferflocken	porridge oats
Hähnchen n (-)	chicken
Halbfettmilch f	semi-skimmed milk
Hauptgericht n (-e)	main course
hausgemacht	home-made
Herr Ober!	Waiter!
Himbeere f (-n)	raspberry
Honig m	honey
Hunger haben	to be hungry
Imbiss m (-e)	snack
Imbissbude f (-n)	snack bar / takeaway
Kakao m	cocoa
Kalbfleisch n	veal
Kännchen n (-)	pot of tea / coffee
Karotte f (-n)	carrot
Karte f (-n)	menu
Kartoffel f (-n)	potato
Käse m	cheese
Keks m (-e)	biscuit
Kellner/in m/f (-/-nen)	waiter / waitress
Kneipe f (-n)	pub
Knoblauch m	garlic
köstlich	delicious
Kotelett n (-s)	pork chop
Lachs m (-e)	salmon
Lammfleisch n	lamb
lecker	tasty
Löffel m (-)	spoon

Magermilch f	skimmed milk
Meeresfrüchte (pl.)	seafood
Mehl n	flour
Messer n (-)	knife
Milch f	milk
Nachspeise f (-n)	dessert
Nachtisch m (-e)	dessert
Nudeln (pl.)	pasta / noodles
Nuss f (-¨e)	nut
Obst n	fruit
Öl n (-e)	oil
Pfeffer m (-)	pepper (spice)
Pfirsich m (-e)	peach
Pflaume f (-n)	plum
Pilz m (-e)	mushroom
Pommes frites	chips
Praline f (-n)	chocolate (in a box)
probieren	to try / taste
Pute f (-n)	turkey
Rechnung f (-en)	bill
Reis m	rice
reservieren	to book
Restaurant n (-s)	restaurant
riechen	to smell
Rindfleisch n	beef
roh	raw
Rührei n (-er)	scrambled egg
Sahne f	cream
salzig	salty
satt sein	to be full up
scharf	hot / spicy
Schaschlik n (-s)	kebab
Schinken m (-)	ham
schmackhaft	tasty
schmecken	to taste
Schnellimbiss m (-e)	snack bar
(Wiener) Schnitzel n (-)	veal / pork cutlet
Schweinefleisch n	pork
Selbstbedienung f (-en)	self-service
Senf m	mustard
Speise f (-n)	dish
Speisekarte f (-n)	menu
Speisesaal m (Speisesäle)	dining hall
Spiegelei n (-er)	fried egg
Spinat m	spinach
Sprudelwasser n	fizzy mineral water
Steak n (-s)	steak
Suppe f (-n)	soup
süß	sweet
Tagesgericht n (-e)	dish of the day
Tagesmenü n (-s)	menu of the day
Teelöffel m (-)	teaspoon
Thunfisch m (-e)	tuna
Tomate f (-n)	tomato
Torte f (-n)	gateau
Trinkgeld n (-er)	tip
Truthahn m (-¨e)	turkey
Vegetarier/in m/f (-/-nen)	vegetarian

Vollmilch f	full-fat milk
vorschlagen	to suggest
Vorspeise f (-n)	starter
Weintraube f (-n)	grape
Wurst f (-̈e)	sausage
würzig	spicy
Zitrone f (-n)	lemon
Zucker m	sugar
Zwiebel f (-n)	onion

Sport (p.22-23)

angeln	to fish
Badeanzug m (-̈e)	swimsuit
Badehose f (-n)	swimming trunks
Basketball m	basketball
begeistert	excited
Bergsteigen n	mountain climbing
Eislaufen n	ice-skating
Fahrrad fahren	to cycle
fechten	to fence
Federball m	badminton
Fitnessstudio n (-s)	gym
Freibad n (-̈er)	outdoor swimming pool
Fußball m	football
gewinnen	to win
Hallenbad n (-̈er)	indoor swimming pool
Hockey n	hockey

joggen	to jog
Kegeln n	bowling (nine-pin)
klettern	to climb
Korbball m	netball
Kricket n	cricket
laufen	to run
Leichtathletik f	athletics
Lust haben, etwas zu tun	to feel like doing something
Mannschaft f (-en)	team
Match n (-es)	match
Mitglied n (-er)	member
nervös	nervous
Olympische Spiele	Olympic Games
Profi m (-s)	professional sportsperson
Rennen n (-)	race
ringen	to wrestle
rodeln	to go sledging
rudern	to row
Rollschuh laufen	to go roller skating
Rugby n	rugby
Schach n	chess
schießen	to shoot
Schlittschuh laufen	ice-skating
Schwimmbad n (-̈er)	swimming pool
schwimmen	to swim
Segelboot n (-e)	sailing boat
segeln	to sail

Ski fahren	to ski
spazieren gehen	to go for a walk
spielen	to play
Sportart f (-en)	type of sport
Sportplatz m (-̈e)	sports field
Sport treiben	to do sport
Sportzentrum n (Sportzentren)	sports centre
springen	to jump
Stadion n (Stadien)	stadium
tauchen	to dive
Tennis n	tennis
Tor n (-e)	goal
ein Tor schießen	to score a goal
trainieren	to train
Training n	training
Trainingsschuh m (-e)	sport shoe / trainer
Turnen n	gymnastics
Verein m (-e)	club
verlieren	to lose
wandern	to hike
werfen	to throw
Wettbewerb m (-e)	competition

Section 4 — Technology in Everyday Life

Technology (p.24-27)

Anrufbeantworter m (-e)	answering machine
anrufen	to call
Anwendungen	applications
App f (-s)	app
(aus)drucken	to print (out)
benutzen	to use
Betriebssystem n (-e)	operating system
Bindestrich m (-e)	hyphen
bloggen	to blog
Blogger/in m/f (-/-nen)	blogger
chatten	to chat online
Computer m (-)	computer
Cyber-Mobbing n	cyber-bullying
Daten (pl.)	data
Drucker m (-)	printer
Einstellung f (-en)	setting
(E-)Mail f (-s)	email
E-Mail-Adresse f (-n)	email address
empfangen	to receive
entwickeln	to develop
erforschen	to research
Forum n (Foren)	forum
Foto n (-s)	photo
funktionieren	to work / to function

Gefahr f (-en)	danger
gefährlich	dangerous
gehören zu	to belong to
Gruppe f (-n)	group
Handy n (-s)	mobile phone
herausfinden	to find out
herunterladen	to download
hochladen	to upload
Internet n	internet
Kamera f (-s)	camera
Klingelton m (-̈e)	ringtone
in Kontakt bleiben	to stay in contact
Konto n (-s)	account
Laptop m (-s)	laptop
löschen	to delete
Medien (pl.)	media
missbrauchen	to abuse / misuse
Nachricht f (-en)	message
Netzwerk n (-e)	network
online	online
Passwort n (-̈er)	password
peinlich	embarrassing
Postfach n (-̈er)	mailbox
praktisch	practical
Privatleben n (-)	private life
Punkt m (-e)	full stop
Risiko n (Risiken)	risk
schicken	to send
Schrägstrich m (-e)	forward slash

schützen	to protect
Sicherheit f	security
simsen	to text
Smartphone n (-s)	smartphone
soziale Medien (pl.)	social media
soziales Netzwerk n (soziale Netzwerke)	social network
speichern	to save (data)
Startseite f (-n)	homepage
streamen	to stream
Suchmaschine f (-n)	search engine
surfen	to surf
Tablet-PC m (-s)	tablet
Technologie f (-n)	technology
teilen	to share
Unterstrich m (-e)	underscore
Veranstaltung f (-en)	event
Video n (-s)	video
Videospiel n (-e)	video game
Website f (-s)	website
Webseite f (-n)	web page
WLAN n	Wi-Fi
Zeit verbringen	to spend time

Section 5 — Customs and Festivals

Customs and Festivals (p.28-30)

Adventskranz m (-̈e)	advent wreath
anzünden	to light
Aprilscherz m (-e)	April fool's trick
Aschermittwoch m	Ash Wednesday
Auferstehung f (-en)	resurrection
auspacken	to unwrap
bekommen	to receive
Chanukka	Hanukkah
Christen	Christians
christlich	Christian
danken	to thank
der erste Weihnachtstag	24th December
der zweite Weihnachtstag	25th December
einladen	to invite
Einladung f (-en)	invitation
Fasching m	carnival
Feier f (-n)	celebration
feiern	to celebrate
Feiertag m (-e)	public holiday
Fest n (-e)	festival / celebration
Festessen n (-)	festive meal
Feuerwerk n (-e)	fireworks display
sich freuen auf	to look forward to
sich freuen über	to be pleased about something
Frohe Weihnachten!	Merry Christmas!
Gans f (-̈e)	goose
Gast m (-̈e)	guest
Gastfreundschaft f	hospitality
Gastgeber/in m/f (-/-nen)	host
Geschenk n (-e)	present / gift
Heiliger Abend	Christmas Eve
Heilige Drei Könige	Epiphany
Hindu m/f (-s)	Hindu
hinduistisch	Hindu
islamisch	Muslim
Jesu Tod	Christ's death
Jude/Jüdin m/f (-n/-nen)	Jew
jüdisch	Jewish
Karfreitag m	Good Friday
Karneval m	carnival
Kerze f (-n)	candle
Kirche f (-n)	church
kirchlich	religious
Lebkuchen m	gingerbread
Lichterfest n (-e)	festival of lights
Maifeiertag m (-e)	May Day
Moslem/in m/f (-s/-nen)	Muslim

Muttertag m (-e)	Mother's Day
Neujahrstag m (-e)	New Year's Day
Osterei n (-er)	Easter egg
Osterhase m	Easter bunny
Ostern n	Easter
Ostersonntag m	Easter Sunday
Pfingsten n	Whitsuntide
religiös	religious
Sankt Nikolaus Tag	St Nicholas' Day
schenken	to give (as a present)
schmücken	to decorate
Sikh m (-s)	Sikh
Silvester	New Year's Eve
Tag der Arbeit	May Day
Tag der Deutschen Einheit	Day of German Unity
Umzug m (-̈e)	procession
Valentinstag m (-e)	St Valentine's Day
sich verkleiden	to dress up
verstecken	to hide
Weihnachten n	Christmas
Weihnachtsbaum m (-̈e)	Christmas tree
Weihnachtskarte f (-n)	Christmas card
Weihnachtslieder	Christmas carols
Weihnachtsmarkt m (-̈e)	Christmas market

Section 6 — Where You Live

The Home (p.31)

Abstellraum m (-̈e)	storeroom
alt	old
Autobahn f (-en)	motorway
Backofen m (-̈)	oven
Badewanne f (-n)	bathtub
Badezimmer n (-)	bathroom
Bauernhaus n (-̈er)	farm house
Baum m (-̈e)	tree
Besteck n (-e)	(set of) cutlery
Bett n (-en)	bed
Bild n (-er)	picture
Blume f (-n)	flower
Dach n (-̈er)	roof
Dachboden m (-̈)	attic / loft
Diele f (-n)	hall
Doppelbett n (-en)	double bed
Doppelhaus n (-̈er)	semi-detached house
Einfamilienhaus n (-̈er)	detached house
im Erdgeschoss	on the ground floor
Esszimmer n (-)	dining room
Etage f (-n)	floor / storey
Etagenbett n (-en)	bunk bed
Flur m (-e)	corridor / hall
Fußboden m (-̈)	floor
Garten m (-̈)	garden
Gerät n (-e)	appliance
geräumig	spacious
Haus n (-̈er)	house
Haushalt m (-e)	household
Hecke f (-n)	hedge
Heizung f	heating
Hochhaus n (-̈er)	high-rise block of flats
Kleiderschrank m (-̈e)	wardrobe
Kochfeld n (-er)	hob
Kommode f (-n)	chest of drawers
Kopfkissen n (-)	pillow
Küche f (-n)	kitchen
Kühlschrank m (-̈e)	fridge
Licht n (-er)	light
Mauer f (-n)	wall (outside)
Mehrfamilienhaus n (-̈er)	house for several families
Miete f (-n)	rent
Mikrowelle f (-n)	microwave
Möbel (pl.)	furniture
Möbelstück n (-e)	piece of furniture
modern	modern
nach oben	upstairs
nach unten	downstairs
Nachbar/in m/f (-n/-nen)	neighbour
Nachttisch m (-e)	bedside table
neu	new
Rasen m (-)	lawn
Regal n (-e)	shelf
Reihenhaus n (-̈er)	terraced house
riesig	huge
Sackgasse f (-n)	cul-de-sac
Schlafzimmer n (-)	bedroom
Schlüssel m (-)	key
Schrank m (-̈e)	cupboard
Schublade f (-n)	drawer
Spiegel m (-)	mirror
am Stadtrand	on the outskirts
im Stadtzentrum	in the town centre
Stuhl m (-̈e)	chair
Tasse f (-n)	cup
Teppich m (-e)	carpet

Tiefkühlschrank m (-¨e)	*freezer*
Treppe f (-n)	*stairs*
umziehen	*to move house*
Vorhänge	*curtains*
Wand f (-¨e)	*wall (inside)*
Wintergarten m (-¨)	*conservatory*
Wohnblock m (-s)	*block of flats*
Wohnung f (-en)	*flat*
Wohnzimmer n (-)	*living room*
Zimmer n (-)	*room*

What You Do at Home (p.32)

Abendessen n	*evening meal*
abwaschen	*to wash up*
sich anziehen	*to get dressed*
aufräumen	*to tidy up*
aufstehen	*to get up*
aufwachen	*to wake up*
den Tisch decken	*to lay the table*
sich duschen	*to have a shower*
frühstücken	*to have breakfast*
Hausaufgaben (pl.)	*homework*
kochen	*to cook*
sich kümmern um	*to look after*
mähen	*to mow*
Mahlzeit f (-en)	*meal / mealtime*
putzen	*to clean*
sauber machen	*to clean*
sich rasieren	*to shave*
sich schminken	*to put on make-up*
Staub saugen	*to vacuum*
Staub wischen	*to dust*
Tagesablauf m	*daily routine*
verlassen	*to leave (the house)*
vorbereiten	*to prepare*
sich waschen	*to have a wash*

Where You Live (p.33)

am Meer	*by the sea*
an der Küste	*on the coast*
auf dem Land	*in the countryside*
Bäckerei f (-en)	*bakery*
Bahnhof m (-¨e)	*train station*
Bauernhof m (-¨e)	*farm*
bergig	*mountainous*
Bibliothek f (-en)	*library*
Brücke f (-n)	*bridge*
Bücherei f (-en)	*library*
Buchhandlung f (-en)	*bookshop*
Busbahnhof m (-¨e)	*bus station*
Denkmal n (-e)	*monument*
Dom m (-e)	*cathedral*
Dorf n (-¨er)	*village*
Drogerie f (-n)	*chemist's*
Einwohner/in m/f (-/-nen)	*inhabitant*
Elektrogeschäft n (-e)	*shop for electrical goods*
Fabrik f (-en)	*factory*
Feld n (-er)	*field*
flach	*flat*
Fleischerei f (-en)	*butcher's*

Fluss m (-¨e)	*river*
Friseur m (-e)	*hairdresser's*
Fußgängerzone f (-n)	*pedestrian zone*
Gebäude n (-)	*building*
Gegend f (-en)	*region*
Großstadt f (-¨e)	*city*
Grünanlage f (-n)	*green space*
Hafen m (-¨)	*harbour*
Hauptbahnhof m (-¨e)	*main train station*
historisch	*historic*
Hügel m (-)	*hill*
im Norden	*in the north*
in den Bergen	*in the mountains*
in der Nähe von	*near to*
Insel f (-n)	*island*
Juweliergeschäft n (-e)	*jeweller's*
Konditorei f (-en)	*confectioner's*
Kunstgalerie f (-n)	*art gallery*
Laden m (-¨)	*shop*
Landschaft f (-en)	*landscape*
lebendig	*lively*
Markt m (-¨e)	*market*
Metzgerei f (-en)	*butcher's*
Park m (-s)	*park*
Parkplatz m (-¨e)	*parking place*
Platz m (-¨e)	*square*
Post f (-en)	*post office*
Reinigung f (-en)	*dry cleaner's*
Spielplatz m (-¨e)	*playground*
Stadt f (-¨e)	*town*
Stadtviertel n (-)	*district / part of town*
tanken	*to fill up with fuel*
Tankstelle f (-n)	*petrol station*
Umgebung f (-en)	*surrounding area*
Vorort m (-e)	*suburb*
Wald m (-¨er)	*wood / forest*
Wohnort m (-e)	*place of living*
Wolkenkratzer m (-)	*skyscraper*

Shopping (p.34-36)

anbieten	*to offer*
Angebot n (-e)	*offer*
anprobieren	*to try on*
ausgeben	*to spend (money)*
Ausverkauf m (-¨e)	*sale*
ausverkauft	*sold out*
Bargeld n (-er)	*cash*
einkaufen gehen	*to go shopping*
Einkaufskorb m (-¨e)	*shopping basket*
Einkaufstasche f (-n)	*shopping bag*
Einkaufswagen m (-)	*shopping trolley*
Einkaufszentrum n (Einkaufszentren)	*shopping centre*
Euro-Schein m (-e)	*euro note*
Euro-Stück n (-e)	*euro coin*
Geld n	*money*
Geldschein m (-e)	*note*
Geldstück n (-e)	*coin*
Geschäft n (-e)	*shop / business*
Gramm n (-)	*gram*

gratis	*free of charge*
Größe f (-n)	*size*
günstig	*good value*
Hemd n (-en)	*shirt*
Hose f (-n)	*trousers*
Jeans f	*jeans*
kaputt	*broken*
mit Karte	*by card*
Kasse f (-n)	*till*
Kaufhaus n (-¨er)	*department store*
Kilo n (-)	*kilogram*
Klamotten	*clothes*
Kleid n (-er)	*dress*
Kleidergeschäft n (-e)	*clothes shop*
Kleingeld n	*small change*
kosten	*to cost*
kostenlos	*free of charge*
Kunde/Kundin m/f (-n/-nen)	*customer*
liefern	*to deliver*
Marke f (-n)	*brand / make*
Münze f (-n)	*coin*
Obst- und Gemüseladen m (-¨)	*green grocer's*
öffentliche Verkehrsmittel (pl.)	*public transport*
Pfund n	*pound*
pleite sein	*to be skint*
Preis m (-e)	*price*
preiswert	*good value*
Pullover m (-)	*sweater*
Quittung f (-en)	*receipt*
Rabatt m (-e)	*discount*
Rock m (-¨e)	*skirt*
Rolltreppe f (-n)	*escalator*
Schaufenster n (-)	*shop window*
Schlange stehen	*to queue*
Schuh m (-e)	*shoe*
Sonderangebot n (-e)	*special offer*
Sonst noch etwas?	*Anything else?*
Sportschuhe	*trainers*
stehen	*to suit*
Taschengeld n	*pocket money*
tragen	*to wear*
T-Shirt n (-s)	*t-shirt*
Warenhaus n (-¨er)	*department store*
Verkäufer/in m/f (-/-nen)	*shop assistant*
verschwenden	*to waste*
wechseln	*to change (money)*

Directions (p.37)

Ampel f (-n)	*traffic light*
auf der rechten Seite	*on the right-hand side*
außen	*outside*
außerhalb von	*outside of*
Bürgersteig m (-e)	*pavement*
draußen	*outside / outdoors*
drinnen	*inside / indoors*
(da) drüben	*over there*

Vocabulary

Ecke f (-n)	*corner*
entfernt	*(far) away*
Fahrkarte f (-n)	*ticket (e.g. bus)*
gegenüber	*opposite*
geradeaus	*straight on*
Haltestelle f (-n)	*stop (bus / tram etc.)*
hin und zurück	*return (ticket)*
Kreuzung f (-en)	*crossroads*
liegen	*to be situated*
(nach) links	*(to the) left*
Meile f (-n)	*mile*
mitten in	*in the middle of*
nah	*near*
neben	*next to*
nehmen	*to take*
(nach) rechts	*(to the) right*
S-Bahn f	*suburban (fast) railway*
Straße f (-n)	*street*
U-Bahn f	*underground train*
überqueren	*to cross (road)*

weg	*away*
weit	*far*
Wo ist...?	*Where is...?*
Zebrastreifen m (-)	*zebra crossing*

Weather (p.38)

bedeckt	*overcast*
Blitz m	*lightning*
Donner m	*thunder*
es donnert	*it's thundering*
feucht	*damp*
frieren	*to freeze*
frisch	*fresh*
Gewitter n (-)	*thunderstorm*
Grad m (-e)	*degree*
Hagel m	*hail*
es hagelt	*it's hailing*
heftig	*heavy / severe*
heiter	*bright / fine*
Himmel m (-)	*sky*
Klima n (-s)	*climate*
kühl	*cool*
Mond m (-e)	*moon*

nass	*wet*
Nebel m (-)	*fog*
nebelig	*foggy*
Niederschlag m (-¨e)	*precipitation*
Regen m (-)	*rain*
es regnet	*it's raining*
Schatten m (-)	*shadow*
schattig	*shady*
Schauer m (-)	*shower*
scheinen	*to shine*
es schneit	*it's snowing*
Sturm m (-¨e)	*storm*
stürmisch	*stormy*
trocken	*dry*
Wetterbericht m (-e)	*weather report*
Wettervorhersage f (-n)	*weather forecast*
Wolke f (-n)	*cloud*
wolkig	*cloudy*

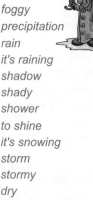

Section 7 — Lifestyle

Health (p.39-40)

abnehmen	*to lose weight*
abstinent	*teetotal*
Ader f (-n)	*vein*
Alkohol m	*alcohol*
Atem m	*breath*
Atembeschwerden	*breathing difficulties*
atmen	*to breathe*
aufgeben	*to give up*
aufhören	*to stop*
ausgewogen	*balanced*
betrunken	*drunk*
Bewegung f (-en)	*exercise*
sich bewegen	*to exercise*
bewusstlos	*unconscious*
Drogen	*drugs*
Drogenhändler/in m/f (-/-nen)	*drug dealer*
Drogensüchtige m/f (-n)	*drug addict*
sich entspannen	*to relax*
Entziehungskur f	*rehab for drug addiction / alcoholism*
Ernährung f	*food / nourishment / nutrition*
fettarm	*low in fat*
fettleibig	*obese*
Fettleibigkeit f	*obesity*
sich fit halten	*to keep oneself fit*
in Form sein	*to be in good shape*
gestresst	*stressed*
gesund	*healthy*
Gesundheit f	*health*
Gesundheits- problem n (-e)	*health problem*

Gruppendruck m	*peer pressure*
magersüchtig	*anorexic*
müde	*tired*
Nahrung f	*food / nourishment*
rauchen	*to smoke*
Raucherhusten m	*smoker's cough*
Rauschgift n (-e)	*drug / narcotic*
regelmäßig	*regular*
schaden	*to damage / harm*
schädlich	*harmful*
schlafen	*to sleep*
Sucht f (-¨e)	*addiction*
süchtig	*addicted*
Süßigkeiten	*sweets*
Überdosis f (Überdosen)	*overdose*
übergewichtig	*overweight*
vermeiden	*to avoid*
Zigarette f (-n)	*cigarette*
zunehmen	*to put on weight*

Illnesses (p.41)

abhängig sein von	*to be addicted to*
Aids n	*AIDS*
allergisch gegen	*allergic to*
Antibiotika	*antibiotics*
Apotheke f (-n)	*pharmacy*
Arzt/Ärztin m/f (-¨e/-nen)	*doctor*
asthmatisch	*asthmatic*
Bauch m (-¨e)	*stomach*
Bauchschmerzen (pl.)	*stomach ache*
Blut n	*blood*
Demenz f	*dementia*
sich erbrechen	*to be sick*

Erkältung f (-en)	*cold*
Erste Hilfe f	*First Aid*
Fieber n (-)	*fever*
gebrochen	*broken*
Gehirn n (-e)	*brain*
Hals m (-¨e)	*neck / throat*
heilbar	*curable*
Herz n (-en)	*heart*
Heuschnupfen m	*hay fever*
Kopf m (-¨e)	*head*
Kopfschmerzen (pl.)	*headache*
krank	*ill*
Krankenhaus n (-¨er)	*hospital*
Krankenwagen m (-)	*ambulance*
Krankheit f (-en)	*illness*
Krebs m	*cancer*
Leber f (-n)	*liver*
Magen m (-)	*stomach*
Medikament n (-e)	*medicine*
mir ist übel	*I feel ill / sick*
ein Mittel gegen...	*a medicine for...*
psychische Probleme	*mental health problems*
Rücken m (-)	*back*
Schmerz m (-en)	*pain*
Spritze f (-n)	*syringe*
sterben	*to die*
Tablette f (-n)	*tablet*
tot	*dead*
Unfall m (-¨e)	*accident*
verletzt sein	*to be injured*
Verletzung f (-en)	*injury*
weh tun	*to hurt*
zuckerkrank	*diabetic*

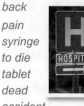

Section 8 — Social and Global Issues

Environmental Problems (p.42-43)

Abfall m (-ˍe)	rubbish / waste
Abfalleimer m (-)	rubbish bin
Abgase	exhaust fumes
Abholzung f	deforestation
alternative Energiequelle f (-n)	alternative source of energy
Altpapier n (-e)	waste paper
anbauen	to grow
aussterben	to die out
bedrohen	to threaten
bekämpfen	to fight / combat
beitragen zu	to contribute to
Benzin n	petrol
Bevölkerung f (-en)	population
biologisch	biological / organic
Biomüll m	organic waste
bleifrei	lead-free
brauchen	to need
Brennstoff m (-e)	fuel
chemisch	chemical(ly)
Dürre f (-n)	drought
Energiequelle f (-n)	energy source
entsorgen	to dispose of
Erdbeben n (-)	earthquake
Erderwärmung f	global warming
Erdrutsch m (-e)	landslide
erheblich	significant
erneuerbare Energie f	renewable energy
extreme Wetter-bedingungen	extreme weather conditions
Fahrradweg m (-e)	cycle lane
Fahrzeug n (-e)	vehicle
FCKWs	CFCs
Folge f (-n)	consequence / effect
fossile Brennstoffe	fossil fuels
führen zu	to lead to
Gebrauch m	usage
Hochwasser n (-)	flood / flooding
Klimawandel m	climate change
Kohle f	coal
Kohlendioxid n	carbon dioxide
Kraftwerk n (-e)	power station
Kunststoff m (-e)	man-made material
Luft f (-ˍe)	air
Luftverschmutzung f	air pollution
Müll m	rubbish / waste
Mülltonne f (-n)	dustbin
Naturkatastrophe f (-n)	natural disaster
Orkan m (-e)	hurricane
Ozonloch n (-ˍer)	hole in the ozone layer
Ozonschicht f (-en)	ozone layer

Pfand n (-ˍer)	deposit
produzieren	to produce
reinigen	to clean
sauber	clean
Sauerstoff m	oxygen
saure Regen m	acid rain
schmutzig	dirty
Solarzelle f (-n)	solar panel
Sonnenenergie f	solar energy
sparen	to save / conserve
Spraydose f (-n)	aerosol
Statt...	Instead of...
Treibhauseffekt m	greenhouse effect
Tsunami m (-s)	tsunami
ultraviolette Strahlen	ultraviolet rays
umstritten	controversial
umwandeln	to convert
Umwelt f (-en)	environment
umweltfeindlich	bad for the environment
umweltfreundlich	environmentally friendly
sich verbessern	to get better
Verbrauch m	consumption
Verkehr m	traffic
Verkehrsmittel n (-)	means of transport
verlangsamen	to slow down
Verpackung f (-en)	packaging
verschmutzen	to pollute
Verschmutzung f	pollution
verschwinden	to disappear
Wasserkraft f (-ˍe)	hydroelectric power
wegwerfen	to throw away
Windpark f (-s)	wind farm
Wirbelsturm m (-ˍe)	tornado
zerstören	to destroy
zusammenarbeiten	to work together

Problems in Society (p.44-46)

arbeitslos	unemployed
Arbeitslosigkeit f	unemployment
arm	poor
Armut f	poverty
Ausländer/in m/f (-/-nen)	foreigner
Bedingung f (-en)	condition
Behinderte m/f (-n)	disabled person
belohnend	rewarding
Bettler/in m/f (-/-nen)	beggar
Deutschkurs m (-e)	German course
Dieb/in m/f (-e/-nen)	thief
Diskriminierung f	discrimination
ehrenamtlich	voluntarily
Einbruch m (-ˍe)	burglary
Eingliederung f	integration
einsam	lonely

Einwanderer/in m/f (-/-nen)	immigrant
Einwanderung f	immigration
erfrieren	to freeze to death
fliehen	to flee
Flüchtling m (-e)	refugee
Gesellschaft f (-en)	society
Gewalt f	violence
gewalttätig	violent
Gleichheit f	equality
Hautfarbe f (-n)	colour of the skin
Ich mache mir Sorgen um...	I'm worried about...
integrieren	to integrate
keinen festen Wohnsitz haben	to have no fixed abode
Kluft f (-ˍe)	gap
Krieg m (-e)	war
Lärm m	noise
laut	noisy
Leben n (-)	life
Lösung f (-en)	solution
Menschenrechte	human rights
menschlich	humane / human
Migrant(in) m/f (-en/-nen)	migrant
Not f	need
obdachlos	homeless
Obdachlosenheim n (-e)	hostel for homeless people
Opfer n (-)	victim
Rasse f (-n)	race
Rassismus m	racism
Rassist/in m/f (-en/-nen)	racist (person)
Regierung f (-en)	government
reich	rich
das Rote Kreuz	the Red Cross
Sexismus m	sexism
Sozialhilfe f	income support
Sozialwohnung f (-en)	council flat
spenden	to donate
stehlen	to steal
Straftat f (-en)	criminal offence
Suppenküche f (-n)	soup kitchen
Tierheim n (-e)	animal shelter
überbevölkert	over-populated
Umfrage f (-n)	survey / opinion poll
unterstützen	to support
Unterstützung f	support
Vandalismus m	vandalism
Verbrechen n (-)	crime
Verbrecher/in m/f (-/-nen)	criminal
Verhältnisse	(living) conditions
vertreiben	to drive out / expel
weltweit	worldwide
wiederverwerten	to recycle
Wiederverwertung f	recycling

Vocabulary

Wohltätigkeit f (-en)	charity	Wohltätigkeits-veranstaltung f (-en)	charity event	ziehen nach	to move to
Wohltätigkeits-konzert n (-e)	charity concert			Zuhause n	home / house

Section 9 — Travel and Tourism

Where to Go (p.47)

die Alpen	the Alps
Amerika	America
Ärmelkanal m	English Channel
Asien	Asia
Ausland n	abroad
Australien	Australia
Bayern	Bavaria
Belgien	Belgium
Bodensee m	Lake Constance
China	China
Deutschland	Germany
Donau f	River Danube
Europa	Europe
Frankreich	France
Genf	Geneva
Griechenland	Greece
Hauptstadt f (-¨e)	capital city
irgendwo	somewhere
Italien	Italy
Kanada	Canada
Köln	Cologne
Land n (-¨er)	country
Mittelmeer n	Mediterranean (Sea)
Mosel f	River Moselle
München	Munich
nirgendwo	nowhere
Österreich	Austria
Ostsee f	Baltic Sea
Polen	Poland
Portugal	Portugal
Reiseziel n (-e)	destination
Rhein m	Rhine
Russland	Russia
Schwarzwald m	Black Forest
die Schweiz	Switzerland
Spanien	Spain
die Türkei	Turkey
Vereinigte Staaten	USA
Wien	Vienna

Preparation (p.48-49)

Aufenthalt m (-e)	stay
Aussicht f (-en)	view
Autovermietung f (-en)	car rental firm
Balkon m (-s)	balcony
bequem	comfortable
Bestätigung f (-en)	confirmation
bleiben	to stay
Blick m (-e)	view / glance
Campingplatz m (-¨e)	campsite
Doppelzimmer n (-)	double room

Einzelzimmer n (-)	single room
Empfang m (-¨e)	reception
Ermäßigung f (-en)	reduction
Formular n (-e)	form
Gasthaus n (-¨er)	guesthouse
gesellig	sociable
Halbpension f	half board
Hotel n (-s)	hotel
Jugendherberge f (-n)	youth hostel
Klimaanlage f	air conditioning
Meerblick m (-e)	sea view
Pension f (-en)	small hotel
Prospekt m (-e)	brochure / leaflet
Reisebüro n (-s)	travel agency
reservieren	to book
Reservierung f (-en)	reservation
Sommerferien	summer holidays
übernachten	to stay overnight
Übernachtung mit Frühstück	B & B
umständlich	inconvenient
Unterkunft f (-¨e)	accommodation
Urlaub m (-e)	holiday
Vollpension f	full board
Wohnwagen m (-)	caravan
Zelt n (-e)	tent
zelten	to camp
Zuschlag m (-¨e)	extra charge
Zweibettzimmer n (-)	twin room

Getting There (p.50)

abfahren	to leave / depart
abholen	to collect / pick up
ankommen	to arrive
aussteigen	to alight / get off bus
Auto n (-s)	car
Bahnsteig m (-e)	platform
sich beeilen	to hurry
Boot n (-e)	boat
Bus m (-se)	bus
Dampfer m (-)	steam boat
dauern	to take (time) / last
einsteigen	to get in / on
entwerten	to stamp / validate a ticket
Fähre f (-n)	ferry
fahren	to travel (in a vehicle)
Fahrkartenautomat m (-en)	ticket machine
Fahrkartenschalter m (-)	ticket office

Fahrpreis m (-e)	fare
Fahrrad n (-¨er)	bicycle
Fahrradvermietung f	bicycle hire
Fahrt f (-en)	journey
fliegen	to fly
Flug m (-¨e)	flight
Flughafen m (-¨)	airport
Flugzeug n (-e)	aeroplane
gehen	to go / walk
Gepäck n	luggage
Gleis n (-e)	platform
herumfahren	to travel around
Koffer m (-)	suitcase
Linie f (-n)	line / number (bus)
Notausgang m (-¨e)	emergency exit
Panne f (-n)	breakdown / puncture
Passagier/in m/f (-e/-nen)	passenger
Platten m	flat tyre
Reise f (-n)	journey
Reisebus m (-se)	coach
reisen	to travel
Reisende m/f (-n)	traveller
Reisepass m (-¨e)	passport
Richtung f (-en)	direction
Rundfahrt f (-en)	round trip / tour
Schließfach n (-¨er)	locker
seekrank	seasick
Sicherheitsgurt m (-e)	safety belt / seat belt
Stau m (-s)	traffic jam
Straßenkarte f (-n)	road map
Überfahrt f (-en)	(sea) crossing
umsteigen	to change (trains)
unterwegs	on the way
Verbindung f (-en)	connection
vermieten	to hire
verpassen	to miss
Verspätung f (-en)	delay
warten auf	to wait for
Wartesaal m	waiting room
Weg m (-e)	way / path
wegfahren	to depart / go away
weiterfahren	to travel on
Zoll m	customs
Zug m (-¨e)	train

What to Do (p.51)

Andenken n (-)	souvenir
sich etwas ansehen	to have a look at something
Ausflug m (-¨e)	excursion
begleiten	to accompany

beliebt	popular	kulturell	cultural
berühmt	famous	Museum n (Museen)	museum
besichtigen	to visit (an attraction)	Öffnungszeiten	opening times
Briefmarke f (-n)	postage stamp	örtlich	local
Burg f (-en)	castle	Schloss n (-¨er)	castle / palace
entdecken	to discover	See m (-n)	lake
sich erinnern	to remember	See f (-n)	sea
Erinnerung f (-en)	memory	sehenswert	worth seeing
erleben	to experience	Sehenswürdigkeit f (-en)	tourist attraction
Erlebnis n (-se)	experience	sich sonnen	to sunbathe
Fotoapparat m (-e)	camera	Sonnenbrand m	sunburn
Führung f (-en)	guided tour		

Sonnencreme f	suntan lotion
Stadtbummel m (-)	stroll through town
Stadtrundfahrt f (-en)	sightseeing tour of the town
Strand m (-¨e)	beach
Strandkorb m (-¨e)	wicker beach chair
verbringen	to spend (time)

Section 10 — Study and Employment

School Subjects (p.52)

Biologie	biology
Chemie	chemistry
Deutsch	German
Englisch	English
Erdkunde	geography
Französisch	French
Fremdsprache f (-n)	foreign language
Geschichte	history
Geografie	geography
Hauswirtschaftslehre	home economics
Klasse f (-n)	class
Kunst	art
Lieblingsfach n (-¨er)	favourite subject
Mathe	maths
Musik	music
Naturwissenschaften	science
Pflichtfach n (-¨er)	compulsory subject
Physik	physics
Prüfung f (-en)	exam
Religion	RE
Schulfach n (-¨er)	school subject
Sozialkunde	social studies / politics
Spanisch	Spanish
Sport	PE
Stunde f (-n)	lesson
Theater	drama
Wahlfach n (-¨er)	optional subject
Werken	design technology
Wirtschaftslehre	business studies / economics

School Life (p.53-55)

1 = sehr gut	very good
2 = gut	good
3 = befriedigend	satisfactory / fair
4 = ausreichend	sufficient / pass (just)
5 = mangelhaft	poor / unsatisfactory / fail
6 = ungenügend	extremely poor / inadequate

Abschlusszeugnis n (-se)	school leaving certificate
abschreiben	to copy
akademisch	academic
Anspitzer m (-)	pencil sharpener
anspruchsvoll	demanding
Antwort f (-en)	answer
Anzug m (-¨e)	suit
aufpassen	to pay attention
Aula f (Aulen)	assembly hall
aus sein	to be over / finished
Auswahl f (-en)	choice / range
beantworten	to answer
bestehen	to pass (exam)
besuchen	to go to (a school)
blau machen	to play truant
Bluse f (-n)	blouse
Direktor/in m/f (-en/-nen)	headteacher
Druck m (-¨e)	pressure
durchfallen	to fail (a test)
Erfolg m	success
erfolgreich	successful
Ergebnis n (-se)	result
erklären	to explain
erzählen	to tell / narrate
Fachschule f (-n)	technical college
fehlen	to be absent
Ferien	holidays
Frage f (-n)	question
Ganztagsschule f (-n)	school that lasts all day
gemischt	mixed (sex)
Gesamtschule f (-n)	comprehensive school
Grundschule f (-n)	primary school
Gymnasium n (Gymnasien)	grammar school
Halle f (-n)	hall
Hauptschule f (-en)	vocational secondary school
Hausmeister/in m/f (-/-nen)	caretaker
Internat n (-e)	boarding school

Klassenarbeit f (-en)	test
Klassenfahrt f (-en)	school trip
klug	clever / intelligent
korrigieren	to correct
Krawatte f (-n)	tie
Kreide f	chalk
Labor n (-s)	laboratory
lehren	to teach
Lehrerzimmer n (-)	staff room
Leistung f (-en)	achievement
Lineal n (-e)	ruler
malen	to paint
Mittagspause f (-n)	lunch break
mündlich	orally
nachsitzen	to have a detention
Note f (-n)	grade
Notendruck m	pressure to get good marks
Pause f (-n)	break
plaudern	to chat
praktisch	vocational / practical
Privatschule f (-en)	private school
Realschule f (-n)	secondary school
rechnen	to calculate
Regel f (-n)	rule
respektieren	to respect
schaffen	to manage / create
Schere f	scissors
schriftlich	written
Schulart f (-en)	type of school
Schüler/in m/f (-/-nen)	pupil
Schulhof m (-¨e)	school yard
schwänzen	to play truant
Seite f (-n)	page
Sekretariat n (-e)	school office
sich setzen	to sit down
sitzen bleiben	to repeat a year
Sprachlabor n (-s)	language lab
Stress m	stress
Stundenplan m (-¨e)	timetable
Tafel f (-n)	black/white board
Turnhalle f (-n)	sports hall

üben	*to practise*
Übung f (-en)	*exercise*
Umkleideraum m (-¨e)	*changing room*
Unterricht m	*lessons / teaching*
unterrichten	*to teach*
Versammlung f (-en)	*assembly*
versetzt werden	*to be moved up a year*
versuchen	*to try*
wissen	*to know*
Wörterbuch n (-¨er)	*dictionary*
Zeugnis n (-se)	*school report*

Education Post-16 (p.56)

Azubi (Auszubildende) m/f (-s)	*apprentice / trainee*
Abitur n (-e)	*A-level equivalent*
Abiturient/in m/f (-en/-nen)	*person doing the Abitur*
arbeiten	*to work*
Arbeitspraktikum n	*work experience*
Ausbildungsplatz m (-¨e)	*vacancy for a trainee*
Berufsberater/in m/f (-/-nen)	*careers adviser*
Berufserfahrung f	*work experience*
Berufsschule f (-n)	*vocational school*
sich bewerben um	*to apply for*
Bewerbung f (-en)	*application*
Chef/in m/f (-s/-nen)	*boss*
einstellen	*to employ*
sich entscheiden	*to decide*
Erfahrung f (-en)	*experience*
fertig	*ready / done*
ein Jahr freinehmen	*to take a year out*
Führerschein m (-e)	*driving licence*
Gelegenheit f (-en)	*opportunity*
Kurs m (-e)	*course*
Lehre f (-n)	*apprenticeship*
Mindestlohn m (-¨e)	*minimum wage*
Nebenjob m (-s)	*part-time job*
Oberstufe f (-n)	*sixth-form equivalent*
Praktikum n (Praktika)	*work placement*
Studienplatz m (-¨e)	*university place*
studieren	*to study*
theoretisch	*theoretical*
auf die Uni gehen	*to go to uni*
Universität f (-en)	*university*
verdienen	*to earn*
Weiterbildung f	*further education*

Career Choices (p.57)

Angestellte m/f (-n)	*employee*
Apotheker/in m/f (-/-nen)	*pharmacist*
Arbeitgeber/in m/f (-/-nen)	*employer*
Arbeitszeit f	*work hours*
Bäcker/in m/f (-/-nen)	*baker*
Bauarbeiter/in m/f (-/-nen)	*construction worker*
bauen	*to build*
Bauer/Bäuerin m/f (-n/-nen)	*farmer*
Beamte m/f (-n)	*civil servant*
Beruf m (-e)	*job / occupation*
berufstätig sein	*to be in work*
beschäftigt sein	*to be employed*
beschließen	*to decide*
besitzen	*to own*
Besitzer/in m/f (-/-nen)	*owner*
Besprechung f (-en)	*meeting / discussion*
Bezahlung f (-en)	*payment*
Briefträger/in m/f (-/-nen)	*postman/woman*
Buchhalter/in m/f (-/-nen)	*accountant*
Büro n (-s)	*office*
Dolmetscher/in m/f (-/-nen)	*interpreter*
erfüllen	*to fulfil*
erfüllend	*rewarding*
Feuerwehrmann/ Feuerwehrfrau m/f (-¨er/-en)	*firefighter*
Fleischer/in m/f (-/-nen)	*butcher*
im Freien	*in the open air*
Friseur/in m/f (-e/-nen)	*hairdresser*
ganztags	*all day*
Gärtner/in m/f (-/-nen)	*gardener*
Gehalt n (-¨er)	*salary*
Halbtagsarbeit f	*part-time work*
Hausmann/Hausfrau m/f (-¨er/-en)	*househusband / housewife*
Informatiker/in m/f (-/-nen)	*computer scientist*
Ingenieur/in m/f (-e/-nen)	*engineer*
Journalist/in m/f (-en/-nen)	*journalist*
Karriere f (-n)	*career*
Kassierer/in m/f (-/-nen)	*cashier / bank clerk*
Klempner/in m/f (-/-nen)	*plumber*

Koch/Köchin m/f (-¨e/-nen)	*cook*
Krankenpfleger m (-)	*(male) nurse*
Krankenschwester f (-n)	*(female) nurse*
kündigen	*to hand in one's notice / to sack someone*
Lebenslauf m (-¨e)	*CV*
LKW-Fahrer/in m/f (-/-nen)	*lorry driver*
Lohn m (-¨e)	*wage*
Maler/in m/f (-/-nen)	*painter / decorator*
Metzger/in m/f (-/-nen)	*butcher*
Pfarrer/in m/f (-/-nen)	*parish priest / vicar*
Polizei f	*police*
Polizist/in m/f (-en/-nen)	*police officer*
Postbote/Postbotin m/f (-n/-nen)	*postman/woman*
Rechtsanwalt/ Rechtsanwältin m/f (-¨e/-nen)	*lawyer*
Rentner/in m/f (-/-nen)	*pensioner*
Schichtarbeit f	*shift work*
Schriftsteller/in m/f (-/-nen)	*writer / author*
selbstständig	*self-employed / independent*
Sozialarbeiter/in m/f (-/-nen)	*social worker*
Stelle f (-n)	*position*
suchen	*to look for / search*
Teilzeitjob m (-s)	*part-time job*
Termin m (-e)	*appointment*
Tierarzt/Tierärztin m/f (-¨e/-nen)	*vet*
Tischler/in m/f (-/-nen)	*carpenter*
Übersetzer/in m/f (-/-nen)	*translator*
vereinbaren	*to agree / arrange*
Vollzeitarbeit f	*full-time work*
Vorstellungsgespräch n (-e)	*job interview*
Werkstatt f (-¨en)	*garage*
Wunsch m (-¨e)	*wish*

Answers

The answers to the translation questions are sample answers only, just to give you an idea of one way to translate them. There may be different ways to translate these passages that are also correct.

Section 1 — General Stuff

Page 1 — Numbers and Quantities

1) Sie sind siebzehn und fünfundzwanzig Jahre alt.

2) Sie ist achtundneunzig Jahre alt.

3) Sie ist neunundsiebzig Jahre älter als Heinrich.

Page 3 — Times and Dates

1) her family

2) very interesting

3) She spent time with her brother.   **or:** She walked through the park with her brother.

4) Not a lot.   **or:** He played handball.

5) every day

6) on Thursday

7) the cinema

Page 9 — Opinions

1) She finds it (very) boring.

2) She never gets a good seat.   **or:** She cannot see what the actors are doing.

3) She finds the theatre interesting.   **or:** You can learn a lot about life.

4) romantic films

5) She's not interested in them.   **or:** She thinks they are unrealistic.

Page 10 — Opinions

1) true   3) false   5) false

2) false   4) true

Section 2 — Me, My Family and Friends

Page 12 — My Family

Hello, I am Joachim and I was born in Leipzig. I live with my wife, her two daughters and my son. He studies / is studying medicine and he wants to be a doctor in the future. One of my stepdaughters has a child, who is called Georg. We will soon celebrate his second birthday.

Page 13 — Describing People

1) one   3) She has brown eyes and wears light blue glasses.

2) dark   4) He thinks it's dreadful because he looks ugly.

Page 16 — Partnership

1) NT   2) R   3) F   4) NT

Section 3 — Free-Time Activities

Page 17 — Music

1) A   2) E   3) F

Page 18 — Cinema

Ich gehe gern ins Kino. Letztes Wochenende bin ich mit meinem Freund / meiner Freundin ins Kino gegangen und wir haben einen Actionfilm gesehen. Ich habe den Film wirklich spannend gefunden, obwohl er ein kleines bisschen gruselig war. Nächste Woche werde ich eine Komödie mit meiner Schwester sehen, weil sie lustige Filme lieber mag. In der Zukunft möchte ich Schauspieler(in) werden.

Page 19 — TV

1) true   2) false   3) false   4) not in the text

Page 20 — Food

1) B   2) A   3) C   4) A

Section 4 — Technology in Everyday Life

Page 25 — Technology

Ich habe ein Handy und einen Tablet-PC. Ich benutze jeden Tag das Internet. Ich benutze es, um meine Hausaufgaben zu machen. Ich lud vor kurzem / neulich viele Filme herunter. Ich simse zwanzig- oder dreißigmal pro Tag. In Zukunft werde ich versuchen, mein Handy weniger / nicht so oft zu benutzen und mehr Sport zu treiben.

Page 26 — Social Media

1) fifty

2) people she knows personally

3) always in the evening

4) They think that she spends too much time on the computer.

Section 5 — Customs and Festivals

Page 28 — Festivals in German-Speaking Countries

1) She makes an advent wreath with four candles.

2) his sister, on Christmas Eve

3) He always buys them a big Christmas tree.

4) everyone

5) gingerbread and biscuits **and:** with (chocolate) stars and hearts on

Page 29 — Festivals in German-Speaking Countries

1) Germany, Switzerland and Austria

2) It's a very colourful and exciting festival.

3) in areas where a lot of Catholics live

4) They put on fancy dress.

Section 6 — Where You Live

Page 31 — The Home

1) under the table
2) Any three from: the bed, the oven, the kitchen, the cupboard, (under) the basin, the clock case
3) the youngest / the one in the clock case

Page 32 — What You Do at Home

I live with my parents in a flat in Berlin. I must help at home every day. That annoys me. After school, I clean the flat. I must also cook for my parents because they come home late. Yesterday, I tidied my room. I hope that I will have more free time at the weekend.

Page 34 — Clothes Shopping

1) Schuhe und eine Jeans
2) Die Verkäuferinnen waren sehr freundlich und hilfsbereit.
3) Sie ist im Moment pleite.
4) ein neues Kleid

Page 37 — Giving and Asking for Directions

A, D, E

Page 38 — Weather

1) falsch 2) nicht im Text 3) richtig 4) falsch 5) falsch

Section 7 — Lifestyle

Page 41 — Illnesses

Last week, my sister was ill. She had a headache, her throat hurt and her cheeks were very red. My father thought that she had a fever. Now, I feel ill and I've had stomach ache for about a week. I must go to the pharmacy. I will buy painkillers.

Section 8 — Social and Global Issues

Page 43 — Environmental Problems

Ich denke, dass wir viele Umweltprobleme verursacht haben. Die Luftverschmutzung ist sehr gefährlich für Menschen und Tiere. Sie kann auch zur Erderwärmung führen. Erneuerbare Energiequellen sind eine mögliche Lösung, weil sie umweltfreundlicher als Kohle sind. Wenn wir nichts machen, werden die Probleme in der Zukunft schlimmer werden.

Page 45 — Problems in Society

1) E   2) C   3) B

Section 9 — Travel and Tourism

Page 47 — Where to Go

1) mit dem Auto
2) todlangweilig
3) in einem Rucksack
4) nach Belgien

Page 48 — Accommodation

1) positiv und negativ 2) positiv   3) negativ

Page 50 — How to Get There

Last week, my father bought a tent. Tomorrow, the whole family is flying to Switzerland, where we will stay on a campsite at Lake Constance. I find that very exciting, but my step-sister doesn't like aeroplanes. We will hopefully have a lovely / beautiful view of the mountains.

Section 10 — Study and Employment

Page 53 — School Routine

1) Der Schultag endet um dreizehn Uhr.
2) Versammlungen morgens
   and: keine Freunde beim Kunstunterricht

Page 54 — School Life

B, C, F, G

Page 56 — Education Post-16

Letztes Jahr habe ich Englisch, Mathe und Geografie / Erdkunde gelernt. Erdkunde hat mir gut gefallen, aber mein(e) Mathelehrer(in) war sehr streng. Nach den Prüfungen werde ich ein Jahr freinehmen. Ich werde einen Job finden, weil ich Geld verdienen will. Danach will ich an die Uni gehen, um Englisch zu studieren. Ich denke, dass es eine interessante Erfahrung / ein interessantes Erlebnis sein wird.

Page 57 — Career Choices and Ambitions

At the moment, I don't know what I want to do in the future. I didn't pass my exams at school and I must find a job. My father is a police officer and in June I did my work experience with him, but I wouldn't like to do that for a living / as a job. I would prefer to be self-employed.

Section 11 — Grammar

Page 58 — Cases — Nominative and Accusative

1) nom. — Der Mann	acc. — Deutsch
2) nom. — Die Stadt	acc. — eine Bibliothek
3) nom. — Ich	acc. — eine Schwester
4) nom. — Er	acc. — Schokolade
5) nom. — Meine Mutter	acc. — ein neues Auto
6) nom. — ich	acc. — einen Rock

Page 59 — Cases — Genitive and Dative

1) gen. — meiner Mutter	4) gen. — meines Vaters
2) dat. — dem Land	5) dat. — dem Zug
3) dat. — meinem Bruder	6) dat. — der Küche

Page 60 — Words for People, Places and Objects

1) die Gesellschaft	4) das Mädchen	7) die Katrin
2) der Mittwoch	5) die Meinung	8) das Schwimmen
3) der Frühling	6) die Polizei	

Page 61 — Words for People, Places and Objects

1) Es gibt viele Autos / Wagen.
2) Die Kinder sind klein.
3) Die Tische sind teuer.
4) Die Ärzte / Die Ärztinnen sind nett.
5) Die alte Frau / Die Alte heißt Renate.
6) Der Jugendliche heißt Ali.

Page 62 — Word Order

You should have ticked: 2), 3) and 6).
You should have crossed: 1), 4) and 5).

Page 63 — Coordinating Conjunctions

Answers may vary, e.g.
1) Ich fahre mit dem Bus und du fährst mit dem Zug.
2) Wir werden in ein Museum gehen oder wir werden Tennis spielen.
3) Ich will Musik hören oder fernsehen.
4) Er ist Vegetarier, aber sie isst Fleisch.
5) Ich liebe Deutsch, aber ich hasse Englisch.

Page 64 — Subordinating Conjunctions

Answers may vary, e.g.
1) Ich mag Lesen, weil es entspannend ist.
2) Komm zu meiner Party, wenn du Zeit hast.
3) Wir waren beste Freunde, als wir Kinder waren.
4) Ich will Lehrer(in) werden, obwohl es anstrengend ist.

Page 65 — 'The', 'A', and 'No'

1) den
2) der
3) eine
4) einen
5) keinen
6) kein

Page 66 — Words to Describe Things

1) Das Pferd ist grau.
2) Ich sehe drei graue Pferde.
3) Er hat zwei graue Pferde.
4) Sie mag das graue Pferd.
5) Welches graue Pferd?
6) Das graue Pferd ist groß.
7) Ich habe ein graues Pferd.
8) Dieses graue Pferd ist alt.

Page 67 — Words to Describe Things

1) Mein Haus ist groß.
2) Ihr Baby ist glücklich / froh.
3) Jeder Job / Jede Stelle ist langweilig.
4) Wer hat meinen neuen Stift / Kugelschreiber?
5) Diese Musik ist toll / super / prima.
6) Ich kaufte dieses schnelle Auto / diesen schnellen Wagen.
7) Welchen Mantel will er?
8) Der Hund meiner Schwester ist lustig / komisch.

Page 68 — Words to Compare Things

1) glücklich, glücklicher, der / die / das Glücklichste
2) langsam, langsamer, der / die / das Langsamste
3) hübsch, hübscher, der / die / das Hübscheste
4) traurig, trauriger, der / die / das Traurigste
5) Das ist das größere Haus.
6) Katrin ist ebenso faul wie Klaus.

Page 69 — Words to Describe Actions

Answers may vary, e.g.
1) Ich gehe sehr schnell.
2) Sie laufen leider wirklich langsam.
3) Er hat kaum gesprochen.
4) Normalerweise helfe ich Lukas viel.
5) Endlich hält das Auto.
6) Wir werden bestimmt gewinnen.
7) Leider kam Stephan etwas spät.
8) Gewöhnlich kostet es fast zwei Euro.

Page 70 — Words to Describe Actions

1) Ich putze mir täglich die Zähne.
2) Andrea erzählt / macht oft Witze.
3) Ich spiele nie dort Tennis.
4) Es gibt überall Vögel.
5) Sie treffen sich manchmal (dort) drüben.
6) Ich werde dich am kommenden Montag hier sehen.

Page 71 — Words to Compare Actions

1) Ich laufe schneller als sie.
2) Sie spielen am besten Fußball.
3) Wir werden langsamer essen.
4) Er springt am weitesten.
5) Der Mann singt am schönsten.
6) Albert malt besser als Liesl.

Page 72 — I, You, He, She, We, They

1) Er sieht sie.
2) Sie sehen uns.
3) Ich spreche mit euch.
4) Sie sprechen mit mir.
5) Ich kenne dich.
6) Sie kennt sie.

Page 73 — Reflexive Pronouns

1) Sie waschen sich.
2) Ich fühle mich glücklich.
3) Er entschuldigt sich.
4) Sie sonnt sich.
5) Du putzt dir die Zähne.
6) Sie wünschen sich einen Hund.
7) Wir ziehen uns um.
8) Ich zog mich um.

Page 74 — Relative and Interrogative Pronouns

1) Die Frau, die einen Hut trägt, ist hübsch.
2) Die Leute, denen ich schreibe, sind nett.
3) Das Kind, dessen Mantel rot ist, lacht.
4) Wen hat er gesehen? / Wen sah er?
5) Nichts, was sie macht, ist einfach / leicht.

Answers

Page 75 — Prepositions

1) zu
2) nach
3) zu
4) zu
5) auf
6) aus
7) in (im)
8) an (am)

Page 76 — Prepositions

1) durch den Wald
2) ohne seinen Stift
3) von ihrem Vater
4) nach dem Film
5) trotz des Regens
6) während der Party
7) Ich lief die Straße entlang.
8) Er steht unter der Brücke.

Page 77 — Verbs in the Present Tense

1) Ich spiele.
2) Wir glauben.
3) Du fragst.
4) Sie tanzen.
5) Ich feire.
6) Sie segeln.
7) Ich gehe laufen / joggen.
8) Jan geht zelten.
9) Ich spiele seit einem Jahr Klavier.

Page 78 — More About the Present Tense

1) Sie hat eine Katze.
2) Wir sind Lehrer(innen).
3) Ich danke meiner Tante.
4) Du folgst dem Mann.
5) Glauben Sie mir?
6) Sie trägt eine Krawatte.

Page 79 — More About the Present Tense

1) Sie macht nichts.
2) Es schneit.
3) Ich sollte etwas sagen.
4) Er gibt es mir zurück.
5) Ich will berühmt sein, um viel Geld zu verdienen.
6) Ich kann nicht weggehen, ohne etwas zu sagen.

Page 80 — Talking About the Past

1) Ich habe Tee getrunken.
2) Wir sind zu Hause geblieben.
3) Er hat mich gesehen.
4) Du hast einen Brief bekommen.
5) Sie haben ihn gefragt.
6) Sie sind hier / hierher gekommen.

Page 81 — Talking About the Past

1) Ich hatte einen Hund.
2) Wir waren sehr traurig.
3) Ich spielte Tennis.
4) Sie waren da.
5) Du hattest eine gute Idee.
6) Sie kauften einen Hund.
7) Er kochte.
8) Sie war jung.

Page 82 — Talking About the Past

1) Ich trank eine Tasse Tee.
2) Ich nahm den Stift.
3) Maria schrieb ein Buch.
4) Wir sahen ihm.
5) Sie halfen seit einem Jahr.
6) Ich aß seit einer Stunde.

Page 83 — Talking About the Past

1) Ich hatte Musik gelernt.
2) Er hatte ein Eis gegessen.
3) Sie hatte sich angezogen.
4) Sie waren zum Park gegangen.

5) Tim war zu Hause geblieben.
6) Wir hatten unsere Hausaufgaben gemacht.

Page 84 — Talking About the Future

1) Ich gehe am Montag ins Kino. / Ich werde am Montag ins Kino gehen.
2) Er erklärt es bald. / Er wird es bald erklären.
3) Angela trifft sich mit uns nächste Woche. / Angela wird sich mit uns nächste Woche treffen.
4) Sie besuchen uns nächstes Jahr. / Nächstes Jahr werden sie uns besuchen.
5) Ich esse morgen Pizza. / Ich werde morgen Pizza essen.
6) Nächstes Mal kaufen wir das Auto. / Nächstes Mal werden wir das Auto kaufen.

Page 85 — Giving Orders

1) Tanz!
2) Seid höflich!
3) Setzen Sie sich!
4) Arbeite!
5) Helft uns nicht!
6) Folgen Sie mir!
7) Gehen wir einkaufen!
8) Entspann dich!

Page 86 — Separable Verbs

1) Ich komme morgen an.
2) Sie geht aus.
3) Er nahm seinen Bruder mit.
4) Du hast abgewaschen.
5) Ich habe es zurückgegeben.
6) Geh weg, Eric!
7) Gehen wir aus!
8) Ich werde aufhören.

Page 87 — Modal Verbs

1) Ich will eine neue Gitarre.
2) Wir mögen Rugby spielen.
3) Ihr dürft euch setzen.
4) Er kann sehr gut Ski fahren.
5) Ich soll gehen.
6) Sie muss bleiben.
7) Jane musste spielen.
8) Sie wollten fliegen.

Page 88 — Would, Could and Should

1) Sie würden mich nicht besuchen.
2) Selma möchte singen.
3) Wir könnten zum Park laufen.
4) Wir könnten unseren Lehrer / unsere Lehrerin fragen.
5) Du solltest warten.
6) Ich sollte ein Sandwich essen.

Page 89 — I would be / I would have

1) Ich wäre ein guter Schauspieler / eine gute Schauspielerin.
2) Er hätte einen Hund.
3) Niklas hätte einen Bruder.
4) Sie wären sehr traurig.
5) Wenn ich ein Auto / einen Wagen hätte, wäre es / er rot.
6) Wenn ich Hunger hätte, würde ich Kartoffeln essen.

Answers

Transcripts

Section 1 — General Stuff

Track 1 — p.3

E.g. **M1:** Hallo Lisa! Hallo Helena!
F1: Guten Tag Jan. Guten Tag Helena. Wie geht's euch?
F2: Sehr gut, danke.
M1: Mir geht's auch gut.
F1: Was hast du am Wochenende gemacht, Helena?
F2: Am Samstag habe ich das Museum besucht.

1) **F2:** Ich bin mit meiner Familie dahin gegangen.

2) **F2:** Die Antiquitäten waren sehr interessant!

3) **F2:** Und vorgestern habe ich Zeit mit meinem Bruder verbracht. Wir sind durch den Park gegangen — es hat so viel Spaß gemacht!

4) **F1:** Wie schön. Und du, Jan? Was hast du am Wochenende gemacht?
M1: Nicht viel, Lisa. Ich habe nur Handball gespielt.

5) **M1:** Ich spiele jeden Tag in einer Mannschaft.

6) **M1:** Aber am Donnerstag gehe ich nicht hin, weil ich Geburtstag habe!

7) **M1:** Kommt ihr zu meiner Party? Ich gehe ins Kino.
F2: Alles Gute zum Geburtstag, Jan. Ja, ich komme zu deiner Party, danke schön.
F1: Ja, ich gehe gern ins Kino. Bis Donnerstag, Helena.
M1: Tschüss Lisa, tschüss Helena.
F1+F2: Tschüss!

Track 2 — p.10

E.g. **M2:** Guten Tag Anja, wie geht's?
F1: Sehr gut, danke Christian. Was machst du heute Abend?
M2: Ich mag Schwimmen, also gehe ich mit Sebastian ins Schwimmbad.

1) **F1:** Das klingt schön. Heute Abend gehe ich mit meiner Schwester einkaufen, aber ich hasse einkaufen gehen! Es interessiert mich nicht, denn es kostet zu viel Zeit.

2) **M2:** Das stimmt. Einkaufszentren gefallen mir auch nicht, weil es immer so viele Leute dort gibt.

3) **M2:** Wie ist es mit Popkonzerten — magst du sie?
F1: Manchmal. Es hängt davon ab, welche Band da spielt.

4) **F1:** Wie findest du Fernsehen?
M2: Ach, ich denke, dass manche Sendungen lustig oder spannend sind, aber ich bin lieber aktiv.

5) **M2:** Was hältst du von Fernsehen?
F1: Im Fernsehen sehe ich am liebsten die Nachrichten. Früher habe ich auch Zeitungen gekauft, aber jetzt lese ich sie im Internet.

Section 2 — Me, My Family and Friends

Track 3 — p.13

1) **M2:** Hallo! Meine Familie ist relativ groß. Ich habe drei Geschwister — einen Bruder, eine Halbschwester und eine Schwester.

2) **M2:** Obwohl meine Mutter und ich blonde Haare haben, hat meine Schwester dunkle Haare.

3) **M2:** Meine Halbschwester Lisa hat braune Augen wie ich und sie trägt eine hellblaue Brille.

4) **M2:** Mein Bruder trägt im Moment einen Schnurrbart, aber ich finde das furchtbar, weil er hässlich aussieht!

Section 3 — Free-Time Activities

Track 4 — p.17

E.g. **F1:** Ich bin Johanna. Letzte Woche war ich auf einem Rockkonzert. Da hat meine Lieblingsband gespielt. Das habe ich richtig toll gefunden und ich habe laut mitgesungen. Es hat total Spaß gemacht.

1) **F1:** Meine Schwester hört aber dauernd Popmusik und zwar immer die gleichen Lieder. Das geht mir richtig auf die Nerven. Sie mag keine Rockmusik und denkt, dass ich verrückt bin.

2) **F2:** Mein Name ist Preethi. Ich finde klassische Musik manchmal langweilig, daher höre ich lieber Rockmusik. Allerdings tanze ich Ballett und dafür ist klassische Musik prima.

3) **M1:** Ich bin Jürgen. Neulich habe ich ein Musikvideo von einem Rapper gesehen, das habe ich schrecklich gefunden. Ich höre lieber Popmusik, die ist nicht so hektisch und ich finde, dass sie mich entspannt.

Track 5 — p.20

E.g. **F1:** Ich bin Elsa. Ich habe beschlossen, überhaupt kein Fleisch und keinen Fisch mehr zu essen. Mir tun die armen Tiere leid.

1) **F1:** Äpfel finde ich langweilig, aber Ananas ist total lecker. Bananen esse ich nur ab und zu.

2) **F2:** Ich heiße Sonja. Mein Lieblingsgericht ist Wurst mit Pommes.

3) **F2:** Sonst esse ich aber nicht so gern Schweinefleisch.

4) **M2:** Mein Name ist Moritz. Ich koche total gern, am liebsten für meine Freunde. Letzte Woche habe ich Fleischlasagne gekocht, die haben alle super gefunden.

Section 5 — Customs and Festivals

Track 6 — p.29

E.g. **M1:** Karneval kann auch „Fasching" oder „Fastnachtszeit" heißen. Es gibt auch viele weitere regionale Namen für das Fest.

1) **M1:** Man feiert Karneval an vielen Orten in Deutschland, in der Schweiz und in Österreich.

2) **M1:** Egal wie er heißt, ist Karneval ein sehr buntes und spannendes Fest. Die Tradition ist sehr alt und man denkt, dass das Wort „Fasching" eigentlich aus dem 13. Jahrhundert stammt.

3) **M1:** Die größten Partys finden in Gegenden statt, wo viele Katholiken wohnen. Zum Beispiel ist die Bevölkerung von Bayern meist katholisch und deswegen gibt es zur Faschingszeit eine ganze Reihe von Veranstaltungen dort.

4) **M1:** Die Festivitäten sind genauso unterschiedlich wie die deutschen Regionen. Jedoch verkleiden sich die meisten Leute.

Transcripts

Section 6 — Where You Live

Track 7 — p.34

E.g. **F2:** Ich war gerade im Kaufhaus in der Stadtmitte, weil ich eine neue Jeans gebraucht habe.

1) **F2:** Aber an der Kasse habe ich schöne Schuhe gesehen – sie waren so süß! Neben den Schuhen waren auch tolle T-Shirts, aber es gab meine Größe leider nicht, deswegen habe ich nur die Schuhe und die Jeans gekauft.

2) **F2:** Die Musik war zu laut und es gab zu viele Kunden, aber die Verkäuferinnen waren sehr freundlich und hilfsbereit, was mir gut gefallen hat!

3) **F2:** Nächsten Samstag muss ich das Kaufhaus wieder besuchen, um einen neuen Pullover zu kaufen. Ich bin im Moment pleite! Obwohl das ein bisschen ärgerlich sein wird, wird es mir hoffentlich eine gute Chance geben, mehr preiswerte Klamotten zu kaufen.

4) **F2:** Ich hätte gern ein neues Kleid für die Geburtstagsfeier meiner besten Freundin, aber das ist momentan leider nicht möglich. Ich brauche einen Nebenjob, um Geld zu verdienen.

Track 8 — p.37

1) **M2:** Entschuldigen Sie bitte, könnten Sie mir helfen? Ich bin hier fremd und muss mich mit Freunden treffen.
   F1: Ja, sicher.

   M2: Ich weiß, wo das Theater ist, aber wir treffen uns vor dem Kino. Wo ist das, bitte?

   F1: Es gibt drei Kinos in der Nähe von hier. Wie heißt es?

   M2: Das Kino heißt „Agora", glaube ich. Ist es weit?

   F1: Nein, das ist gar nicht weit – Sie sind nur einen Kilometer entfernt. Nehmen Sie da drüben die dritte Straße links, gehen Sie über die Brücke und es liegt auf der rechten Seite.

Section 8 — Social and Global Issues

Track 9 — p.45

1) **F2:** Ich heiße Sofia. Ich habe in der Zeitung gelesen, dass es gleichen Lohn für gleiche Arbeit jetzt gibt und ich freue mich darauf. Früher haben Frauen weniger verdient als Männer.

2) **M1:** Mein Name ist Peter. Ich mache mir Sorgen um die Gewalttätigkeit. Manchmal, wenn Menschen zu viel Alkohol trinken, kämpfen sie abends auf der Straße. Das ist sehr gefährlich.

3) **M2:** Ich bin Lionel. Es gibt so viele Menschen, die aus Syrien nach Deutschland fliehen. Sie können in Deutschland Asyl bekommen. Unser Stadtviertel ist jetzt sehr multikulturell, aber die Einwanderer sprechen nur sehr wenig Deutsch.

Section 9 — Travel and Tourism

Track 10 — p.48

1) **F1:** Ich heiße Monika. Letztes Jahr haben meine Freundinnen und ich in einer Jugendherberge gewohnt. Ich hatte ein bisschen Angst, aber es war auch gleichzeitig ziemlich spannend.

2) **M1:** Ich bin Ben. Ich übernachte immer in einer Pension, weil ich sie normalerweise günstig und bequem finde.

3) **M2:** Mein Name ist Anton. Hotels kann ich nicht leiden. Sie sind für mich einfach zu groß und unpersönlich.

Section 10 — Study and Employment

Track 11 — p.53

1) **F1:** Hallo Mutti. Ich habe endlich meinen Stundenplan für das neue Schuljahr. Im Allgemeinen ist es ganz angenehm. Ich habe viermal in der Woche Geschichte, was für mich perfekt ist. Ich muss sehr fleißig arbeiten, aber das stört mich nicht. Außerdem ist die Schule sehr früh aus. Um dreizehn Uhr endet für uns der Schultag.

2) **F1:** Leider ist aber nicht alles ideal. Dieses Jahr müssen wir uns morgens zur Versammlung treffen und das finde ich eine Zeitverschwendung. Molly lernt freitags in der sechsten Stunde Musik, aber ich habe das nicht gewählt – ich habe also beim Kunstunterricht keine Freunde dabei.

Index

Index

DAR41